ATLA Monograph Series
edited by Dr. Kenneth E. Rowe

1. Ronald L. Grimes. *The Divine Imagination: William Blake's Major Prophetic Visions.* 1972.
2. George D. Kelsey. *Social Ethics Among Southern Baptists, 1917-1969.* 1973.
3. Hilda Adam Kring. *The Harmonists: A Folk-Cultural Approach.* 1973.
4. J. Steven O'Malley. *Pilgrimage of Faith: The Legacy of the Otterbeins.* 1973.
5. Charles Edwin Jones. *Perfectionist Persuasion: The Holiness Movement and American Methodism, 1867-1936.* 1974.
6. Donald E. Byrne, Jr. *No Foot of Land: Folklore of American Methodist Itinerants.* 1975.
7. Milton C. Sernett. *Black Religion and American Evangelicalism: White Protestants, Plantation Missions, and the Flowering of Negro Christianity, 1787-1865.* 1975.
8. Eva Fleischner. *Judaism in German Christian Theology Since 1945: Christianity and Israel Considered in Terms of Mission.* 1975.
9. Walter James Lowe. *Mystery & The Unconscious: A Study in the Thought of Paul Ricoeur.* 1977.
10. Norris Magnuson. *Salvation in the Slums: Evangelical Social Work, 1865-1920.* 1977.
11. William Sherman Minor. *Creativity in Henry Nelson Wieman.* 1977.
12. Thomas Virgil Peterson. *Ham and Japheth: The Mythic World of Whites in the Antebellum South.* 1978.
13. Randall K. Burkett. *Garveyism as a Religious Movement: The Institutionalization of a Black Civil Religion.* 1978.
14. Roger G. Betsworth. *The Radical Movement of the 1960's.* 1980.
15. Alice Cowan Cochran. *Miners, Merchants, and Missionaries: The Roles of Missionaries and Pioneer Churches in the Colorado Gold Rush and Its Aftermath, 1858-1870.* 1980.
16. Irene Lawrence. *Linguistics and Theology: The Significance of Noam Chomsky for Theological Construction.* 1980.
17. Richard E. Williams. *Called and Chosen: The Story of Mother Rebecca Jackson and the Philadelphia Shakers.* 1981.
18. Arthur C. Repp, Sr. *Luther's Catechism Comes to America: Theological Effects on the Issues of the Small Catechism Prepared In or For America Prior to 1850.* 1982.
19. Lewis V. Baldwin. *"Invisible" Strands in African Methodism.* 1983.
20. David W. Gill. *The Word of God in the Ethics of Jacques Ellul.* 1984.

"INVISIBLE" STRANDS IN AFRICAN METHODISM:

A History of the *African Union Methodist Protestant* and *Union American Methodist Episcopal* Churches, 1805-1980

by
LEWIS V. BALDWIN

ATLA Monograph Series, No. 19

The American Theological Library
Association and
The Scarecrow Press, Inc.
Metuchen, N.J., & London • 1983

BX
8471
.A4
B34
1983

Library of Congress Cataloging in Publication Data

Baldwin, Lewis V., 1949–
   "Invisible" strands in African Methodism.

   (ATLA monograph series ; no. 19)
   Includes bibliographical references and index.
   1. African Union Methodist Protestant Church (U.S.)
--History.   2. Union American Methodist Episcopal
Church--History.   3. Methodist Church--United States--
History.   I. Title.   II. Series.
BX8471.A4B34   1983   287'.8   83-15039
ISBN 0-8108-1647-4

Dedicated to the memory of my clergy forebears

Rev. Eli Baldwin, Sr. (paternal great-grandfather)
Rev. Clay Holt (maternal great-grandfather)
Rev. Lacy Leon Holt (maternal grandfather)

and to my parents

Rev. and Mrs. L. V. Baldwin, Sr.

CONTENTS

LIST OF ILLUSTRATIONS

ACKNOWLEDGMENTS

The immediate inspiration for this study came from Sara Gardner and the Reverend Hervey W. Greer. Both are actively involved in black Methodism in Wilmington, Delaware, the birthplace of the African Union Methodist Protestant and Union American Methodist Episcopal Churches. Prior to meeting them in 1976, I was totally unaware of the existence of these churches. I have benefited tremendously from their assistance in the conception and preparation of this book.

I am under deep obligation to many others who freely put their sources and resources at my disposal. The members of the Mother A. U. M. P. Church in Wilmington were quite generous in contributing financially to this effort. Individual members of the A. U. M. P. Conference placed me permanently in their debt by sharing documents and useful information through private interviews. Elizabeth Brown, the charming widow of the late Bishop George F. Brown, did not hesitate to make letters, manuscripts, newspaper clippings, pamphlets, and pictures available to me. The Reverend George A. Woodards, the conference secretary for some thirty years, made his papers accessible. The late Bishop Reese C. Scott, who embodied every level of competence and dedication, was a constant source of help and inspiration. I deeply regret that his death on January 3, 1981, robbed him of an opportunity to see this study in published form. Bishop Robert F. Walters, the present bishop of the A. U. M. P. Conference, also made available a wide range of source materials. The difficulties of an initial work of this kind would have been insurmountable without the assistance of these people.

Several leaders and members of the U. A. M. E. Conference were quite generous in supplying source materials, insight, and encouragement. Bishop John P. Predow donated valuable papers on the history of African Union Methodism. Bishops David E. Hackett and Earl L. Huff were helpful, as was Presiding Elder George W. Poindexter. The papers of the late Bishop David M. Harmon, which remain in private

hands at his home in Camden, New Jersey, could have perhaps added significantly to the quality of this study, but his
widow, to my regret, simply refused to open his library for
use. The Reverend Etta Robertson, the conference local
preacher, was always willing to offer support and encouragement.

I am deeply indebted to many staff persons and librar-
ians of the Wilmington Public Library and the Wilmington-
based Historical Society of Delaware for their assistance in
locating sources. Files of information on the Spencer Churches
and the Big Quarterly festival would have been lost had it not
been for their diligence.

Marc D. Pevar of Cultural Encounters, Inc., a minority
media company headquartered in Kennett Square, Pennsylvania,
shared with me the few primary sources he discovered. He
and his associates are presently producing a documentary
film about the Peter Spencer movement in Delaware for the
Association for the Study of Afro-American Life and History.
This film, which will focus on the Spencer Churches and the
Big Quarterly festival, is based largely on this study. Pevar's criticisms and suggestions have been quite helpful in
making this story come alive.

Special thanks are due to Reverends Hervey W. Greer,
Harvey Kelley, George M. McMillan, and Edward "Stonewall"
Williams, who burned tanks of gas driving me to parts of
Delaware, Maryland, and Pennsylvania during the period of
my research.

Hearty words of acknowledgment are extended to two
of my dissertation advisors, Drs. Frederick A. Norwood and
Sterling Stuckey, for their constant encouragement, support, and
influence. Dr. Norwood, who directed my dissertation while
teaching at Garrett-Evangelical Theological Seminary, gra-
ciously accepted the offer to write the Foreword. He and
Dr. Carl H. Marbury, the Dean and Vice President of Academic Affairs at Garrett, were quite generous in recommending this study for publication to Dr. Kenneth E. Rowe, editor
of the American Theological Library Association Monograph
Series. Dr. Stuckey, who teaches in the History Department
at Northwestern University, has profoundly influenced me as
a writer. The influence of both Dr. Stuckey and Dr. Norwood is evident throughout this work.

My abiding appreciation goes to my parents, Reverend

and Mrs. L. V. Baldwin, Sr., whose prayers have sustained me during the course of my research and writing. As a child in the cotton fields of Wilcox County, Alabama, I was taught by them that humility, faith in God, and perseverance were the master keys to success.

I acknowledge with thanks my wife, Jacqueline, who frequently offered constructive criticisms and gave me the encouragement to work to completion.

Finally, my sincere appreciation to Dr. Rowe and the American Theological Library Association for their interest in this work and for agreeing to publish it.

L. V. Baldwin
Wooster, Ohio
January 1982

EDITOR'S NOTE

Since 1972 the American Theological Library Association has undertaken responsibility for a modest dissertation series in the field of religious studies. Our aim in this series is to publish two dissertations of quality each year at reasonable cost. Titles are selected from studies in a wide variety of religious and theological disciplines nominated by graduate school deans. We are pleased to publish Lewis V. Baldwin's study of several independent black Methodist churches in America as number 19 in our series.

Following undergraduate studies in Talladega College, Talladega, Alabama, Dr. Baldwin studied theology at Colgate-Rochester Divinity School and took the doctorate in church history at Northwestern University in 1980. His articles on black church studies have appeared in Methodist History and Delaware History. Following a one-year appointment in the department of religion at the College of Wooster, Dr. Baldwin currently serves as Assistant Professor of Religion and Philosophy at Colgate University in Hamilton, New York.

Kenneth E. Rowe
Series Editor

Drew University Library
Madison, New Jersey

FOREWORD

Frederick A. Norwood

In any brood or family the youngest or smallest is likely to be left behind or ignored. This might be said of the black denominations that are discussed in this work of original research by Lewis V. Baldwin, except that the roots of these "Spencerian" Churches are as deep as those of any of the larger denominations of black Methodism. The difference is not so much antiquity as extent. The African Methodist Episcopal Church, the African Methodist Episcopal Zion Church, and the Christian Methodist Episcopal Church all grew not only large but national in scope, whereas the groups that derived from Peter Spencer remained both small and regional.

To say this is not the same as saying that they are insignificant in the understanding of black Methodism. On the contrary, they exemplify some of the unique characteristics of this racial minority in that tradition. One may cite on the one hand the early leadership of Spencer and on the other hand the spectacular expression of both culture and worship known as the Big Quarterly. These churches, for all of their smallness, also reveal the common tendency to contention and schism.

Baldwin has collected from many scattered sources, both oral and written, materials that enable him for the first time to tell the story of all that began with Peter Spencer in Wilmington, Delaware.

INTRODUCTION

One of the most serious gaps in our knowledge of Afro-American religious history is our almost total ignorance of the story of the African Union Methodist Protestant and Union American Methodist Episcopal Churches. Although these small bodies have existed primarily in the mid-Atlantic region of the United States since the early years of the nineteenth century, they have received virtually no attention from black and white scholars alike. Most professional church historians, sociologists, and theologians remain curiously unaware of their existence. This is partly because these churches, known also as the Spencer Churches or the Union Churches, have survived throughout their histories as "invisible branches" within the larger sphere of African Methodism. Consequently, they have not yet been provided a space on the ever-expanding agenda of American Church historiography.

This book is the result of pioneering research into an unexplored area of African Methodism. It is aimed at interweaving the story of the A. U. M. P. and U. A. M. E. Churches into the tapestry of Afro-American religious history. More specifically, the work focuses largely on three important aspects of the development of these denominations. First, it explores their origins as the products of a "dissenting movement" within the context of Episcopal Methodism in America. Second, it addresses the question as to why these churches have languished over the years in the backwaters of African Methodism. Finally, particular notice is taken of the special or unique expression these churches found through addressing some of the economic, moral, and political problems that have confronted black people since their arrival on these shores. The years within which the study is focused, 1805-1980, were chosen because nothing is presently available which attempts a comprehensive chronological overview of the A. U. M. P. and U. A. M. E. Churches for the benefit of students of Afro-American religious history. [1]

What is especially new in the treatment offered in "Invisible" Strands in African Methodism is the thesis that the Union Church of African Members, the parent body of the A. U. M. P. and U. A. M. E. denominations, was the first branch of African Methodism to effect both de facto and de jure separation from the predominantly white Methodist Episcopal structure. [2] This church signaled the culmination of a movement toward independence among African Methodists in Wilmington, Delaware. The movement began in 1805 when Peter Spencer and William Anderson, two black lay preachers, led forty or so blacks out of the predominantly white Asbury Methodist Episcopal Church to demonstrate their opposition to discrimination in worship. They soon organized Ezion Methodist Episcopal Church, a black church which was to function as a mission under the direction of the M. E. Conference. They worshiped there for about seven years before the blatant arrogance and paternalism of a white elder compelled them to break with the M. E. Conference. [3]

In 1813, Spencer and Anderson took the lead in organizing the Union Church of African Members, which was variously called the African Union Church, the African Union Methodist Church, the Union Church of Africans, and the Union Methodist Connexion. The new church was incorporated at Dover, Delaware, in September of that year. It soon assumed connectional form with the addition of small congregations in New York and Pennsylvania. [4] In 1851, a major dispute occurred which eventually split the body, resulting in two denominations; namely, the African Union Church and the Union American Methodist Episcopal Church. [5] In 1866, the African Union Church, the smallest of the two, merged with the First Colored Methodist Protestant Church. The resulting body was called the African Union First Colored Methodist Protestant Church of the United States of America or Elsewhere, ordinarily known as the African Union Methodist Protestant Church. [6]

Historians of the black church, both lay and professional, have long disagreed over which of the several branches of African Methodism was first to establish its unconditional independence from white Methodism. J. Harvey Anderson, who was a prominent African Methodist Episcopal Zion minister and author at the beginning of this century, attributed that distinction to his denomination:

> October, 1796--about 60 of the colored members from the First Methodist Episcopal Church established in America, John Street, New York City, New York, and led by James Varick, formed the first Negro Methodist Society in America. [7]

Anderson was obviously mistaken in his assertion. A wide range of sources present evidence to the contrary. Even the works of most of the authorities on A. M. E. Zion Church history, dating from as far back as 1843, reveal findings that challenge Anderson's account. David Bradley, J. W. Hood, John J. Miller, John J. Moore, Christopher Rush, and William J. Walls have all produced histories which show unmistakably that the A. M. E. Zion Church was not organized as a legal corporate body until 1821.[8] Both the A. M. E. Church and the Union Church of Africans had achieved this status at least five years prior to that date.

Most historians claim that the African Methodist Episcopal Church, under the leadership of Richard Allen, predated all separate and independent black Methodist Churches in America. Proponents of this thesis, such as J. Curtis Foster and Harry V. Richardson, have suggested that the A. M. E. Church developed in stages, beginning with the African prayer band Allen organized at St. George's M. E. Church in Philadelphia in 1786. According to this line of reasoning, the founding of the Free African Society in 1787, the departure from St. George's six years later, and the dedication of Bethel Church in 1794 simply represented a series of developments which found final institutional expression in the officialization of the A. M. E. Church in 1816.[9] Even though Allen's movement began with the African prayer band and passed through these various stages in its development, the A. M. E. Church was not organized and incorporated until 1816, three years after the Union Church of Africans had assumed this form. Thus, the history of African Methodist denominations in the United States should be rewritten based on the chronological priority of the Union Church of Africans.

The foregoing observations are not made with the intention of minimizing the importance of Richard Allen as the father of African Methodism. To be sure, African Methodism was born in the mind of Richard Allen. As early as 1786 he conceived the idea of a separate organization for African Methodists:

> I thought I would stop in Philadelphia a week or two. I preached at different places in the city. My labor was much blessed. I soon saw a large field open in seeking and instructing my African brethren, who have been a long forgotten people and few of them attended public worship.[10]

When Allen led his followers out of St. George's in

Philadelphia, Spencer was only eleven years old, and James Varick had not emerged as a leader of the A. M. E. Zion movement in New York. Both Spencer and Varick were virtually unknown to those who became their followers when Allen took the lead in erecting Bethel Church in 1793. Allen began the movement, but Spencer was first to succeed in organizing and incorporating a fully independent African Methodist denomination. Hence, Spencer played a far more important role in furthering the cause of African Methodism than is usually known or imagined.

Despite the importance of figures like Allen, Spencer, and Varick, they were not solely responsible for giving character, direction, and scope to African Methodism in America. Morris Brown, Daniel Coker, and a host of little-known Africans made contributions. They were the people who threw the weight of their support behind Allen, Spencer, and Varick, and who strengthened African Methodist movements, which sprung up in cities such as Baltimore, Charleston, New York, Philadelphia, Wilmington, Attleborough (Pennsylvania), and Salem (New Jersey). In a word, they were the people who made these movements.

This study is new and different from previous treatments of Afro-American religious history not simply because it concentrates on untouched dimensions of African Methodism, or because it sets forth the chronological priority of the Union Church of Africans, but also because it seeks to establish a comparative context with the various branches of African Methodism. It illustrates at a number of points that the movements led by Allen, Spencer, and Varick had much in common. They were products of the same social and theological forces in that they developed because of the refusal of white Methodists to respect the full personhood of African Methodists under God. The movements produced churches which were all essentially Methodistic, with articles of religion, general rules, and disciplines. [11] There were also elements that distinguished them from each other. As this book will demonstrate, the early leaders of the A. M. E. Church, the A. M. E. Zion Church, and the Union Church of Africans took slightly different approaches to church polity and organization. The three churches have also differed in terms of their numerical strength, influence, and geographical scope. [12]

Another distinctive feature of this study is its consideration of black public worship and devotional styles as they

developed from antebellum days to the present. Two chapters are devoted to a discussion of Wilmington, Delaware's
Big August Quarterly, a black religious festival inaugurated
by Peter Spencer in connection with the Union Church of
Africans in 1814. [13] This annual festival, which still takes
place on the last Sunday in August, has traditionally marked
a time when blacks on the Delmarva Peninsula came together
to celebrate their faith in styles more congenial to their own
spirit. It clearly documents African cult behavior as it found
expression in dancing, shouting, footstomping, hand-clapping,
and testifying, particularly in the nineteenth century. By
examining what took place at these celebrations, one gains
keen insight into what W. E. B. Du Bois meant when he referred to "the inner spirit and motive of that marvelous faith
and unreason which made a million black folk on the shores
of exile dance and scream and shout the Sorrow Song. "[14]
What is offered in this book concerning black worship styles
may lead to a more indepth study of the black worship tradi-
tion--perhaps a study which focuses on Big Quarterly as a
microcosm of a larger picture.

A combination of observational and historical methods
were used in gathering source materials for this work. The
use of oral history techniques proved highly rewarding in
that information was acquired which does not normally find
its way into books and other publications. In a somewhat
different and more extensive form, the material on which
this volume is based was presented as a dissertation in par-
tial fulfillment of the requirements for the Degree of Doctor
of Philosophy at Northwestern University, and in that connection was awarded a grant by the American Theological
Library Association for the year 1981. A copy of the original manuscript is on file in the Northwestern University
Library and is available to anyone having legitimate need of
it. However, I hasten to admit that parts of it are flawed.
Obviously, considerable pruning and a more critical focus
were necessary to make this study a worthy contribution to
Afro-American religious history. This book is the result of
an attempt to fulfill those needs. For the sake of historical
accuracy and integrity, major revisions were undertaken
based on more recent findings.

NOTES

1. Lewis V. Baldwin, "The A. U. M. P. and U. A. M. E.
Churches: An Unexplored Area of Black Methodism, " Meth-

odist History, Vol. XIX, No. 3 (April 1981), pp. 175-178.
The term "African Union Methodism" is commonly used to
refer jointly to the A. U. M. P. and U. A. M. E. denominations.

2. Ibid. The word "connection" has been used widely in historical works on Episcopal Methodism in America.
It has reference to two or more congregations associating to
form a single body or church. The Union Church of Africans became a connection soon after its founding. For a
brief discussion of the meaning of connection, see Frederick
A. Norwood, The Story of American Methodism: A History
of the United Methodists and Their Relations (Nashville and
New York: Abingdon Press, 1974), p. 20.

3. Daniel J. Russell, Jr., History of the African
Union Methodist Protestant Church (Philadelphia: The Union
Star Book and Job, 1920), pp. 4-9; The Discipline of the Union
Church of Africans, for the State of Delaware, Second Edi-
tion Enlarged (Wilmington, 1841), pp. iii-v; The Discipline
of the African Union Church in the United States of America
(Wilmington: Porter & Eckel, 1852), pp. 1-8; and Colored
American, New York (May 20, 1837), p. 2. The title
"Union Church of Africans" will be used most commonly in
this work.

4. Articles of Association of the African Union
Church at Wilmington, State of Delaware (Wilmington, 1813),
pp. 1-4; and Incorporation in the Office for Recording Deeds,
New Castle, Del., Book M, Vol. III, p. 470. The corner-
stone of the old African Union Church of New Garden Township, Pennsylvania, which still exists, reveals that this
church affiliated with the mother church in Wilmington in
1813. Old records of the Official Board of Elders of the
African Union Church, which are housed in the Historical
Society in Wilmington, also suggest that this church, and
the church started in New York by Isaac Barney in 1801,
became affiliates of the African Union Church soon after
it was legally recorded in September 1813. These records were used in the preparation of Our Heritage: The
History of the Union American Methodist Episcopal Church
(Hackensack, N. J.: Custombook, 1973), pp. 12 and
34.

5. The Case of the Union Church of Africans, in
Wilmington, Before the Superior Court for New Castle County,
Comprising the Petition of Ellis Saunders for a Mandamus,
the Return Thereto; Brief Notes of the Argument and Re-

Argument of Counsel, and the Final Decision of the Court
Awarding the Mandamus, 1852-53 (Wilmington: Henry Eckel,
1855), pp. 1-24.

6. The Doctrine and Discipline of the African Union
First Colored Methodist Protestant Church in the United
States or Elsewhere, First Edition (Wilmington: Henry Eck-
el, 1867), pp. 5-11.

7. Quoted in Crawford Brady, "Black Folks and Religion: Who Moved First to Separate?" The Racine Star
Times, Racine, Wisc. (February 14, 1976), Section II,
p. 2.

8. Ibid.

9. J. Curtis Foster, The African Methodist Episcopal Church Makes Its Mark in America (Nashville: The
A. M. E. Book Concern, 1976), pp. 1 ff.; and Harry V.
Richardson, Dark Salvation: The Story of Methodism as It
Developed Among Blacks in America (New York: Doubleday,
1976), Chapter VI. Milton Sernett argues, and rightly so,
that the Allenite walkout from St. George's could not have
occurred in 1787 as commonly held because the gallery of
that church, which was the center of the controversy that
prompted the walk-out, was not completed until 1791.
A. M. E. leaders reported to Colored American in 1837 that
the walk-out took place in 1793. See Milton C. Sernett,
Black Religion and American Evangelicalism: White Protestants, Plantation Missions, and the Flowering of Negro
Christianity, 1787-1865 (Metuchen, N. J.: Scarecrow Press,
1975), pp. 117 and 218-220; and Colored American (May 20,
1837), p. 2.

10. Richard Allen, The Life, Experience and Gospel
Labors of the Rt. Reverend Richard Allen (Philadelphia,
1793; reprinted, New York: Abingdon Press, 1960), p.
14.

11. Norwood, The Story of American Methodism,
pp. 171-174.

12. Ibid.; and Baldwin, "The A. U. M. P. and
U. A. M. E. Churches," pp. 177-178.

13. Alice Dunbar-Nelson, Big Quarterly in Wilmington (Wilmington: the author, 1932), pp. 1-5.

14. Quoted in Herbert Aptheker, ed., Book Reviews by W. E. B. Dubois (New York: Kto Press, 1967), p. 68. Cult behavior among black people, which also occurred in the clandestine meetings of slaves in the South, is discussed at some length in studies like Miles Mark Fisher's Negro Slave Songs in the United States (Ithaca, N. Y.: Cornell University Press, 1953); and Zora Neale Hurston's Mules and Men (Philadelphia: J. P. Lippincott, 1935).

Chapter I:

THE AFRICAN AND METHODISM PRIOR TO AFRICAN METHODIST BEGINNINGS

> Notwithstanding we had been violently perse-
> cuted by the elder, we were in favor of being
> attached to the Methodist Connexion, for I was
> confident there was no religious sect or de-
> nomination that would suit the capacity of the
> colored people as well as the Methodists, for
> the plain and simple Gospel suits best for any
> people, for the unlearned can understand, and
> the learned are sure to understand; and the
> reason that the Methodists are so successful
> in the awakening and conversion of the colored
> people is the plain doctrine and having a good
> discipline.
>
> --Richard Allen[1]

No examination of the history of independent black religious
institutions in America can be valid and complete if it ig-
nores the cultural milieu out of which African slaves came.
The slaves who were brought to North America during the
four centuries of the African slave trade came from West
African societies where they had been steeped in religious
traditions that drew no sharp dichotomy between religion and
other areas of life. They came from intensely religious cul-
tures where religion, in the words of Leroi Jones, "was a
daily, minute-to-minute concern, and not something relegated
to a specious once-a-week reaffirmation."[2]

Upon reaching the shores of the New World, these
African imports found that they could no longer adhere openly to the highly developed religious values and systems which
had been so inextricably linked to every aspect of their cul-
tures. Consequently, they not only had to reach out for new
gods, but also had to appropriate new methods of worshiping
those gods. This resulted in spiritual pain of untold dimen-

sions--a spiritual turmoil that represented one of the many processes of change and adaptation that African slaves inevitably endured in the New World. W. E. B. Du Bois displayed tremendous insight into the depth of that spiritual pain in 1903 as he assessed the breakdown of African religious values and systems in The Souls of Black Folk:

> By the middle of the eighteenth century the black slave had sunk, with hushed murmurs, to his place at the bottom of a new economic system, and was unconsciously ripe for a new philosophy of life. Nothing suited his condition better than the doctrines of passive submission embodied in the newly-learned Christianity.... Courtesy became humility, moral strength degenerated into submission, and the exquisite native appreciation of the beautiful became an infinite capacity for dumb suffering. The Negro, losing the joy of this world, eagerly seized upon the offered conceptions of the next; the avenging spirit of the Lord enjoining patience in this world, under sorrow and tribulation until the Great Day when He shall lead His dark children home, -- this became his comforting dream. [3]

Even though African slaves were spiritually transformed by their experiences in the New World, this in no way means that they completely abandoned all of the rituals and practices which had characterized their religious ceremonies in their ancestral homeland. The works of Du Bois, Melville J. Herskovits, Newbell Niles Puckett, and others, allowing for differences in method and purpose, reveal that the process of enslavement, despite the radical social disruption which accompanied it, was not so traumatic that it robbed bondsmen of every vestige of their cultural heritage. [4] Du Bois was far ahead of Herskovits and other scholars in asserting that the African religious experience as a critical dimension of culture, far from being completely obliterated in the New World, was simply merged with theological insights which slaves gathered from personal experiences and exposure to Christianity, thereby producing a hybrid which was neither completely African nor completely Christian:

> It was not at first by any means a Christian Church, but a mere adaptation of those heathen rites which we roughly designate by the term Obe worship, or "Voodooism." Association and missionary effort soon gave these rites a veneer of Christianity, and

gradually, after two centuries, the Church became Christian, with a simple Calvinistic creed, but with many of the old customs still clinging to the services. [5]

Though we do not know enough about the early secret plantation meetings to determine with great precision the true nature of slave religion, there are substantial reasons for believing that the African presence was significant enough to influence the character of religion among bondsmen. The prevalence of the "ring shout" ceremony in the Georgia-South Carolina sea coast areas and the persistence of Vodun as a cultic element in black religion in Louisiana serve as prime examples of how the African presence in the New World contributed to non-European elements in slave religion. Furthermore, the lingering presence of these elements adds substance to Charles Long's claim that "the image of Africa has had an enormous impact on the development of religion among Afro-Americans."[6]

Whatever may be said concerning the primary sources of slave religion, the Christian faith, as redefined and reshaped by bondsmen, became the historic base of black religion. In a real sense, whites did not introduce Christianity to the slaves; the slaves introduced Christianity to the whites. Rejecting the racistic religion of white society and culture, Africa's transplanted children took the faith that had been delivered to the early saints and gave powerful and creative expression to it in dance, prayer, sermon, and song. They fashioned a neo-Christianity which valued personhood more than materialism--a faith that found chief institutional embodiment in the black church. But long before the rise of this magnificent institution, Protestant groups from New England to Georgia devoted an immense amount of time and energy to evangelizing blacks. This chapter discusses the efforts of one of those groups, the Methodists, and offers an appraisal of the black response to those efforts.

John Wesley and Africans

Black people have had an enduring relgionship with Episcopal Methodism for over two centuries. That relationship began at least as far back as 1737, when John Wesley, the father of Methodism, gave spiritual advice to African slaves in South Carolina. In November, 1758, he baptized two Africans and recorded the following in his diary:

> I rode to Wandsworth and baptized two Negroes
> belonging to Mr. Gilbert, a gentleman lately from
> Antiqua. One of these was deeply convinced of
> sin; the other is rejoicing in God her Saviour, and
> is the first African Christian I have known. But
> shall not God in his own time, have these heathens
> for His own inheritance?[7]

Wesley's action in this case takes on great significance when
one considers the fact that it was indicative of his willingness to include black people in his movement. On the other
hand, his use of the word "heathen" in reference to the two
Africans he baptized was highly unfortunate in that it fore-
shadowed the kind of narrow cultural thinking which later
gave impetus to a movement of African dissent in American
Methodism. Yet one must be clear as to what Wesley was
saying and why. Apparently, his position was largely religious and not so much racial. The primary concern for
him was not the racial background of Africans, but, rather,
the fact that they were unenlightened as to the guiding tenets
of the Christian faith. This is evident from a substantive
passage in Wesley's The Imperfections of Human Knowledge
(II, 5), where he used the Hottentots as examples of human
nature in its fallen state. Wesley felt that African traditional religions and other non-Christian expressions of faith
among Africans constituted heathenism, a conviction shared
by the vast majority of Europeans and Euro-Americans in
his day. [8]

Wesley lived in an age when prejudice against people
of African descent was commonplace, but he was remarkably liberal in his attitude toward Africans. [9] In his celebrated Thoughts upon Slavery, issued in 1774, Wesley vehe-
mently denounced the notion that Africans were inherently
inferior to Europeans and emphasized strong, genuine qualities in the character of African peoples which he thought
Europeans would do well to emulate:

> Upon the whole, therefore, the Negroes who in-
> habit the coast of Africa, from the River Senegal
> to the Southern bounds of Angola, are so far from
> the stupid, senseless, brutish, lazy barbarians,
> the fierce, cruel, perfidious savages they have
> been described, that, on the contrary, they are
> represented, by them who have no motive to flat-
> ter them, as remarkably sensible, considering the
> few advantages they have for improving their under-

standing; as industrious to the highest degree, perhaps more so than other natives of so warm a
climate; as fair, just and honest in all their deal-
ings, unless where white men have taught them to
be otherwise; and as far more mild, friendly, and
kind to strangers than any of our forefathers were.
Where shall we find at this day, among the fair-
faced natives of Europe, a nation generally practicing the justice, mercy, and truth which are
found among these poor Africans? We may [have
to] leave England and France, to seek genuine honesty in Benin, Congo, or Angola. 10

In suggesting that "We may [have to] leave England and
France, to seek genuine honesty in Benin, Congo, or Angola, "
Wesley was seemingly implying that Africans were capable of
assuming a leading role in the shaping of a new humanity.
Perhaps he was envisioning the possibility of Africans fulfilling a messianic role in the world. Wesley's vision of
Africa, which bordered on the "Noble Savage" idea, was
more sympathetic and positive than even that of some black
preachers in his time. It is interesting that black ministers,
particularly those of the Methodist persuasion, were not influenced by his vision of contemporary African societies. 11

    Impelled by the conviction that blacks were the human
equals of whites, Wesley frequently lashed out at all forms
of racism and discriminatory practices. On February 24,
1791, a week before his death, he wrote William Wilberforce,
the great English emancipator, expressing displeasure because
Africans in the British colonies were victims of an unjust legal system:

> Reading this morning a tract, written by a poor
> African, I was particularly struck by that circum-
> stance that a man who has a black skin, being
> wronged or outraged by a white man, can have no
> redress; it being a law in our colonies that the
> oath of a black against a white goes for nothing.
> What villainy is this!12

    Wesley's views on slavery offer more insights into
his attitude toward people of African descent. He was
among the first generation of staunch opponents of slavery
and the African slave trade. Some fifteen years before
Thomas Clarkson, William Wilberforce, and Granville Sharp
began their agitation for the abolishment of the slave system,

John Wesley, the celebrated father of Methodism (from The Letters of the Rev. John Wesley, ed. by John Telford).

Wesley organized "A Society for the Suppression of the Slave Trade. "13   He became adept at using his oratorical skills in leveling attacks against the system.   He openly attacked it in 1788 in Bristol, one of the principal strongholds of slave traders.   Few religious leaders of his day equaled him in sheer boldness when speaking out against the evils of human bondage. 14

In communicating his deep-rooted hostility toward slavery, Wesley relied most heavily upon the pen.   In 1743 he wrote the General Rules of his societies, in which he attacked "the buying or selling of the bodies and souls of men, women, and children, with an intention to enslave them. "15 In 1771 Wesley read an antislavery tract written by the American Quaker leader Anthony Benezet a few years earlier. As it turned out, Benezet was a powerful influence on Wesley's views concerning Africa and African peoples. In 1772 Wesley boldly criticized the slave trade as "the sum of all villainies. "16 His Thoughts upon Slavery constituted a rousing denunciation of both slavery and the African slave trade. In this piece he scoffed at the idea of "the enslavement of the noble by barbarous and inferior white men. " He wrote encouragingly to the newly-organized Abolition Committee in 1787, admonishing it to work not only on behalf of the abolition of the slave trade, but also against that "shocking abomination of slavery itself. "17 The historical record reveals that Wesley surpassed most white church leaders of his day when it came to making persistent attacks on the slave system through speeches and publications.

For Wesley, the slave system not only amounted to an economic liability for the enslaved, but also a frustrating hindrance to the unity of humankind. As he explained it, "It is impossible that it should ever be necessary for any reasonable creature to violate all the laws of Justice, Mercy, and Truth. " Wesley continued, "No circumstances can make it necessary for a man to burst asunder all the ties of humanity. "18

Toward the end of his life, Wesley was confronted with the painful realization that slavery would not end soon because too many enslavers were obsessed with satisfying their pecuniary motives. Thus, he, like most perceptive men of his time, doubted that abolitionists could muster the necessary support to rid England and her possessions of the evils of slavery and the trade. He expressed this doubt in his final letter to his old friend, William Wilberforce:

> My Dear Sir, --Unless the Divine Power has raised you up to be as Athanasius, Contra Mundum, I see not how you can go through your glorious enterprise in opposing that execrable villainy which is the scandal of religion, of England, and of human nature. Unless God has raised you up for this very thing, you will be worn out by the opposition of men and devils; but if God be for you, who can be against you?19

In the closing lines of this same letter, Wesley placed before Wilberforce a challenge: "Oh, be not weary in welldoing. Go on in the name of God and in the power of His Might, till even American slavery, the vilest that ever saw the sun, shall vanish away before it."[20]

Wesley's zeal and influence were undoubtedly instrumental in shaping the antislavery policy and sentiments of the People Called Methodists. Methodists in England and America were exposed to his antislavery works. Although he never devised a plan for abolishing the slave system, he did provide early Methodists with a strong antislavery principle as well as the moral urgency to put it into effect.[21]

Early Beginnings of Africans in Methodism

Africans were involved in the Methodist movement in America from the outset. When Philip Embury, an Irish Methodist layman, held the first Methodist society meeting in his home in New York in 1766, a slave woman named Betty was among those present.[22] Though very little is known about her, it is certain that her appearance at this meeting represented the beginning of African presence and participation in a formal way in American Methodism.

The participation of Africans in early Methodist societies was significant to the point of eliciting reactions from some of the leading white Methodist preachers in America. Richard Boardman and Joseph Pilmore, who were sent to America by Wesley in 1769, marveled at the number of Africans they encountered in society meetings. A year after arriving in America, Pilmore, reporting to Wesley on black presence and involvement in societies in New York, wrote, "The number of blacks that attend the preaching affects me much."[23] The traveling preacher Thomas Rankin, who came to America in 1773, was highly impressed by the support given by Africans to societies in and around Philadelphia. In 1777 he expressed great concern because the resistance of slavemasters was preventing more bondsmen from joining Methodist societies.[24] Nathan Bangs, a pioneer Methodist historian and theologian, often alluded to the contributions made by Africans to societies, noting particularly their involvements at Lovely Lane Meeting House in Baltimore and at the log chapel on Sam's Creek.[25]

Equally significant was the part played by Africans in

the development of early Methodist class meetings. The class meeting system, which became a defining character- istic of early Methodism, attracted scores of Africans of both slave and non-slave status. [26] There seems to have been variety in black-white relations at such meetings from the beginning. Africans frequently formed all-black classes, but it was not unusual for them to join white classes. Sev- eral Africans in New York joined a class which had grown out of the society started by Philip Embury in 1766. This marked the beginning of the John Street Methodist Episcopal Church. [27] Francis Asbury, Joseph Pilmore, William Col- bert, and Richard Whatcoat were among those early Method- ist leaders who recorded other instances of African involve- ment in racially-mixed class meetings. Pilmore was deeply touched by the devotion shown by some Africans to the class meeting system. In November 1771 he received a letter from a slave who complained that his enslavement prevented his active participation at class meetings. The letter read in part:

> Dear Sir,--these are to acquaint you, that my bondage is such I cannot possibly attend with the rest of the Class to receive my ticket, therefore beg you will send it. I wanted much to come to the Church at the Watchnight, but could not get leave; but, I bless God that night, I was greatly favoured with the spirit of prayer, and enjoyed much of His Divine Presence. I find the enemy of my soul continually striving to throw me off the foundation, but I have that within me which bids defiance to his delusive snares. I beg an interest in your prayers that I may be enabled to bear up under all my difficulties with patient resignation to the will of God. [28]

William Colbert's accounts of the African commitment to class meetings are equally touching and descriptive. Once while traveling along the banks of the Potomac, he came upon a group of Africans who had organized a thriving class on their own. Being remarkably pleased, he wrote,

> They not only have their Class meetings, but their days of examination in order to find out anything that may be amiss among them and if they can set- tle it among themselves they will, if not, as the Elder of Israel brought matters which they con- ceived were of too great importance for them to de-

cide on before Moses, so would these people bring matters of the greatest moment before the preacher. 29

It was not uncommon for Africans, despite their slave status, to make impressive monetary contributions toward the maintenance of societies and classes. According to Richard Allen, who later became the father of the African Methodist movement, slaves frequently worked in little gardens until midnight to earn extra money to give to the Methodist preachers. 30 Rachel and Margaret, two female servants, contributed considerably to the building of the chapel which later became the John Street M. E. Church in New York. 31 While traveling through parts of Virginia and Maryland, William Colbert encountered a society of Africans who, in his view, were more generous in their giving than the white society members he knew:

> Their society is very numerous, and very orderly, and to their great credit with pleasure I assert, that I never found a white Class so regular in giving their Quarterage, as these poor people are, and the greater part of them are slaves, of whom never request anything. But they will enquire when the Quarterly meetings are from time to time, and by the last time the preacher comes around before the Quarterly meeting, they will have five dollars tied up for him. 32

Several reasons apparently accounted for the strong support given by Africans to Methodism in these early years. First, Methodist preachers, many of whom were circuit riders, showed an abiding concern for the spiritual lives of black people. Convinced that all people stood in need of God's saving grace, they actively sought black converts on farms, plantations, and in households. They were so dedicated to their task until it became a proverbial saying on cold winter days that "there is nothing out today but crows and Methodist preachers. "33 Leroy F. Beaty's poignant statement concerning the untiring devotion of Francis Asbury and other Methodist preachers to black spiritual welfare is compelling enough to deserve quotation:

> Stirred by the sight of the large number of these wandering sheep without a shepherd, they doubtless did all they could to encourage their attendance on the public worship of God in the hope that the truth might find lodgment in their hearts. 34

Second, the evangelical style and ethos so endemic to Methodism appealed to Africans. Methodist preachers such as Francis Asbury and George Whitefield engaged in fiery, Bible-based preaching as they endeavored to spread scriptural holiness throughout the land. Blacks with little or no education were made to understand because of the simplicity of the preaching and the lack of ritual in Methodist services. Richard Allen undoubtedly spoke for the vast majority of African Methodists when he suggested that the Methodist approach to faith and discipline was more amenable to people of African descent. [35]

Third, Africans were obviously impressed by the Methodist policy which allowed for the acceptance, though limited in nature, of their services in ministry. Richard Allen and Harry "Black Harry" Hoosier, two of the earliest black Methodist preachers, were often given opportunities to address racially-mixed congregations. In 1800 "A Regulation Respecting the Ordination of Colored People to the Office of Deacon" was approved by the Methodist Episcopal Church despite opposition from pro-slavery advocates. This measure permitted the ordination of blacks as local deacons under certain conditions. Aside from being "qualified for that office," Africans had to "obtain an election of two-thirds of the male members of the society" to which they belonged and were required to have "a recommendation from the minister who has the charge, and his fellow-laborers in the city or circuit."[36] Considering their state of existence, it was not easy for Africans to meet these conditions. A few were successful in doing so and went on to become dynamic preachers in the M. E. Church. No other denomination in the country at that time, with the possible exception of the Baptists, provided such an opportunity for Africans to exercise their homiletical gifts.

Finally, the early stance taken by the Methodists against slavery pleased Africans. As stated previously, John Wesley provided much of the incentive for this position among Methodists with his denunciations of slavery and the African slave trade. His example was followed by Francis Asbury, Thomas Coke, Freeborn Garrettson, William Colbert, Thomas Rankin, and other Methodist preachers in charge of the work in America. Asbury was particularly disturbed by the immoral and unChristian character of slavery, declaring on one occasion that "The Lord will certainly hear the cries of the oppressed, naked, starving creatures."[37] The dynamic Doctor Coke ran into trouble many times be-

cause of his attacks on slavery in sermons and private conversations. Angry mobs threatened him at times, and re-
wards were offered to those who took steps to silence him.[38]
Freeborn Garrettson's preachments against the institution
provoked similar reactions. After freeing his own slaves,
he became an active opponent of the system. While preaching in Virginia and North Carolina in 1775 he "endeavored
frequently to inculcate the doctrine of freedom in a private
way, and this procured me the ill will of some, who were
in that unmerciful practice."[39] William Colbert and Thomas
Rankin were equally vocal in their criticisms of slavery
and the trade. The excitement generated by the antislavery
propaganda of such men had the effect of casting suspicion
upon all Methodists during the period of the American Revolution.[40]

The strong opposition to slavery on the part of the
early Methodists was caused not only because the institution
contradicted the principles upon which Wesley founded Methodism, but also because it was inconsistent with the goals of
the American Revolution. Thomas Rankin was perplexed by
what he saw as the paradox of a new nation born in freedom
while thousands of Africans were held in bondage. During
his many conversations with congressmen in the Philadelphia
area in 1775, he often pointed to this startling paradox:

> I found liberty to speak my mind with freedom and
> so far as I could see they were not offended. I
> could not help telling many of them, what a farce
> it was for them to contend for liberty, when they
> themselves, kept some hundreds of thousands of
> poor blacks in most cruel bondage? Many con-
> fessed it was true, but it was not now the time to
> set them at liberty.[41]

Methodist mission work among slaves was conceivably
hurt because of the antislavery position of the denomination
before and immediately after the American Revolution. Francis Asbury complained that gaining access to bondsmen had
been made more difficult because of the attacks of Methodists
upon slavery:

> We are defrauded of great numbers by the pains
> that are taken to keep the blacks from us. Their
> masters are afraid of the influence of our princi-
> ples. Would not an amelioration in the condition
> and treatment of slaves have produced more prac-

tical good to the poor Africans, than any attempt at their emancipation? The state of society, unhappily does not permit this: besides, the blacks are deprived of the means of instruction; who will take the pains to lead them into the ways of salvation, and watch over them that they may not stray, but the Methodists? Well; now their masters will not let them come to hear us. [42]

Asbury, Coke, and others soon accepted the fact that reaching the slaves through missions was easier when the emphasis was placed on conversion and personal salvation instead of human equality and freedom. Thus, in time they softened their opposition to slavery and ceased to attack it with great regularity and vigor. This increasingly relaxed stance was also reflected at the general church level. Between 1780 and 1800, the M. E. Church had taken a firm stand against slavery by passing resolutions attacking it, by vowing to discipline preachers who became involved with it, and by calling for its abolishment in statements issued in various editions of the M. E. Discipline. However, from 1800 to 1828, the printed minutes of the church did not reveal a single action taken against slavery. [43] Apparently, the church had slowly receded from the radicality of its earlier stance for the sake of maintaining unity within the general body.

In the latter 1820s, a militant phase of abolitionism began to engulf parts of the nation, and the M. E. Church found that it could not maintain a neutral and submissive position with regard to the slavery issue. Attempts at appeasing the southern element of the church by keeping silent on the issue would prove unsuccessful. Orange Scott, La Roy Sunderland, and other rising abolitionists within the church refused to let the issue die. Matters came to a head when the General Conference of the M. E. Church met in New York City in May 1844. Two cases involving slavery became the center of much attention and debate. Francis A. Harding, a preacher from Baltimore, had been suspended by his annual conference for his refusal to free several slaves acquired by marriage. The General Conference refused to honor his appeal and upheld the decision of his annual conference. The southern delegates were angered by this action. They were further outraged when Bishop James O. Andrew of Georgia was reprimanded for his failure to free slaves passed on to him from his first wife's estate. A strongly worded resolution was adopted ordering Andrew

"to desist from the exercise of this office so long as this
impediment remains. " Andrew's offer to resign his post was
rejected by the southern delegates, who insisted that slavery
was a civil matter which did not fall under the jurisdiction
of the church. Furious debates continued and when the conference adjourned on June 11, 1844, there was little doubt
about the prospect of a major split in the church along sec-
tional lines. One year later, the M. E. Church, South was
born in Louisville, Kentucky. [44] The body was to remain divided until 1939.

The Nature of the African Response

Africans responded in a traditional African fashion to the appeal of Methodism. An inherently spiritual and emotional
people, they had come from West African societies where
call-and-response, music, prayer, and rhythmic movement
and dance were acceptable ways of expressing one's emotions
and faith. Such African cult behavior was widespread among
Africans who joined the Methodist movement in this country.
In their journalistic accounts, early Methodist preachers referred to the intense emotionalism which characterized the
African response to their preaching. While on a preaching
tour in the vicinity of Philadelphia in May 1740, George
Whitefield recorded an incident which typified that response:

> Near fifty Negroes came to give me thanks, for
> what God had done to their souls. How heartily
> did those poor creatures throw in their mites for
> my poor orphans. Some of them have been ef-
> fectually wrought upon, and in an uncommon man-
> ner. I have been much drawn out in prayer for
> them, and have seen them exceedingly wrought upon
> under the Word preached. [45]

Thomas Rankin was far more descriptive in his accounts of the manner in which Africans responded. In 1776,
while on one of his preaching missions along the east coast,
he witnessed hundreds of Africans who were freely and collectively caught up in emotional excitement: "We saw nothing but streaming eyes and faces bathed in tears; and nothing
but groans and strong cries after God and the Lord Jesus
Christ. " He went on to write:

> I preached from Ezekiel's vision of dry bones; and
> there was a great shaking. I was obliged to stop

again and again, and beg of the people to compose
themselves. But they could not; some on their
knees, and some on their faces, were crying
mightily to God all the time I was preaching.
Hundreds of Negroes were among them with the
tears streaming down their faces. [46]

The "uncommon manner" in which Africans expressed
themselves at Methodist society and class meetings disturbed
some whites who considered dancing, rhythmic motions, and
other expressions of emotionalism grotesque and idolatrous.
The Africans obviously thought differently. They engaged in
weeping, groaning, shouting, jumping, and dancing because
of a deeply-felt need to celebrate the fact that they, too,
were subject to the saving grace of God. This kind of emotional outlet undoubtedly provided a context of meaning for a
people who could not easily find meaning in their existence.

Some of the early Methodist leaders accepted the ec-
static religious practices of Africans as evidence that their
faith was genuine and sincere. They were further convinced
by the noticeable changes in the everyday lives of African
slaves. For example, Rankin, while visiting a Brother Hyn-
son's house in Maryland in July 1775, was pleased to learn
that their slaves had been spiritually and morally transformed
by the Methodist style of faith:

> There has been a most blessed work among the
> black people in this part of the country. Mrs. Hyn-
> son observed to me, that before the Gospel was
> brought among them by the Methodist preachers,
> they could scarce keep anything (even under lock
> and key) but more or less was stolen by the slaves.
> Whereas, now, they could leave every kind of food
> exposed and none touched by any of them. I ob-
> served to her, that the Gospel in its power and
> purity could perform that which the laws faintly
> attempted to do. [47]

Evidence of such changes in the daily lives of Africans attests further to the nature and extent of the African
response to Methodism. It also illustrates the depth and
sincerity of the black Christian commitment as it was during
this age of intense black oppression.

The Rise of the Black Methodist Preacher

A significant development in the history of African involvement in American Methodism was the emergence of the black
Methodist preacher. This figure had appeared on the scene
by the middle of the eighteenth century and, in the course of
time, achieved recognition among black and white Methodists
alike. Often endowed with natural ability and eloquence, this
personality was occasionally given the chance to preach to
racially mixed congregations. At times he was allowed to
speak from the pulpit, but was often forced to address his
hearers from the floor.

        The first black preacher to gain eminence in Methodist
circles for his homiletical gifts was Harry "Black Harry"
Hoosier, who was born a slave in North Carolina around
1750. He became free at a young age and was con-
verted to Methodism under the preaching of Francis Asbury,
whom he later assisted as a traveling companion. He soon
accepted the call to preach and, through sheer ability, earned
a reputation as a dynamic preacher. He traveled extensively
with Asbury, Thomas Coke, Freeborn Garrettson, Richard
Whatcoat, and Jesse Lee. Harry was described by one contemporary as "a small, very black, powerful, keen-eyed
man possessing great volubility of tongue. " Dr. Benjamin
Rush, the distinguished Quaker, called him "the greatest
orator in America. " Thomas Coke referred to him as "one
of the best preachers in the world. "[48] Such compliments
can only be considered remarkable, especially since Hoosier
could not read or write.

        Richard Allen was another black Methodist preacher
who achieved a position of prominence very early. Like
Hoosier, he was known to accompany white Methodist preachers on preaching missions. He traveled with Whatcoat on
the Baltimore Circuit and accompanied Peter Morratte and
Irie Ellis on the Lancaster Circuit in Pennsylvania. Before
settling in Philadelphia in 1786, he traveled on various circuits in Delaware, Maryland, and New Jersey, frequently
preaching to both black and white Methodists.[49] Considering
the limitations placed on them as to function, movement, and
opportunities of leadership, Allen and Hoosier should be
ranked among the greatest circuit riders of their day.

        The names of Henry Evans and John Stewart also ap-
pear among that cadre of early black Methodist preachers.
Evans, who was born free in Virginia, organized a Methodist

Church in Fayetteville, North Carolina, as early as 1790.
Despite opposition mounted against him by the town council,
he continued to serve that church until his death in 1810.
Stewart, also born of free parents in Virginia, became widely
known in the M. E. Church because of his successful mission work among the Wyandott Indians in Upper Sandusky,
Ohio. In the face of bitter opposition from white traders, he
was probably the first Methodist preacher to achieve great success in evangelizing the Wyandotts. Indeed, he may have been
the first preacher of any denomination to attain success on a
high level in mission work among Native Americans. He
continued his work until his death during the second decade
of the 1800s. [50]

Other pioneer black Methodist preachers included William Anderson, Morris Brown, Daniel Coker, Absalom Jones,
Christopher Rush, Peter Spencer, Abraham Thompson, and
James Varick. Even though all of these creative geniuses of
black religion began their ministerial careers in the M. E.
Church, they became best known because of their connection
with the independent African Methodist movement which swept
parts of the country in the late eighteenth and early nineteenth centuries. [51]

Much of the authority of these preachers resulted
from the fact that they were tremendously important in shaping the spiritual destiny of their people. They gave their
people a vision of God and of their own humanity which kept
them from sinking into the abyss of hopelessness. Furthermore, these preachers had a great degree of African consciousness, and they went among their people advancing the
cause of race pride and African consciousness. This is
why they became prime movers in the establishment of Free
African Societies and separate African Methodist Churches.

Segregation in Early Methodism

One of the unfortunate developments in early American Methodism was the beginning of discriminatory policies and practices in its societies and classes. It is clear that from the
outset the issue of race was not a crucial consideration in
the acceptance of members. In Delaware, Maryland, Pennsylvania, New Jersey, New York, and Virginia, it was quite
common for black and white Methodists to assemble together
for Watch Night meetings, love feasts, testimonial services,
and other ceremonies. However, such assemblies were never

meant to suggest freedom and equality for black Methodists.
Most white Methodists did not assume that the freedom and
equality denied at other levels of society should be available
at the ecclesiastical level. [52]

As the number of Africans in societies and classes
multiplied, the tendency was toward segregation. Early
Methodist preachers made numerous references to this growing tendency in Methodism in their diaries. Benjamin Abbott remembered that Africans were restricted to the kitchen
area of the meeting house at one particular society meeting
he attended: "We soon fell into conversation on the things
of God. At the time of family worship, an abundance of
black people assembled in the kitchen, and the door was set
open that they might hear without coming into the parlor."[53]
In a letter to John Wesley, dated August 12, 1792, Joseph
Pilmore called attention to a similar situation: "As the
ground was wet they persuaded me to try to preach within
and appointed men to stand at the door to keep all the Negroes out till the white persons were got in, but the house
would not near hold them."[54]

The interesting note about such segregated practices
is that they existed in both the North and the South. Most
white Methodists simply refused to entertain the thought that
there was something terribly immoral and unChristian about
such social arrangements. It was always clear to black
Methodists that segregation in worship was contrary to divine
principles as set forth in the Bible. Yet some African
Methodists, displaying a high tolerance for the contradictory,
were willing to remain in communion with white Methodists.

To avoid the indignity of being segregated in Methodist
meetings, some blacks in the Methodist Church formed their
own classes and societies. As stated earlier, Methodist
preachers like William Colbert and Joseph Pilmore occasionally encountered all-black classes and societies on their
preaching missions. In 1780, four years before the Methodist Episcopal Church was formally organized, the Methodists adopted a resolution establishing the legality of all-black
meetings on the condition that "proper white persons" be selected to oversee them. [55] Such an arrangement was obviously designed to discourage discontent and rebellion, but it
also had a restraining effect upon black religious expression. [56]

Africans and the M. E. Church

The formation of the Methodist Episcopal Church did not take place apart from the active involvement of African Methodists. Harry "Black Harry" Hoosier, the outstanding black preacher, was among those sent out to call the traveling preachers together for the great Christmas Conference, which was scheduled to meet in Baltimore on December 24, 1784. [57] When this historic conference began, Hoosier and Richard Allen were present as representatives of the African Methodists. [58]

As the conference proceeded, it became apparent that the African presence would again be a critical issue. Question 41 of the Book of Discipline, which were raised before the delegates, read as follows: "Are there any directions to be given concerning the Negroes?" The answer was contained in the following statement:

> Let every preacher, as often as possible, meet them in class, and let the assistant always appoint a proper white person as their leader. Let the assistants also make a regular return to the Conference on the number of Negroes in society in their respective circuits. [59]

According to L. M. Hagood, a late-nineteenth-century Methodist historian, "It was the reluctance of some to accept the situation of Negro equality in the Church that led to the discussion of the question, 'What shall we do with the Negro?'"[60] It was clear after the M. E. Church had been officialized that white Methodists would continue to practice discrimination against their African brethren. Patterns of segregation, in the words of one Methodist historian, "not only continued but crystallized."[61] Separate galleries, balconies, and "nigger pews" were introduced in M. E. Churches in the North and South for the expressed purpose of seating black members. [62] Soon the situation became depressing to the point of causing frustration and anxiety among African Methodists. Signs of a movement of African dissent in American Methodism became evident as early as 1786, when Richard Allen sought to unite African Methodists for prayer and instruction in Philadelphia. In subsequent years, the movement spread to other cities as African Methodists united and walked out of white Methodist Churches in search of their own places of worship. By 1818, at least nine separate African Methodist Churches had been organized in Delaware, Maryland, New Jersey, New York, Pennsylvania, and South Carolina.

Many Africans chose to remain in the M. E. Church
despite racially proscriptive policies and practices. Harry
V. Richardson lists five reasons for this apparent preference
on the part of some Africans, all of which are open to question. First, Richardson suggests that some blacks chose
not to break with the M. E. Church and join the African Methodist movement because "in their beginnings the black denominations were small and unimpressive."[63] While it is
true that African Methodist Churches were small at the outset, it is doubtful that this was a major consideration that
compelled most Africans to decide against joining them.
After all, the Methodist movement itself was also small and
unimpressive from the start, but this did not discourage those
countless numbers of Africans who associated with it during
the immediate years after the First Great Awakening. Furthermore, it is difficult to understand how the African Methodist Churches could be so "unimpressive," especially when
one considers the problems Africans faced in the predominantly white M. E. Churches. Certainly, it would seem that
the African Churches were no less impressive than the white
M. E. Churches, with their segregated seating arrangements.

Second, Richardson contends that "the efforts at ecclesiastical independence on the part of two black groups
(A. M. E. and A. M. E. Zion) to many persons white and black
seemed ludicrous, to say the least."[64] Here he engages in
pure guesswork, neglecting to cite convincing sources to
support his contention. Some white Methodists undoubtedly
regarded the work of Allen, Spencer, Varick, and other
African Methodist leaders as ludicrous, failing to realize
that their racist practices were even more so. Most Africans viewed the work of these men as a daring attempt, but
to say that they regarded them as "ludicrous" is incompre-
hensible, particularly in light of the strained relations which
existed between Africans and whites in the M. E. Church.
If attempts at African ecclesiastical independence seemed
ludicrous, then remaining in the M. E. Church and accepting
the unwarrantable abuses meted out by racist elements could
only be regarded as ridiculously absurd.

A third reason for some Africans remaining in the
M. E. Church, declares Richardson, "was that separate meetings among Negroes, even religious ones, were publicly disapproved and often legally forbidden."[65] This statement
bears some truth, particularly when applied to the situation
in the slave South. But it is a known fact that in the North,
where the independent movement among African Methodists

began, more opportunities were offered for blacks to hold separate meetings. The record clearly shows that the followers of Richard Allen, Peter Spencer, and James Varick often met separately from the white Methodists long before they took steps to build their own churches. Some whites disapproved, but others went along with the leaders of the independent African Methodist movement. In 1800, the General Conference of the M. E. Church not only officially endorsed the separation of Allen's group from St. George's in Philadelphia, but also agreed to the ordination of black preachers who were affiliated with the movement. Whites in the M. E. Church in New York gave some support to Varick's movement. Spencer's church in Wilmington, Delaware, was built with the help of whites from the Asbury M. E. Church. 66 Apparently, some white Methodists were willing to support the idea of separate African Methodist Churches rather than to sit and drink from the same cup with black people.

Fourth, Richardson charges that many Africans refused to sever ties with the M. E. Church because "this provided an opportunity for wholesome association with whites, at least the most wholesome association possible at that time. "67 This argument is not at all persuasive. It is evident that the best opportunity possible for wholesome association during those early years was afforded when Africans got together among themselves and worshiped God according to the dictates of their own feelings. It occurred when they constructed their own meeting houses and determined their own spiritual destiny. That opportunity was not available in situations where Africans were confined to separate galleries and balconies, or where they were required to wait for communion until after the white Methodists had been served. Richardson, himself, acknowledges that "these discriminations were irritating and humiliating to the black members. "68 To follow this up with the suggestion that the atmosphere in the M. E. Church made for the most wholesome relationship possible between Africans and whites appears to be a contradiction of the highest order.

Finally, Richardson argues that the largest percentage of blacks stayed in the M. E. Church because "this church was one of the friendliest of all the major Protestant bodies toward Negroes, and was one of, if not the most vigorous and effective spokesman for Negro rights and freedom. "69 Even though the M. E. Church took an early position in favor of African rights and freedom, it acted, at the same time, to implement policies of segregated worship. Furthermore, by the time the independent African Methodist movement had begun in full-swing, the M. E. Church had receded from its earlier stance as an advocate of African liberation in order to appease the southern wing of its white membership. This change in direction was indicative of the vacillating character of white Christianity. Richardson, for reasons best known to himself, fails to point to the gross inconsistency which characterized the M. E. Church's position on equal rights and black freedom during the late eighteenth and early nineteenth centuries.

Contrary to what Richardson has written, it appears that those Africans who remained in the M. E. Church had enduring hopes that this church, in the spirit of John Wesley, would relinquish its increasing tendency toward racial discrimination and accept black people as the human equals of whites. Through great men like Wesley, Francis Asbury, Thomas Coke, and Thomas Rankin, Methodists had demonstrated in the past that they could accept blacks as children of God irrespective of their color and social status. Those Africans who believed in the possibility of a return to those days refused to give up on St. George's, John Street, and Asbury. They remained with these churches. However, their hopes were frustrated time and time again because many issues regarding equity and intra-church race relations would remain unresolved for years to come. Those Africans who left St. George's, John Street, Asbury, and other white Methodist Churches were convinced that they could only be free and happy in their own separate and independent churches.

NOTES

1. Richard Allen, The Life, Experience and Gospel Labors of the Rt. Rev. Richard Allen (Philadelphia, 1793; reprinted in New York, Abingdon Press, 1960), p. 29.

2. Leroi Jones, Blues People: Negro Music in White America (New York: William Morrow, 1963), p. 34. Jones' contention is clearly borne out by the works of African scholars. See John S. Mbiti, African Religions and Philosophy (New York: Doubleday, 1969), Chapter I; and E. Bolaji Idowu, African Traditional Religion (New York: Orbis Books, 1973), Chapter IV.

3. John Hope Franklin, ed., The Souls of Black Folk in Three Negro Classics (New York: Avon Books, 1975; originally published in 1903), p. 344. Du Bois is, with the exception of Howard Thurman, the only scholar who has made significant references to the deep spiritual anguish African slaves underwent in the New World. This spiritual trauma--the act of calling on African gods and finding that they were not answering--must have been inevitable. One gets suggestive insights into the nature of that spiritual pain by studying African-American folklore, especially the spirituals and folktales, as revealed in the works of J. Mason Brewer, William John Faulkner, Lawrence Levine, Sterling Stuckey, and others.

4. W. E. B. Du Bois, The Negro Church: A Social Study Done Under the Direction of Atlanta University (Atlanta: Atlanta University Press, 1903), pp. 2ff.; Melville J. Herskovits, The Myth of the Negro Past (Boston: Beacon Press, 1958), Chapter VII; and Newbell Niles Puckett, Folk Beliefs of the Southern Negro (Chapel Hill: The University of North Carolina Press, 1926), pp. 1ff. Similar conclusions are given in the works of Carter G. Woodson, Lorenzo D. Turner, Roger Bastide, Leroi Jones, Charles Long, Janheinz Jahn, Gayraud Wilmore, Albert Raboteau, Ulysses D. Jenkins, and others.

5. Du Bois, The Negro Church, p. 2.

6. Charles H. Long, "Perspectives for a Study of Afro-American Religion in the U.S., History of Religions, University of Chicago, Vol. II, No. 1 (August, 1971), p. 58.

7. John Wesley, The Works of the Reverend Mr. John Wesley, First American Edition (Philadelphia: D. & S. Neall and W. S. Stockton, 1826), II, p. 412.

8. Winthrop Jordan, in a monumental work, has shown how Englishmen, from the sixteenth century through the early years of the American Republic, tended to associate African religious beliefs and practices with "heathenism." Wesley was a product of his culture, and could not entirely escape this ethnocentric tendency. Even though he was not maliciously racist, he was nevertheless capable of promoting biases as unedifying as those propagated by John C. Calhoun, George Fitzhugh, and other American theorists of the nineteenth century. See Winthrop D. Jordan, White Over Black: American Attitudes Toward the Negro (Baltimore: Penguin Books, 1968), Chapter I.

9. In sharp contrast, Wesley's view of Native Americans (Indians) was not so liberal. He characterized most Native Americans as "drunkards, thieves, dissemblers, and liars," probably because they were not as responsive as Africans to the Christian missionary thrust. See Nehemiah Curnock, ed., The Journal of the Rev. John Wesley, A. M., 8 Vols. (London: Epworth Press, 1938), I, p. 407.

10. John Emory, ed., Thoughts upon Slavery in the Works of Rev. John Wesley (New York: John T. Waugh, 1835; originally issued by Wesley in 1774), VI, pp. 278-293. Interestingly enough, Wesley, in suggesting that people of African descent were capable of fulfilling a messianic role, was setting forth a point of view which later found popularity among black nationalist figures such as David Walker, Robert Alexander Young, Edward Wilmont Blyden, John E. Bruce, W. E. B. Du Bois, Paul Robeson, and Martin Luther King, Jr.

11. Ibid.

12. John Telford, The Life of John Wesley (London: The Wesleyan Methodist Book Room, 1899), p. 347.

13. Charles B. Swaney, Episcopal Methodism and Slavery with Sidelights on Ecclesiastical Politics (Boston: The Gorham Press, 1926), p. 1.

14. Richard M. Cameron, Methodism and Society in Historical Perspective, 2 Vols. (New York and Nashville: Abingdon Press, 1961), I, p. 53.

15. Donald G. Mathews, Slavery and Methodism: A Chapter in American Morality, 1780-1845 (Princeton, N. J.: Princeton University Press, 1965), pp. 5-6.

16. Curnock, ed., The Journal of the Rev. John Wesley, V, pp. 445-446.

17. Mathews, Slavery and Methodism, p. 6.

18. Emory, ed., Thoughts upon Slavery, pp. 278ff.

19. Telford, The Life of John Wesley, p. 347.

20. Ibid.

21. Mathews, Slavery and Methodism, p. 6.

22. Mason Crum, The Negro in the Methodist Church (New York: The Editorial Department of the Board of Missions and Church Extension of the Methodist Church, 1951), p. 11.

23. Quoted in Nathan Bangs, A History of the Methodist Episcopal Church, 2 Vols. (New York: T. Mason and G. Lane, 1838), I, pp. 63ff.

24. Thomas Rankin, The Diary of the Rev. Thomas Rankin, One of the Helpers of John Wesley (Evanston, Ill.: unpublished manuscript in the library collection of Garrett-Evangelical Theological Seminary, 1790), p. 219.

25. Bangs, A History of the Methodist Episcopal Church, I, pp. 63ff.

26. For brilliant discussions of societies and classes as distinguishing marks of early Methodism, see Cameron, Methodism and Society in Historical Perspective, I, pp. 35-38; and Frederick A. Norwood, The Story of American Methodism: A History of the United Methodists and Their Relations (New York and Nashville: Abingdon Press, 1974), p. 33.

27. David H. Bradley, A History of the A. M. E. Zion Church, 2 Vols. (Nashville: Parthenon Press, 1956), I, pp. 23-25; and Harry V. Richardson, Dark Salvation: The Story of Methodism As It Developed Among Blacks in America (New York: Doubleday, 1976), p. 36.

28. Frederick E. Maser, et al., eds., The Journal of Joseph Pilmore, Methodist Itinerant (Philadelphia: The Historical Society of the Philadelphia Annual Conference of the United Methodist Church, 1969), pp. 26ff.

29. William Colbert, A Journal of the Travels of William Colbert, 1790-1837, 13 Vols. (Evanston, Ill.: unpublished manuscripts in the library collection of Garrett-Evangelical Theological Seminary, 1837), I, pp. 5ff.

30. Allen, The Life, Experience and Gospel Labors, p. 26; and Richardson, Dark Salvation, p. 75.

31. Bradley, A History of the A. M. E. Zion Church, I, pp. 23-25; William J. Walls, The African Methodist Episcopal Zion Church (Charlotte, N. C.: The A. M. E. Zion

Publishing House, 1974), pp. 39-42; and Richardson, Dark Salvation, p. 43.

32.   Colbert, A Journal, I, pp. 5, 7, 12, 17, and 155.

33.   Quoted in Lars P. Qualben, A History of the Christian Church (New York: Thomas Nelson, 1942), p. 541, note 13.

34.   Leroy F. Beaty, "The Work of South Carolina Methodism among the Slaves," An Address Presented before the Historical Society of the South Carolina Annual Conference (November 26, 1901), p. 4.

35.   Allen, The Life, Experience and Gospel Labors, p. 29.

36.   L. M. Hagood, The Colored Man in the Methodist Episcopal Church (Cincinnati: Cranston & Stowe; New York: Eaton & Hunt, 1890), p. 29; and Minutes of the Annual Conferences of the Methodist Episcopal Church, 1773-1828 (New York: Mason & Lane, 1840), pp. 1ff.

37.   Elmer T. Clark, ed., The Journals and Letters of Francis Asbury, 3 Vols. (Nashville and New York: Abingdon Press, 1958), I, p. 293.

38.   Swaney, Episcopal Methodism and Slavery, pp. 2-3; and Thomas Coke, A Journal of the Reverend Dr. Coke's Fourth Tour on the Continent of North America, 3 Vols. (London: the author, 1792), I-II, pp. 1ff.

39.   Freeborn Garrettson, The Experience and Travels of Mr. Freeborn Garrettson (Philadelphia: Parry Hall, 1791), pp. 76ff.

40.   Norwood, The Story of American Methodism, Chapter VII.

41.   Rankin, Diary, pp. 149ff.

42.   Clark, ed., Journals and Letters, II, pp. 151, 284, and 591.

43.   W. D. Weatherford, American Churches and the Negro (Boston: The Christopher Publishing House, 1957), pp. 85ff.

44. Norwood, The Story of American Methodism, pp. 197ff.; and Richardson, Dark Salvation, pp. 59-61.

45. William V. Davis, et al., compilers, George Whitefield's Journals, 1737-1741 (Gainesville, Fla.: Scholars Facsimiles & Reprints, 1969), p. 420.

46. Quoted in Bangs, History of the Methodist Episcopal Church, I, pp. 11ff.

47. Rankin, Diary, pp. 149ff.

48. Quoted in Abel Stevens, History of the Methodist Episcopal Church, 2 Vols. (New York: Eaton & Mains, 1866), II, pp. 174-176.

49. Allen, Life, Experience and Gospel Labors, pp. 19-23.

50. Crum, The Negro in the Methodist Church, pp. 24-25; and J. Beverly F. Shaw, The Negro in the History of Methodism (Nashville: Parthenon Press, 1954), pp. 16-19.

51. Richardson, Dark Salvation, p. 170; and Grant S. Schockley, "Negro Leaders in Early Methodism, 1766-1966," Forever Beginning: Methodist Bicentennial Historical Papers (Lake Junaluska, N.C.: Reprint by the Commission on Archives and History, The United Methodist Church, 1968), pp. 45-46.

52. Gayraud S. Wilmore, Black Religion and Black Radicalism: An Examination of the Black Experience in Religion (New York: Doubleday, 1973), pp. 103ff.

53. John Firth, Experiences and Gospel Labors of the Rev. Benjamin Abbott (New York: Hunt and Eaton, 1801), p. 120; and Richardson, Dark Salvation, p. 64.

54. Maser, et al., eds., The Journal of Joseph Pilmore, pp. 26-199.

55. Minutes of the Annual Conferences of the Methodist Episcopal Church, 1773-1828, p. 12; and Dwight W. Culver, Negro Segregation in the Methodist Church (New Haven, Conn.: Yale University Press, 1953), p. 43.

56. Wilmore, Black Religion and Black Radicalism, pp. 103-104.

57. Allen, The Life, Experience and Gospel Labors, p. 13; and Harry V. Richardson, "Early Black Methodist Preachers, " The Journal of the Interdenominational Theological Center, Vol. III, No. 1 (Fall 1975), pp. 1ff.

58. Schockley, "Negro Leaders in Early Methodism, " pp. 45-46.

59. Robert Emory, History of the Discipline of the Methodist Episcopal Church (New York: G. Lane & P. P. Sanford, 1844), pp. 42-43; and Crum, The Negro in the Methodist Church, pp. 11ff.

60. Hagood, The Colored Man in the Methodist Episcopal Church, p. 13.

61. Richardson, Dark Salvation, pp. 157ff.

62. Ibid.; Culver, Negro Segregation in the Methodist Church, pp. 43ff.; and Wilmore, Black Religion and Black Radicalism, pp. 103-104.

63. Richardson, Dark Salvation, p. 149.

64. Ibid.

65. Ibid., pp. 149-150.

66. Charles H. Wesley, Richard Allen: Apostle of Freedom (Washington, D. C.: Associated Publishers, 1935), pp. 71-73; Daniel J. Russell, Jr., History of the African Union Methodist Protestant Church (Philadelphia: The Union Star and Job, 1920), p. 7; and Christopher Rush, A Short Account of the Rise and Progress of the African Methodist Episcopal Zion Church in America (New York, 1843; reprinted in 1866), p. 13.

67. Richardson, Dark Salvation, p. 150.

68. Ibid., p. 158.

69. Ibid., pp. 150-151.

Chapter II:

AFRICAN DISSENT IN AMERICAN METHODISM:
THE RISE OF THE UNION CHURCH OF AFRICANS

> We then saw that, if we did not let that church
> go, we might look for nothing but lawing, un-
> less we could comply, and let the preacher do
> as he pleased. For the sake of peace and
> love, and nothing but that, we all soberly came
> away, and we mean that all shall see that we
> want nothing but peace. We can appeal to Him,
> that knows all things, that we had no thought
> of pursuing this course, until we saw no other
> way; no one directed us in this but the Lord,
> and to Him be glory forever and ever.
>
> > --Peter Spencer
> > William Anderson[1]

A significant event for American religious history, and
for Afro-American religious history in particular, was
the rise of African Methodism. The movement actually began in 1786 when Richard Allen organized an African prayer
band in St. George's M. E. Church in Philadelphia. Seven
years later, discriminatory practices in worship compelled
him and his followers to leave St. George's in search of a
church of their own. [2] In time, the movement spread as
blacks walked out of white M. E. Churches in Baltimore,
Charleston, New York, Wilmington, Attleborough (Pennsylvania), and Salem (New Jersey). By 1813, at least six
separate African Methodist Churches had been organized.
Between 1813 and 1821, the movement assumed institutional
form with the organization and incorporation of the Union
Church of Africans and the African Methodist Episcopal and
African Methodist Episcopal Zion Churches. [3]

Though obviously influenced by the Wesleyan and
Methodist tradition, these separate and independent black religious institutions, because of the very nature of the black

37

situation in America, found a special or unique expression.
The mere organization of the Union Church of Africans, and
the A. M. E. and A. M. E. Zion Churches, was, as James H.
Cone has observed, "A visible manifestation of Black Theology. "[4] These churches began as "protest institutions, " or
"dissenting movements, " and by their very existence challenged a system of social arrangement which stood in stark
contrast to divine principles and the dignity and worth of all
human beings. Richard Allen, Peter Spencer, James Varick,
and the other black pioneers who took the lead in organizing
these churches were unalterably convinced that the God of the
Bible was opposed to racism. This was the key to their refusal to accept the abuses visited upon them by the white
Methodists.

These churches were also unique in that they represented a classic example of black nationalism--of black people building institutions to effect their own liberation. The
early leaders of African Methodism obviously believed in the
development and maintenance of black institutions. They
perceived that such institutions were indispensable if blacks
were to elevate themselves from a condition of oppression
and dependency to one of liberation and self-sufficiency. [5]

Peter Spencer and the Movement in Wilmington

Sometime during the 1790s a young black man named Peter
Spencer arrived in Wilmington, Delaware. Spencer had been
born a slave in Kent County, Maryland, in 1782, but had
been granted his freedom upon the death of his master. [6]
Being born in slavery and having watched his people grope
under the heavy yoke of bondage must have left a permanent
mark upon his personality. Yet he grew up in touch with
himself as a human being, and as a person of African ancestry. He soon found that Wilmington, at close inspection,
offered very little in terms of freedom and opportunities for
people of African descent. Blacks throughout Delaware were
subject to a variety of discriminatory legal and social barriers. From the time of their introduction into the state in
the early 1600s, they faced the brutal reality of slavery.
After the Dutch conquered the Swedes in 1655, more and
more Africans were brought to Delaware, and slavery slowly
gained social acceptability as Africans, unlike white inden-
tured servants, could be held for life. [7]

A small free black population emerged very early in

Delaware, but there is no indication that it fared any better than the slave population. Free black men frequently suffered flagrant abuses as they worked on boats between Wilmington and Philadelphia. A law of 1700 for the trial of black people signaled the beginning of more than a century and a half of discriminatory legislation against both slaves and free blacks. The law allowed severer penalties for black people than whites for certain offenses, forbade blacks from carrying weapons and from gathering in great numbers on any day of the week, and set up a special system of trial for blacks whereby, instead of the usual judicial procedure, they were tried and executed on the spot by six freeholders and two justices of the peace. [8]

Spencer's desire to achieve was not stifled by the situation of racial inequality in Wilmington. He enrolled in a private school, probably supported by Quakers, and received an education that was quite impressive in his day. In time, he became a teacher and a very capable mechanic. [9]

Soon after becoming established in Wilmington, Spencer affiliated with the Asbury Methodist Episcopal Church, "the so-called Mother of Methodism in the State of Delaware." [10] Africans in search of Christian light and truth aligned themselves with this church from the beginning. They were represented at the corner-stone laying ceremonies in the summer of 1789. When Bishop Francis Asbury, for whom the church was named, dedicated Asbury Church in October of that year, the black membership stood at nineteen, or more than one-third of the total membership. Harry "Black Harry" Hoosier, the dynamic black preacher who traveled with Asbury, had the privilege of preaching there. When Spencer joined Asbury, the black membership constituted a growing but forgotten segment of the church. In 1805, the number of black members reached about one hundred, accounting for nearly half of Asbury's total membership. Due to his leadership qualities, Spencer soon obtained privileges as a lay preacher. He and William Anderson, another black lay preacher, became class leaders for the black members. [11] These men provided the leadership and instruction that Asbury's black contingent so desperately needed in those early days.

Although the white members at Asbury had demonstrated their willingness to accept blacks into the church, this was not to suggest that they considered them their human equals. From the time the church was organized, As-

Peter Spencer (from History of the African Union Methodist Protestant Church, by Daniel J. Russell, Jr.).

bury's whites subscribed to the general custom of segregating people of African descent in worship. This early reference to what transpired at the dedicatory services at Asbury in 1789 clearly proves that this was the case:

> On the lower floor most of the 43 white members were gathered, thrilled with the eloquence of the occasion, scarcely believing that the church was really theirs, while up in the little gallery, not less interested and perhaps more demonstrative, were the 19 colored members who had cast in their lot with the despised Methodists. 12

As the number of black members increased, racial tension intensified. A regulation was adopted requiring black people to wait for communion until after the whites had been served. Such practices of overt racism and discrimination did not reflect well on the church, which claimed "to give to all men an equal right to a place during Divine Worship. "13 As early as 1800 there were clear signs that some of the black members were becoming more disgusted with the insults to their human dignity. They began to meet separately and autonomously in their homes. On February 6, 1805, the following notice appeared in The Mirror of the Times, a Wilmington newspaper:

> African Church--The people of color, of this Borough being desirous of building a house of worship, but not possessing funds sufficient, contemplate soliciting donations to assist them in the undertaking. For this purpose subscription papers will be shortly presented to the public whose generous aid they respectfully solicit to enable them to accomplish this laudable purpose. 14

The Exodus from Asbury

The racial situation at Asbury took a turn for the worst in June 1805, when the emotional fervor of some of the black members "ran so high" until several benches were broken on the main floor of the church. On June 19, Asbury's trustees issued several complaints, charging the black members with the abuse of church property. A formal allegation was worded as follows:

> Whereas, in consequence of meeting the classes of

black people on the lower seats of this Church, a
number of the benches have been broken, and the
house so defiled by dirt, etc., as to render it un-
fit to meet in, and if any longer tolerated, more
injury may be sustained. [15]

In response to this complaint, the following resolution was
enacted:

Resolved, that no black classes shall hereafter
meet on the lower floor of Asbury Church, and if
they refuse to meet in the gallery, the sexton shall
inform them that the door will not be opened for
their reception, and furthermore, the leaders of
the same are requested to respect this resolution
and govern themselves accordingly. [16]

This resolution forced forty or so of the black members, under the leadership of Spencer and Anderson, to take
a course of action similar to those taken by Richard Allen
and his followers in Philadelphia in 1793 and by the Zionites
in New York in 1796. They walked out of Asbury in search
of a place where "nigger pews" and separate balconies would
not restrain their efforts to worship God and to freely practice Christian brotherhood and sisterhood. Spencer and Anderson later described this event in words which perfectly
expressed their courage and careful defiance:

In the year 1805 we, the colored members of the
Methodist Church in Wilmington, thought that we
might have more satisfaction of mind than we then
had if we were to unite together and build a house
for ourselves, which we did in the same year.
The Lord gave us the favor and the good will of
all religious denominations, and they all did freely
lend us help, and by their good graces we got a
house to worship the Lord in. [17]

For a short time after leaving Asbury, this small
band of African men and women, in a manner strikingly
similar to the early Christians, worshiped in private homes.
They still considered themselves a part of the Methodist
Episcopal structure, and desired only to build a black church
that would function in that connection. They soon secured
enough money to build a church at Ninth and Walnut Streets
in Wilmington. [18] The new church became known locally as
"the old Stone Church," but was dedicated as "Ezion," a

name derived from Ezion Gaber, a town in the Land of Edom where Solomon's vessels were built. It was also commonly referred to as "The African Methodist Episcopal Church," a name adopted earlier by the Allenites in Philadelphia. 19 Frederick A. Norwood has shown convincingly that the background of Ezion was similar in some ways to that of Bethel Church in Philadelphia, Zion Church in New York, and other separate churches formed by African Methodist dissenters in Baltimore, Charleston, Attleborough (Pennsylvania), and Salem (New Jersey). The same process of segregation passed through stages to separate meetings and separate houses. The churches also shared a similarity in that they all remained under the tutelage of white M. E. Churches for some time. 20

Ezion was to operate as a "mission church" in connection with Asbury and under the auspices of the M. E. Conference. Spencer and Anderson were led to believe that the arrangement allowed both black and white preachers, authorized by the conference and approved by the blacks at Ezion, to exercise ministerial rights and responsibilities at the new church. The following statement was recorded in Ezion's deed record to guarantee black participation in church governance:

> And it is hereby further provided that none but persons of colour shall be chosen as trustees of the said African Methodist Episcopal Church ..., nor shall any person be eligible to the office of trustee of the said church but such as are received and acknowledged to be members thereof by the resident elder and trustees of the aforesaid church in Wilmington. 21

In accord with this provision, seven blacks were chosen to serve as trustees at Ezion; Peter Spencer, Joseph Nicholson, Frances Bailey, Jacob Morgan, Scotland Hill, Stephen Harris, and Thomas Brown. 22

For about seven years worship took place at Ezion without serious incident. By 1812, however, Spencer and the other blacks at Ezion found themselves confronting the same problems, legal and otherwise, that black Methodists were facing in Philadelphia, New York, and Baltimore. A white elder from Philadelphia named James Bateman, who apparently did not want to honor the agreement previously made between Ezion's blacks and the M. E. Conference, was placed in charge at the church. Dispute after dispute arose, sometimes over the rights of the elder, but often over the rights of the black members. A portion of Ezion's membership, including all of its trustees, came to disagree with the method of selecting preachers to preach at the church and was angered by the elder's efforts to control church property and finances. [23] The conflict over property control must be understood in the context of the Wesleyan and Methodist principle of lodging trusteeship in the annual conference. By seeking to control Ezion's properties and finances, and by insisting on whom he desired to preach at the church, elder Bateman believed that he was simply following the Book of Discipline of the M. E. Church. But he apparently refused to understand the complexity of the matter. Here the black members' willingness to control their own affairs ran into conflict with Bateman's understanding of Methodist polity. No one seemed to understand the other side or to find an acceptable compromise. Spencer and Anderson correctly diagnosed the sentiments of the majority of the blacks at Ezion:

> We thought that we could have the rule of our church, so as to make our own rules and laws for ourselves; only we knew that we must help to support the preachers that were stationed in Wilmington to preach at both churches [Ezion and Asbury], which we were willing to do. We then thought that we had the power to refuse any that were not thought proper persons to preach for us; but the preacher that was stationed in Wilmington to preach, told us plainly that we had no say, and that he must be the entire judge of all. [24]

The dispute would have been settled had Spencer and Anderson directed the black members to bow to the wishes of Batemen, but this their proud spirits could not brook. As Colored American reported less than three decades later, "they were not content to allow their white brethren to ride over them rough shod." [25] In the heat of the dispute, Spencer emerged as the main spokesman for the dissident group. His position was characteristic of early African Methodist leaders--not that of a fanatical dissenter, but certainly unwilling to compromise his dignity and freedom as a human being. He and his followers merely wanted to be respected and to worship their God with full liberty of conscience. When this was denied them, tempers exploded and the situation reached crisis proportions. Bateman moved to disqualify the black trustees and class members, and the two sides ended up in a Wilmington court. Spencer and Anderson later described the events as they unfolded in the winter of 1812:

> Then that body of us who built the meeting house could not see our way clear, to give up all say, and for that reason our minister said we had broken the Discipline and turned out all the Trustees and Class leaders, and never allowed us a hearing. This was done in December, 1812, and after many sorrowful times, and amongst all the rest a small party, the most of them strangers, that knew but little of the cause that we built a house for, told the elder they were willing to be governed by the Discipline, and do what he told them; and then things went on worse and worse, till at length, we were brought before the court, which cost us much loss of time and money. 26

Spencer's protesters did not win the case. The disenchantment, anger, and heightened awareness born out of this dramatic confrontation in a Wilmington court coalesced in a movement among the majority of Ezion's members for complete ecclesiastical independence. The indignities to which Spencer and his followers were subjected cannot but have increased their sensitivity to the centrality of racial prejudice within the United States, and particularly within the white churches of this country. Having a thirst for human dignity, personal fulfillment, and truth similar to that proclaimed in modern times by Martin Luther King, Jr. and Malcolm X, they withdrew in 1813 and declared themselves to be completely independent of the M. E. Conference. 27

A minority of black members, siding with the elder Bateman, retained the church property for the M. E. Conference. They witnessed a slight improvement in their relationship with Asbury and the M. E. Conference as time passed. The church was reorganized and two blacks, Michael Stirling and Ralph Harding, were named trustees. One year after the walk-out Ezion's membership, which stood at thirty-nine, was organized into three classes with Stirling, Harding, and Jacob Pindergrass as leaders. Pindergrass was licensed as a local preacher and placed as a sub-pastor over the black members. 28 After the death of Pindergrass, other black preachers were placed in charge at the church at various times, and the church experienced steady growth. In 1864 it was formed into the Delaware Colored Conference, which embraced black Methodist Churches in New Jersey, New York, Maryland, and Virginia. 29

Since the Civil War, Ezion has maintained a developing relationship with the M. E. (United Methodist) Church and has continued to progress in terms of growth and activity. Several small "mission churches" were organized under its direction in the latter nineteenth century. [30] The church grew substantially during the first five decades of this century, primarily because of strong black leadership. Projects aimed at the economic, educational, and political advancement of black people have been traditionally supported by Ezion. In the early years of this century, the church's leadership was quite active in the Colored Interdenominational Ministerial Union of Wilmington, which called upon the nation's colleges and universities to open their doors to black students in 1920. [31] In the 1960s and early 1970s, in the midst of a changing scene of social and political activism in America, leaders such as O. H. Spence and Felton E. May emerged to thrust Ezion to the center of the movement. In 1971 the church merged with Mount Carmel United Methodist Church, and the resulting body, Ezion-Mount Carmel United Methodist Church, came into being. [32] This church, which is currently a part of the Peninsula Conference of the United Methodist Church, still stands as a reminder of the struggles that Peter Spencer and a small band of black men and women endured almost two centuries ago.

The First Independent African Methodist Church

The struggle for ecclesiastical independence in Wilmington was essentially a lay movement, since neither Peter Spencer nor William Anderson were ordained clergymen. In this sense the Wilmington movement was different from those led by the Allenites in Philadelphia and the Zionites in New York. After the break with the M. E. Conference, Spencer and his followers moved rapidly to establish an African Church where they could, as they put it, "enjoy more spirituality and do more good amongst their own race. "[33] They purchased a pigeon coop from a man in Hedgeville, a small community in south Wilmington. "The old pigeon coop, " as it was called, served as the first place of worship for them. It was situated in the vicinity of Tatnall Street. [34] On July 21, 1813, a church site on French Street between Eighth and Ninth Streets in Wilmington was purchased from Thomas Gilpin, who was associated with the Quakers. By the first week of September, a building had been completed, and the Union Church of African Members was fully organized with due forms and ceremonies. The charter members could now sing with loud voices and high spirits the marvelous hymn arranged by Spencer:

> Let Zion and her sons rejoice,
>   behold the promised hour.
> Her God hath heard her mourning voice,
>   and comes to exalt His power.
>
> It shall be known when I am dead,
>   and left on long record.
> That ages yet unborn may read and trust,
>   and praise the Lord. [35]

The new African Methodist Church, established not very far from Ezion, was legally recorded at Dover, Delaware, under the Delaware law of 1787 which authorized religious bodies. This occurred on September 18, 1813. The trustees named in the Articles of Association included Peter Spencer, John Kelly, John Simmons, Scotland Hill, David Smith, Jacob March, and Benjamin Webb (four of whom were listed as "labourers" and two as "blacksmiths" in the Wilmington directory). [36] The Union Church of African Members, which became the mother church to a large number of independent black churches throughout the Middle Atlantic area, soon became an ecclesiastical compact with the addition of small congregations in New York and Pennsylvania. [37]

The new denomination was and remained essentially a Methodist Church with articles of religion, general rules, and discipline. The system of classes and class leaders, along with the method of trustee election, conformed to the Wesleyan and Methodist tradition. The earliest editions of the African Union Hymnal, assembled in 1822 and 1839, included numerous selections from John and Charles Wesley. [38] The hymnals also included hymns arranged by Spencer, which were put together to suit every aspect of religious thought and experience. There were some notable exceptions which set the Union Church of African Members apart from the Methodist Episcopal Church. The multiple conference system of Episcopal Methodism was adopted with the exception of the practice of holding general conference. Annual, district, and quarterly conferences were adopted, but there was no apparent need for general conferences. The annual big meeting, known as Big Quarterly, adequately served the purpose of a general conference in that it always attracted representatives from the various congregations in the Union Church of Africans to Wilmington for a weekend of business transactions, festivity, and celebration. [39]

The Union Church of Africans was Methodist in polity
with two major exceptions. The episcopacy and presiding
eldership were abolished because Spencer and Anderson felt
that such offices would prevent the practice of democracy in
the church. They had learned well from their experiences
at Asbury and Ezion and were determined to form a body that
would allow for the active participation of both the clergy and
laity in its affairs. "The preachers instead of being bishops
and masters," reported an early edition of Wilmington's
Morning News, "were servants of the people."[40]

The first edition of the Discipline of the Union Church
of Africans, compiled in September 1813, specifically stated
that the church's hierarchy would consist of one lay order,
called ruling or lay elders, and three orders of preachers:
elder ministers, deacons, and licensed preachers.[41] Ultimate
authority rested with the local congregations composing the
body in that they elected ruling elders and gave approval or
disapproval to the ordination of elder ministers and deacons
and to the licensing of preachers. Lay elders comprised a
central policy-making board in the church. Elder ministers
were similar to M. E. bishops in that they were invested
with the general superintendence of all the congregations in
the Union Church of Africans. Spencer and William Anderson were "set apart" as the first elder ministers. In time,
Spencer assumed the title of Senior Elder. His church retained the ordination of deacons, who could preach and bap-
tize in the absence of an elder minister, but could not administer the Lord's Supper or church discipline. Licensed
preachers merely had the right to preach. Both men and
women could function in this capacity.[42]

The style and title of the early Union Church of Africans are also suggestive of how this church broke with the
Wesleyan and Methodist model. Article I of its charter
specified, "The style and title of this corporation should be
the Union Church of African Members at Wilmington, Delaware." The term "Methodist," or "Methodist Episcopal,"
was deliberately excluded from the church's title probably
out of fear that it might suggest a link with the predominantly white M. E. Conference. Spencer and Anderson needed
added assurance that their people could have religious freedom without further encroachment and interference from the
white Methodists.[43]

The itinerant system of Methodism was rejected off-
hand in favor of the stationed pastorate. Spencer opposed

the idea of his preachers traveling from place to place covering circuits partly because of the undue burden this would
have placed upon their families and because such a system
would have compelled them to sacrifice all means of acquir-
ing property.   Instead, preachers in the Union Church of
Africans were encouraged to serve congregations zealously
without a set salary and without any limit to the period of
their service. [44]

The Methodist brand of connectional authority, which
placed all church property under conference control, was
abolished in the case of the Union Church of Africans.   Local autonomy was stressed more than connectionalism.   A
policy was introduced giving local trustees authority over
church properties and finances.   Laymen gained equal representation at all church conferences and meetings.   Under
this policy, other congregations could organize, own their
own property, and participate in every level of church government in a congregational-style polity.   By allowing for black
control of local churches, the leaders of the Union Church of
Africans gained what had been disallowed them in the M. E.
Church. [45]

After all is said, a major question surfaces: Did
Spencer and Anderson take the lead in forming a voluntary
association, or did they organize a connection?   It is more
correct to say that the Union Church of Africans had some
of the characteristics of both.   Its style of organization was
very similar to the accommodational or associational plan
adopted in 1801 by the Presbyterian General Assembly and
the Congregational General Association and to the plan of
union embraced in 1830 by the "Associated Methodist
Churches, " which formed the Methodist Protestant Church. [46]
Hence, it is understandable why an early source characterized the Union Church of Africans as being "neither Presbyterian, Episcopal, or Congregational, but from its origin
Associated. "[47]   Even so, each of the congregations forming
this body, despite having a degree of local autonomy, were
ultimately answerable to and under the authority of Spencer
and Anderson.   Thus, the connectional system was preserved,
although in a weakened form.

Spencer evidently borrowed from a number of traditions in planning the organization of his church.   The Union
Church of Africans amounted to an institutional blend of
Presbyterian, Congregational, Quaker, and Methodist influences.   The offices of elder minister and ruling elder seemed

to suggest a Presbyterian influence. The emphasis on congregational autonomy was clearly in accord with the principles of early New England Congregationalism. The custom
of accepting women as preachers and the idea of an annual
"big meeting," known as August Quarterly, were furnished
by the Quakers. The influence of the Wesleyan and Methodist tradition, already discussed, was more pronounced.
Despite being influenced by other religious traditions, Spencer
and his followers were Methodists, constitutionally and emphatically. They had been nurtured in the Methodist faith
and had a special affinity for it. They realized that the
Methodist style of polity and organization had been somewhat
modified in the case of their church, but the doctrines and
system of faith of the Methodists, as they understood them,
remained intact. [48]

Another subject to be considered is the degree to
which the Union Church of Africans compared to the other
early African Methodist denominations; namely, the African
Methodist Episcopal and African Methodist Episcopal Zion
Churches. The churches had much in common with regard
to doctrine. They were and remained, in effect, Methodist
Churches with the M. E. general rules, articles of religion,
and discipline. The early leaders of these churches were
in agreement that the Methodist ethos or form of faith was
more amenable to their people. [49] Less than three decades
after they were established, Colored American related that
"the tenets and discipline of the Union Methodist Connexion
are substantially the same as that of the Bethel and Zion
Connexions." [50]

In the matter of style, organization, and polity, there
were both important similarities and profound differences.
The charters of all the churches contained provisions that
limited leadership to "Africans and the descendants of the
African race," and that stipulated, "no person shall have
any vote, sway, or rule in or be elected a trustee of said
church but Africans and the descendants of the African
race." [51] The nationalist implications of such provisions
are unmistakable. Only two of the churches, the A. M. E.
and A. M. E. Zion denominations, included the title "Methodist Episcopal" in their names and Articles of Incorporation.
They also, unlike the Union Church of Africans, embraced
the itinerant ministry and the traditional Methodist system
of connectional authority.

The governmental structures of these churches provide

a basis for more interesting comparisons. Deacons and traveling preachers, orders of ministers in the M. E. tradition, were included by all three bodies. Their spiritual supervisors were equal in terms of influence and authority, but functioned under different titles. The Union Church of Africans, having rejected the episcopacy and the presiding eldership, applied the title "elder minister" to its spiritual heads. The A. M. E.'s, who adopted the episcopacy and abolished the office of presiding elder, chose the title "bishop" for their spiritual supervisors. The A. M. E. Zion Church officially accepted the presiding eldership, but used the title "general superintendent" in reference to its spiritual heads. In 1852 the word "general" was dropped. In 1864 the general conference of this church adopted the title "bishop. "52

Spencer's Involvement in Other Movements

The involvements of Spencer in the early African Methodist movement extended beyond the limits of his own church. Between 1813 and 1816, he and Anderson participated in a movement in Attleborough, Pennsylvania, which resulted in a separate African Methodist Church. 53 One can imagine the great sympathy he had for other movements which developed among African Methodists in Baltimore, Charleston, Philadelphia, New York, and Salem (New Jersey). Spencer remained at the vortex of the swirling concerns of those African Methodists who faced the realization that they could only be free in their own churches.

When Richard Allen called for a general meeting of African Methodists in Philadelphia in 1816, Spencer was among those invited. An editor of Colored American noted two decades later that the Philadelphia conference was planned by the Allenites in an attempt to unite all African Methodists who seceded from white Methodist Churches under the banner of the African Methodist Episcopal Church:

> It was desired on the part of many, at the time that the final separation from the white Methodists in Philadelphia took place, that the seceding brethren in all parts of the country, and particularly in Wilmington, Baltimore, and New York, should unite with them and consolidate a large and powerful combination. 54

At the outset, it appeared that all would go well at the meeting. On April 9, representatives arrived, with six delegates from Baltimore; five from Philadelphia; three from Attleborough, Pennsylvania; one from Wilmington, Delaware; and one from Salem, New Jersey. [55] As it turned out, representatives from Charleston were not able to attend, and the Zionites in New York declined to appear supposedly because "they preferred to go on by themselves." [56] Spencer was present as the lone delegate from the Union Church of Africans, but in the end chose not to unite with the Allenites. Reuben Cuff, the Salem delegate from Mt. Pisgah Church, also refused to join Allen's group. His church became a part of Spencer's denomination. The delegates from the other churches did decide in favor of union, but the large and powerful connection previously dreamed of did not meet with an unqualified success. [57] The reasons for its failure were never fully revealed, since no one kept a detailed record of what transpired at the meeting.

The critical question for this study is, Why did Spencer decide against union with the Allenites? Attempts have been made to answer this question. Levi J. Coppin, the Maryland ex-slave who became the thirtieth bishop of the A. M. E. Church and who lived in close contact with the Spencer Churches for a time during the pre-Civil War and post-Civil War eras, reported that "Spencer did not go with Allen in his movement because he opposed the itineracy." [58] Charles H. Wesley, one of Allen's biographers, alleged that "Spencer failed to agree with Allen and his followers concerning the episcopacy, the itineracy, and the detailed matter of the Discipline." [59] Milton Sernett has charged that Spencer "was rebuffed in his attempt to include the presiding eldership in the new organization." [60] Harry V. Richardson merely concludes, "Peter Spencer was not in accord with some of the actions in Philadelphia [so] he returned to Wilmington and tried to make his Union American Methodist Episcopal Church into a denomination." [61]

A careful look at the outcome of the Philadelphia conference raises suspicion that union between Spencer and the Allenites did not materialize for a number of important reasons, some of which have not been mentioned. First, it is conceivable that Spencer and Allen, as Coppin and Wesley have indicated, differed over matters relating to church organization and polity. The two men had different views concerning the episcopacy and the itinerancy and, understandably, could have disagreed on certain details of the Methodist Disci-

Left: the Rev. Richard Allen, father of the A. M. E. Church; right: the Rev. James Varick, first bishop of the A. M. E. Zion Church (from The History of the Negro Church, by Carter G. Woodson).

pline. However, it is unlikely that Spencer was rejected in an effort to include the presiding eldership in the new church, as Sernett suggests. Both Spencer and Allen were opposed to the idea of including the office of presiding elder in the church. [62] Richardson is certainly not wide of the mark in noting that Spencer objected to some of the actions taken by the Allenites in Philadelphia, but he is clearly mistaken in asserting that Spencer simply returned to Wilmington after the A. M. E. organizing conference and "tried to make his Union American Methodist Episcopal Church into a denomination." Spencer's church had already been organized and incorporated, and it was called the Union Church of Africans, not the Union American Methodist Episcopal Church.

Second, Spencer may have felt that it was more incumbent upon Richard Allen and the other black Methodists to join his movement. The Union Church of Africans had already settled upon a Discipline and form of church government. It would have made little sense to Spencer to abandon his church for the sake of uniting with a new African Methodist connection which would have to prove its chances of survival, growth, and development. Obviously there were risks involved. As a reporter of Colored American pointed out a few years later, "Spencer and his followers had no intention of unshipping matters a second time, but preferred to remain as they were. "[63]

Third, political considerations probably made a merger highly unlikely, if not impossible. It was soon apparent that all who joined the new organization had to submit to the authority of Richard Allen, who was strong-willed and determined to be its first bishop. [64] Such an arrangement would not have appealed to Spencer because it would have forced him to take a back seat in the movement. His authority and influence as the popular leader of his own church were well-established, to say the least. In reality, it would have been politically inexpedient to sacrifice his role and authority in the Union Church of Africans to follow Allen.

The tactics used by the Allenites to consummate the planned grand connection could have been a key factor. They had called for the Philadelphia meeting, constituted a sizeable number of the delegates in attendance, and apparently tried to control its outcome. Largely because of pressure exerted by them, a resolution was adopted requiring all who joined the movement to unite under the banner and style of the A. M. E. Church. It read in part: "That the people of Philadelphia, Baltimore, and all other places who should unite with us, shall become one body under the name and style of the African Methodist Episcopal Church."65 Spencer's decision not to join places in bold relief the possibility that he had problems with not only the style of the church (with its episcopal office, itinerant ministry, and system of connectional authority), but also its name, which included the title "Methodist Episcopal."

Finally, Allen's personality could have been unappealing to Spencer. Allen was undoubtedly a strong and important figure in the early African Methodist movement, but there is reason to believe that he was not an easy person with whom to work. He has been labeled "authoritative," "dogmatic," and "egotistical." His rise to the episcopacy, a day after the capable Daniel Coker had been elected to that post, may have been related in part to these aspects of Allen's personality. Coker had been forced to step down in favor of the man who had started the movement in Philadelphia and who had first called for the general meeting of African Methodists there. Charles Wesley has suggested that there may be some basis for the charge that Allen's personality was a factor in preventing unity and understanding among African Methodist leaders, "for he does seem tenaciously to follow his own views. Neither Absalom Jones nor Peter Spencer, nor the Zionists could turn him aside."66

After being convinced that he could not in good faith support the plan of union worked out by the Allenites, Spencer returned to Wilmington to work toward the further growth and expansion of the Union Church of Africans. The possibility that he may have made a mistake in not affiliating with the A. M. E. Church looms greatly, especially in light of the fact that the churches which sprung from his movement have never grown and expanded with effectiveness.

Church Growth and Expansion Under Spencer and Anderson

When the Union Church of Africans was incorporated in September 1813, the extent of its limits was Wilmington, Delaware. 67 By the end of the first year, the mother church in Wilmington had joined with a congregation in New York and another in Pennsylvania to start denominational connections. In 1815 new congregations were organized in Christiana and New Castle, Delaware. 68 There were five congregations in the Union Church of Africans when Richard Allen formed his ecclesiastical compact in Philadelphia in 1816. In that year, the Mt. Pisgah M. E. Church of Salem, New Jersey, a black church which decided against affiliating with Allen's group, was organized into the Union Church of Africans. 69 Between 1816 and 1836 congregations were formed in Welsh Tract, Delaware; Chester, Pennsylvania; Baileytown, New Jersey; Philadelphia, Pennsylvania; Summit, Delaware; and Pennsboro, Pennsylvania. 70 All of these congregations were started by small groups of free blacks who had very little in terms of organizing ability and financial resources. Hence, most of the congregations, which developed out of house-to-house prayer meetings, remained small and weak. Such developments were to have an enormous impact on the future of the Union Church of Africans as far as growth and extent of influence were concerned. 71

The early development of the Union Church of Africans occurred slowly and regionally in the adjoining states of Delaware, Pennsylvania, New Jersey, and New York. Congregations were irregularly and sporadically settled within a hundred-mile radius of Wilmington, with most being in Delaware and Pennsylvania. In Delaware, congregations were thinly planted mostly in the north, out from Wilmington near the Pennsylvania and New Jersey borders. In Pennsylvania they were largely concentrated in the south and southeast, in and around the city of Philadelphia. Very few congregations were established eastward into New Jersey and northward into New York.

In the late 1820s and early 1830s, the church almost succumbed to a host of problems. It continued to grow at a snail's pace. There was an inadequate supply of strong, dedicated preachers to serve the local congregations. Institutional weaknesses became more apparent and the church incurred a very heavy debt. When all seemed lost, the church was held together because of the diligence of three elements within it. First, Spencer and Anderson, the elder ministers, met the challenge in a reasonable manner. Frequent meetings with the ruling elders of various congregations were held, and rallies were sponsored to raise funds and to garner other means of support. 72 Second, there were a few devoted preachers like Isaac Barney, Moses Chippey, James Hill, Ralph Gilmore, and Daniel J. Russell, Sr., who were willing to serve the various congregations for almost nothing in return. Levi J. Coppin, who knew some of these preachers, wrote the following concerning the great dedication they displayed:

> His [Spencer's] preachers would work in the field
> all the week and preach on Sunday, sometimes after
> walking many miles, and only receive the few pen-
> nies that would be thrown into the collection basket.
> They were encouraged to be very "spiritual," with
> the idea that "the letter killeth, but the spirit makes
> alive." I often heard them preach during my resi-
> dence in Wilmington, Del., the original home of
> Father Spencer, and his church. 73

Finally, the female component in the church responded well
to the urgency of the situation. A group of loyal women
from the congregations walked from Woodstown, New Jersey,
to New York City in 1835 and met in the home of "Sister
Polke." Here they banded together and started their own
campaign to secure monies for mission efforts and the general upkeep of the church. Their efforts apparently met with
a measure of success and contributed to the survival of
congregations which were already a part of the Union Church
of Africans. This marked the beginning of the Spencer United
Daughters of Conference, a female conference auxiliary. 74

More immediately important for the development of
the Union Church of Africans was the question of Spencer's
and Anderson's authority. Although the two men were essentially equal in terms of their titles, and the privileges
and responsibilities which those titles entailed, Spencer clearly emerged as the more popular and powerful of the leaders.
He was apparently the better trained of the two, and his personality seemed to have been more attractive to most in the
Union Church of Africans. In 1837 Colored American featured a discussion of the Union Church of Africans in which
Anderson's name was not even mentioned. The following was
written concerning Spencer:

> The Rev. Peter Spencer of Wilmington is looked
> up to as their Presiding Elder. He is the Patri-
> arch of the connexion, having obtained this consid-
> eration among his brethren, more by his useful-
> ness, and zeal, and science, and fervent piety,
> than by any formal appointment to office. 75

Additional evidence of Spencer's outstanding reputation, influence, and involvement within his denomination was presented by one of his contemporaries, a Wilmington historian,
who wrote eight years after Spencer's death:

Daniel J. Russell, Sr., one of Peter Spencer's associate ministers who became well-known for his preaching ability (from History of the African Union Methodist Protestant Church, by Daniel J. Russell, Jr.).

> For years Peter Spencer, an exemplary colored
> man, was their ruler. His tact to govern was
> wonderful, and his influence unbounded. When
> death summoned him from his useful sphere, all
> classes of citizens lamented his departure. 76

The influence and leadership wielded by Spencer and
Anderson were not sufficient to deter their church from its
course of slow growth and expansion. Scattered regional
development continued in the mid-Atlantic area after 1835.
The A. M. E. and A. M. E. Zion Churches also developed
slowly, but the Union Church of Africans did so with even
less authority. Spencer gave the first firm statistics on the
church to Colored American in 1837, and they revealed the
following: 1) there were twenty-one churches having places
of worship erected, and three missions which had not yet
been organized into congregations; and 2) Delaware and
Pennsylvania had more than half the total membership. 77
The figures in the table on page 60 show how the development of the Union Church of Africans measured in comparison
with the A. M. E. and A. M. E. Zion Churches in 1837. Between 1837 and 1843, congregations and small missions were
started in Connecticut, Rhode Island, Springfield Township
(Pennsylvania), Oxford (Pennsylvania), and in the Wilmington
area. Isaac Barney of New York was "set apart" as a third
elder minister to assist in supervising the churches. 79 He
was given charge of the congregations in New York and New
England, while Spencer and Anderson supervised those in
Delaware, Pennsylvania, and New Jersey. Some Delaware
historians have claimed that Barney and Spencer were made
bishops in 1841, but not a single reference was made to
this in the 1852 issue of the Book of Discipline of the Union
Church of Africans, an historical note that cannot be ignored. 80

Both Spencer and Anderson died in 1843, leaving a
small regional denomination comprising thirty-one congregations. They also left behind many perplexing questions which
may never be answered completely: Why did the Union
Church of Africans grow and spread so slowly? How can
the strange pattern of growth in the Middle Atlantic region
of the United States be explained? This author does not
have all of the answers, but several factors seem worth
noting.

First, complications of origin interfered with the
usual course of growth and expansion. All of the congrega-

THE UNION CHURCH OF AFRICANS
(Union Methodist Connection)[78]

Presiding Officers	Conferences	Members
Peter Spencer (Wilmington)	Wilmington (Delaware-Pennsylvania)	887
William Anderson (Wilmington)	(New York-New Jersey)	376

TOTAL IN CONNECTION = 1, 263

THE AFRICAN METHODIST EPISCOPAL CHURCH
(Bethel Methodist Connection)

Morris Brown (Philadelphia)	Philadelphia	3, 476
Edward Waters (Baltimore)	Baltimore	2, 006
	New York	810
	Ohio	996

TOTAL IN CONNECTION = 7, 288

THE AFRICAN METHODIST EPISCOPAL ZION CHURCH
(Zion Methodist Connection)

Christopher Rush (New York)	New York	2, 147
William Miller (Philadelphia)	Philadelphia	737

TOTAL IN CONNECTION = 2, 884

tions in the early Union Church of Africans were small and weak from their beginnings and did not progress to any great extent with the passing of time. Some even became weaker due to mismanagement, poor planning, and insufficient financial resources. Conflicting interests often led to disputes, dissension, and even rivalries between the relatively autonomous congregations that made up the Union Church of Africans. These internal problems surfaced in a painful way when the controversy involving Ellis Saunders and his supporters came to a head in the 1850s. [81]

Second, problems of organization contributed to institutional weaknesses which, in turn, restricted the development of the church. Local autonomy gave individual congregations an excessive amount of freedom in making decisions pertaining to church properties and finances, thereby weakening connectional authority and control. The lack of an itinerant ministry complicated matters. Despite having a head start, the Union Church of Africans failed to move along the frontier into Western Pennsylvania and beyond the Alleghenies into Ohio and Illinois, as did the A. M. E. Church.

Finally, the dearth of vigorous leadership was a key factor. There is little doubt that men like Spencer, Anderson, and Barney were strong and charismatic leaders who proved themselves to be capable church organizers and builders. However, after struggling to get congregations started, they lacked the necessary support to keep them growing and progressing. There were a few strong and dedicated preachers aside from these men in the church, but certainly not enough to meet the challenge of developing a strong national denomination in that day. Furthermore, critical mistakes of an organizational nature were made by Spencer and his associates from the beginning. They exercised bad judgment in refusing to embrace the itinerant ministry and the traditional Methodist connectional system. By opposing the notion of a hired ministry, they decreased their chances of attracting young, vigorous preachers into the church. There was always an inadequate supply of energetic preachers to serve the local congregations. This problem remained to haunt the Spencer Churches throughout their long histories.

The Church and the Freedom Movement

The Union Church of Africans was born to serve the spiritual and temporal needs of a people who were misplaced, misun-

derstood, and despised. These people had special needs,
substantive and ritualistic, which only a black church could
satisfy. They were an emotional people who needed a context in which to express their emotions freely and collectively. Many of them could not read and write and did not feel
comfortable handling disciplines, prayer books, and hymnals.
They needed basic education as well as religious training.
Spencer had great sensitivity and insight into the nature of
those needs. Thus, it was no accident that he advocated the
same concerns that were stressed by the Negro Convention
Movement between 1830 and 1860--concerns such as education, temperance, moral reform, frugality, race pride, and
self-help. [82]

Four important aspects in the rise of the Union Church
of Africans gave it a special or unique character. First,
the denomination, in a way similar to the early A. M. E. Zion
Church, breathed life into and nourished a strong tradition
of lay involvement. This mattered much to black men and
women who were denied full entry into the mainstream of
American political and institutional life. In the Union Church
of Africans they could exercise a voice and control their own
properties and finances. Their political aspirations found a
measure of fulfillment as they conducted their own meetings,
served on various boards and committees, and held positions
as superintendents, trustees, class leaders, ruling elders,
and conference delegates.

Second, the place of women in the church was given
serious consideration from the start. Women had been a
very strong part of the Spencer movement from the time of
the Asbury walk-out. The thirteen women listed among the
organizers of the African Union Church were Margaret Allen,
Deborah Anderson, Hannah Benton, Amelia Butch, Maggie
Debberty, Lydia Hall, Sarah Hall, Ferreby Draper, Susan
Hicks, Grace Powell, Annes Spencer, Anna Trunn, and Ellen
Weeks. Six of these women were among the signatories of
the Church's articles of association. [83] The question of what
role women should play in the ministry of the church was
faced forthrightly. Being favorably impressed with the manner in which the Quakers had resolved the issue of women
preachers, Spencer and Anderson agreed that women who had
the divine call should be given equal opportunity with men to
serve as licensed preachers. The Union Church of Africans
became the first black denomination in this country to state
categorically in its Discipline that women could exercise this
privilege. The provision made in the 1813 and 1841 editions

of the church's Discipline was included in the 1852 issue of its Discipline:

> Concerning women preachers, the Quaker Friends have always spoken for us, that being their way, they shall always preach for us when they have a mind, and none but them. [84]

Thus, women in the Union Church of Africans were given an opportunity very early to fill a role that was not so readily available to females in the A. M. E., A. M. E. Zion, and other black denominations. There is no record of the number of females who actually applied for a preaching license in the Union Church of Africans in the pre-Civil War years. However, it is known that women such as "Mother" Ferreby Draper, Araminta Jenkins, and Annes Spencer did perform duties traditionally associated with ministry. They visited the sick, spoke at churches, offered wise counsel to the young, served as missionaries and church extension workers, and undertook exhortation and religious teaching in their homes. The importance of "Mother" Draper as a spiritual force in the early Union Church of Africans is best illustrated by the fact that she was mentioned a number of times by nineteenth- and twentieth-century Wilmington newspapers in that regard. "Mother" Lydia Hall, who lived to be 102 years old, was also mentioned in this connection by nineteenth- and twentieth-century Wilmington historians and newspapers. [85] All of these women were not only strong spiritual forces, but also instrumental in determining the general direction of their church. In 1861 they organized the Grand Body of the Daughters of Conference, a conference auxiliary designed to help meet the challenge of church building and maintenance. This society replaced the then defunct Peter Spencer United Daughters of Conference and was symbolic of the extent to which women were allowed to function within the Union Church of Africans in the nineteenth century. [86]

Third, the church took a strong stand against racism and slavery from the beginning. The A. M. E. and A. M. E. Zion Churches did likewise, and so did separate and independent black churches of other denominational backgrounds. Spencer knew firsthand of the sorrows and hardships of human bondage because he had served as a slave himself. Even after moving to Wilmington, reminders of what the institution was like confronted him. The Union Church of Africans was established only a short distance from a slave auction block, which was situated near Market Street in Wil-

mington. This was undoubtedly a source of great irritation
for Spencer. Everything he wrote suggested that he believed
dearly in human equality, freedom, and Christian fellowship.
This is why he could not remain at Asbury Church. Furthermore, he advocated the preservation of the family structure
and the right of every individual to own property, privileges
that were clearly undermined by slavery and the African slave
trade. [87]

Spencer was quite active in black and white protest
groups against slavery and colonization. The Mother Union
Church of Africans, pastored by him for thirty years, became a center of antislavery activities. In July 1831 the
church went on record for having sponsored a rally to attack
the colonization scheme, which was aimed at firmly establishing slavery by ridding the United States of its so-called free
African population. At this meeting of free blacks, Spencer
and Abraham Shadd, another black Delawarean who was active
in the Negro Convention Movement, gave fiery speeches and
declared, "We are natives of the United States; our ancestors
were brought to this country by means over which they had
no control; we have our attachment to the soil, and we feel
that we have rights in common with other Americans."[88]

Some of the local congregations in the denomination
joined in a lateral assault on the slave system by functioning
as antislavery meeting houses and stations on the Underground
Railroad. The Hosanna African Union Church, formally organized in Oxford Township, Pennsylvania, in 1843, but with
an older history as "The African Meeting House," was the
focal point of numerous antislavery meetings. This church,
now located on U.S. Highway 1, adjoining the campus of predominantly black Lincoln University, is known to generations
of black people as an important station on the Underground
Railroad. A tunnel underneath it, in which links of chain
were found a few years ago, served as a haven for many
weary fugitives. Frederick Douglass and Sojourner Truth
spoke on occasions in the Hosanna Church, and Harriet Tubman is said to have conducted one or more of her famous
"underground trains" along this route. [89] The mother church
in Wilmington was also connected to a degree in this underground freedom movement. For years this church was the
object of much suspicion on the part of slaveholders, slave
catchers, constables, and U.S. Marshalls because it was the
main point of attraction for pre-Civil War Big Quarterly
festivals, which were regarded as major excursions on the
Underground Railroad. The activities of the African Union

Churches in Wilmington, Delaware, and Oxford, Pennsylvania, on behalf of abolitionism were nothing short of amazing, considering that they existed so close to the institution of slavery. [90]

Finally, the work of Spencer and Anderson was an early example of black nationalism because they were actively engaged in the establishment of black institutions geared toward moving their people from a condition of oppression and dependency to one of liberation and independency. Like the early A. M. E. and A. M. E. Zion leaders, they fostered the ideals of self-help and group consciousness and solidarity. [91] Statements in the early Books of Discipline of the Union Church of Africans suggest that its leaders believed that the long road to freedom and independence was first and foremost the struggle of black people and that the outcome of this struggle depended heavily upon black unity:

> Let us be deeply sensible (from what we have known) of the evil of a division in principle, spirit, or practice, and the dreadful consequences to ourselves. If we are united, what can stand before us? If we divide, we shall destroy ourselves, the work of God, and the souls of our people. What can be done in order to effect a close union with each other? Let us be deeply convinced of the absolute necessity of it. [92]

Typical of Spencer and Anderson's efforts on behalf of black autonomy was the lead they took in building their own church. [93] Their decision to do so had nothing to do with a belief in racism or separation; it had everything to do with race pride and self-reliance. They accepted friendship and support from whites, but were determined to be self-governing. The demeaning and heinous treatment which had been meted out to them by the white Methodists convinced them that they had no other choice. Additionally, their people needed an "all-comprehending institution," as some have called it, which could be adapted to their own needs. [94] Both Spencer and Anderson understood the magnitude of those needs, and so did Barney, Ellis Saunders, and the other leaders who followed them. Through their part in organizing and supporting the Union Church of Africans, they showed their people that they were indeed capable of controlling their own lives and destinies. [95] The charter of the church evidenced a very definite sense of group awareness and acknowledgment of African ancestry, ingredients that are essential to any full-blown ideology of black nationalism. The body was "to be known and distinguished by the name of the Union Church of Africans, and by this name alone we and our successors in office may forever hereafter be so known and distinguished."[96]

This emphasis on black autonomy also extended to the building of schools for the education of black people. It has been supposed by some that Spencer was not progressive-minded in matters relating to education and that he was not in favor of an educated ministry.[97] This claim must be weighed against vital evidence to the contrary. Spencer constantly stressed the positive value of education for all blacks, including preachers, as long as it was not an impediment to the basic mission of the church, which is that of winning souls for Christ. Spencer opposed an unconverted clergy, not a trained clergy. He and Anderson impressed upon their people that the church should be used to exploit every possible educational medium, and they set out to organize a school in connection with each congregation they started. In so doing, they gave further proof of their conviction that black people must take primary responsibility for their own liberation:

> Some may make light of this small advice, but this we know, that we feel for our colored friends; and our white friends may try to raise up schools time after time, but we well know, that if we colored people do not unite and try to help ourselves, all that our best friends will do for us, will fail; and as this is the case, while they, our best friends are trying, let us try, and by their help, and we helping ourselves, and the Lord helping all, we shall be a people.[98]

In the thinking of leaders like Spencer, Anderson, and Barney, basic education had to be emphasized in conjunction with moral and religious training. Specifically, church doctrine and the Disciplines not only placed high priority on reading, writing, and knowledge of scriptural teachings, but also on chastity, piety, monogamy, and fidelity of family life.[99] On rare occasions, appeals were even made to white Christians for support in advancing the cause of basic and Christian education among people of African descent. In February 1837 Isaac Barney joined Christopher Rush, Timothy Eato, and James Simmons of the A. M. E. Zion Church, Samuel E. Cornish and Theodore S. Wright of the Presbyterian Church, and several black ministers of other denominations in New York in calling for:

> The active benevolence and sympathy of the Christians among whom blacks live, to be manifested towards them in acts of Christian kindness and love--in visiting them--inducing them to attend Sabbath School and Bible classes--and upon the preaching of the Gospel--collecting adults in evening classes to teach them to read and write--securing schools where children can attend--and by precept and kindness, making the parents to feel how important it is always to send them. 100

Insisting that "we look for assistance and protection, to plead our cause, to advocate our claims, " the black clergymen went on to declare:

> There is a work which the most exalted and untiring philanthropy cannot effect for us. Religion may prompt, intelligence may devise, and moral heroism may accomplish, but if we remain inactive or indifferent, the work cannot be done. The breach will be wide, and not only wide, but most dishonorable to ourselves. 101

The role of the Union Church of Africans in encouraging forms of economic cooperation among its constituents is yet another indication of how much its leaders valued black autonomy. Spencer was a strong advocate of the wisdom of practicing economy and of the need for people of African descent to pool their resources, physically as well as financially, to purchase land and buildings. Land ownership was for him the first step in the direction of economic security and freedom. The economic blueprint proposed by him for all who affiliated with the Union Church of Africans attached great importance to the necessity for race consciousness, corporate responsibility, and cooperation. That blueprint encouraged the following:

1. Be industrious.
2. Avoid dealing in lotteries.
3. Be prompt in paying debts.
4. Be saving with your means.
5. Deal fairly with one another.
6. Buy from one another.
7. Support one another in business ventures. 102

The economic teachings and organizing efforts of Spencer were intimately linked to his religious and nationalistic advocations for the amelioration of the black condition. Apparently, the emphasis placed by him on hard work, thrift, and the accumulation of wealth met with listening ears among some of his followers. It is worth noting that the properties and buildings owned by the Union Church of Africans at the time of Spencer's death were worth thousands of dollars. [103]

The Church After Spencer and Anderson

The year 1843 signaled the climax of a great era in the Union Church of Africans. In March of that year, William Anderson passed on to his reward. Exactly four months later, on July 25, Spencer died. For more than thirty years the two men had known and worked with each other in the general service of spreading the Christian Gospel and building churches. The news of Spencer's death caused great sorrow among his church people throughout the Mid-Atlantic area, and was the subject of much conversation throughout the entire community of Wilmington. The Delaware Gazette and The Delaware State Journal carried notices of his death which will form an enduring tribute to the 61-year-old ex-slave who became the father of African Union Methodism. [104] The Delaware State Journal, dated August 1, 1843, offered an assessment of the impact of Spencer's death upon his church and his people:

> The "Union" deeply deplores this loss which they consider almost irreparable. Peter Spencer has long been active in this church, exercising his great influence for the improvement of people of his own color, and acting with great decision and wisdom, in all the vicissitudes to which his charge were subject. [105]

The combined impact of the deaths of Spencer and Anderson left little hope concerning the future of the small, struggling Union Church of Africans. A serious vacuum had been created in the leadership of the church, and doubts surfaced as to whether capable leaders were available to keep the church united. James Hill and Ralph Gilmore replaced Spencer and Anderson, and Isaac Barney remained in charge of the congregations in New York and New England. Daniel Bailey, who had served as a deacon under Spencer, was chosen to replace Spencer as pastor of the mother church in Wilmington. Isaac Parker, a licensed preacher under Spencer, became Bailey's assistant. 106 By 1846 Hill had died and Gilmore had been forced into retirement, and the need for elder ministers had become crucial once again. In April 1846 Barney and a select group of ruling elders "set apart" Ellis Saunders, a deacon from the African Union Church in Christiana, Delaware, to assist Barney in presiding over the congregations. While Barney and Saunders were undeniably capable leaders, their work did not meet with great success. Only five years after Saunders became an elder minister, internal bickering erupted and eventually led to a schism in the Union Church of Africans which was never healed. The details surrounding this schism, and its long-term effects on the Spencer Churches, are treated in the next chapter. 107

NOTES

1. The Discipline of the Union Church of Africans for the State of Delaware, Second Edition (Wilmington, 1841), pp. iii-v; and The Discipline of the African Union Church in the United States of America and Elsewhere, Third Edition Enlarged (Wilmington: Porter & Eckel, 1852), pp. iii-v.

2. Richard Allen, The Life, Experience and Gospel Labors of the Rt. Reverend Richard Allen (Philadelphia, 1793; reprinted, New York: Abingdon Press, 1960), pp. 26ff.

3. Frederick A. Norwood, The Story of American Methodism: A History of the United Methodists and Their Relations (Nashville and New York: Abingdon Press, 1974), pp. 171-174; and Harry V. Richardson, Dark Salvation: The Story of Methodism as It Developed Among Blacks in America (New York: Doubleday, 1976), pp. 76ff.

4. James H. Cone, Liberation: A Black Theology (Philadelphia and New York: J. B. Lippincott, 1970), p. 59.

5. Norwood, The Story of American Methodism, p. 171; Alain Rogers, "The African Methodist Episcopal Church, A Study in Black Nationalism," The Black Church, I (1972), pp. 17-43; and Sterling Stuckey, ed., The Ideological Origins of Black Nationalism (Boston: Beacon Press, 1972), pp. 1-29. I am highly indebted to Sterling Stuckey for my concept of black nationalism. In a brief but perceptive statement,

Stuckey describes black nationalism as it is understood within the context of this study:

"A consciousness of a shared experience of oppression at the hands of white people, an awareness and approval of the persistence of group traits and preferences inspite of a violently anti-African society, a recognition of bonds and obligations between Africans everywhere, an irreducible conviction that Africans in America must take responsibility for liberating themselves--these were among the pivotal components of the world view of the black men who finally framed the ideology."

6.   Daniel J. Russell, Jr., History of the African Union Methodist Protestant Church (Philadelphia: Union Star Book and Job, 1920), pp. 5ff.; Jacob F. Ramsey, Father Spencer, Our Founder: His Work for the Church and the Race (Camden, N.J.: The General Conference of the Union American Methodist Episcopal Church, 1914), pp. 3-4; and The Delaware State Journal, Wilmington, Del. (July 28, 1843), p. 3. Russell and Ramsey dated Spencer's birth at "around the year 1779." The Delaware State Journal, a nineteenth-century newspaper which "had business transactions with him for a long time and to a considerable amount," and which was certainly in a better position to know the exact time of Spencer's birth, indicated at the time of his death that he was born early in 1782.

7.   John A. Munroe, "The Negro in Delaware," The South Atlantic Quarterly, Vol. LVI, No. 4 (Autumn 1957), pp. 428ff.

8.   "The Negro in Delaware: Legal Status," in H. Clay Reed, ed., Delaware: A History of the First State, 3 Vols. (New York: Lewis Historical Publishing, 1947), II, pp. 572-573; Pauline A. Young, "The Negro in Delaware, Past and Present," in Ibid., pp. 605ff.; and "The Kidnapping of Delaware Free Negroes," The Delaware Gazette, Wilmington, Del. (July 23, 1817), p. 3.

9.   Russell, History of the African Union Methodist Protestant Church, pp. 5 and 17; Ramsey, Father Spencer, Our Founder, pp. 3-14; and Thomas Scharf, History of Delaware, 1609-1888, 2 Vols. (Philadelphia: L. J. Richards, 1888), II, p. 730.

10.   Russell, History of the African Union Methodist

Protestant Church, p. 5; and Rev. John D. C. Hanna, ed.,
The Centennial Services of Asbury Methodist Episcopal
Church, Wilmington, Delaware, October 13-20, 1889 (Wil-
mington: Delaware Printing, 1889), p. 141.

11. Hanna, ed., Asbury Centennial, pp. 137-146;
John P. Predow, A Brief History of the Spencer Movement
(Wilmington: unpublished paper, The Predow Collection, The
Boulden Academy and Seminary, 1979), p. 1; and Carol E.
Hoffecker, Wilmington, Delaware: Portrait of an Industrial
City, 1830-1910 (Richmond: The University of Virginia
Press, 1974), pp. 74-75.

12. Hanna, ed., Asbury Centennial, p. 141.

13. Ibid., p. 147.

14. The Mirror of the Times, Wilmington, Del.
(February 6, 1805), p. 2; and Scharf, History of Delaware,
II, p. 729.

15. Hanna, ed., Asbury Centennial, p. 146.

16. Ibid.

17. The Discipline of the Union Church of Africans,
1841, pp. iii-v; The Discipline of the African Union Church,
1852, p. iii; and Colored American, New York (October 21,
1837), p. 2. Most of the black members remained at Asbury. Throughout the nineteenth century, the church maintained a sizeable black membership despite its racist policies and practices.

18. Deed Record to the Property of Ezion Methodist
Episcopal Church (Wilmington: New Castle County Recorder
of Deeds, June 25, 1805), C3, p. 226; Hanna, ed., Asbury
Centennial, pp. 173-174; Scharf, History of Delaware, II, p.
729; and Frank R. Zebley, The Churches of Delaware (Wilmington: the author, 1947), p. 103.

19. Russell, History of the African Union Methodist
Protestant Church, pp. 5-11; Hanna, ed., Asbury Centennial,
pp. 173-174; Scharf, History of Delaware, II, p. 729; Zebley,
The Churches of Delaware, p. 103; Deed Record to the
Property of Ezion Methodist Episcopal Church, pp. 226ff;
and Norwood, The Story of American Methodism, p. 174.

20. Norwood, The Story of American Methodism, pp. 171-174.

21. Deed to the Property of Ezion Methodist Episcopal Church, pp. 226ff.

22. Ibid.

23. Russell, History of the African Union Methodist Protestant Church, pp. 5ff.; The Discipline of the Union Church of Africans, 1841, pp. iii-v; and The Discipline of the African Union Church, 1852, pp. iii-v.

24. Colored American (October 21, 1837), p. 2; The Discipline of the Union Church of Africans, 1841, pp. iii-v; and The Discipline of the African Union Church, 1852, pp. iii-iv.

25. Colored American (October 21, 1837), p. 2.

26. The Discipline of the Union Church of Africans, 1841, pp. iv-v; The Discipline of the African Union Church, 1852, pp. iv-v; Colored American (October 21, 1837), p. 2.

27. Eldridge Walters, Historical Sketch of Ezion-Mount Carmel United Methodist Church (Wilmington: unpublished paper, Collection of Ezion Mount-Carmel United Methodist Church, 1980), pp. 1-2.

28. Eldridge Walters, et al., Ezion United Methodist Church, 1805-1970 (Wilmington: the authors, 1970), pp. 3-5.

29. Hanna, ed., Asbury Centennial, pp. 174ff.; Walters, et al., Ezion United Methodist Church, pp. 3ff; and Scharf, History of Delaware, II, p. 729.

30. Walters, et al., eds., Ezion United Methodist Church, pp. 3-5; Hanna, ed., Asbury Centennial, pp. 174-176 and 239-242; and Zebley, The Churches of Delaware, pp. 103-105.

31. Henry C. Conrad, History of the State of Delaware: From the Earliest Settlements to the Year 1907, 3 Vols. (Wilmington: the author, 1908), II, p. 791; Walters, et al., eds., Ezion United Methodist Church, pp. 3ff.; and The Evening Journal, Wilmington, Del. (April 28, 1920), p. 6.

32. Walters, Historical Sketch of Ezion-Mount Carmel United Methodist Church, pp. 1-2; James Davis, et al., compilers, Ten Years Later: The Merger of the Delaware and Peninsula Conferences (New York: The National Division, Board of Global Ministries, The United Methodist Church, 1976), pp. 1ff.; and Norwood, The Story of American Methodism, pp. 169-172.

33. Hanna, ed., Asbury Centennial, p. 178.

34. Ibid., p. 173; and "The Mother A. U. M. P. Church," The Vawter's Day Booklet (Wilmington: T. E. Bolden, printer, 1947), p. 5.

35. Deed Record to the Property of the African Union Church in Wilmington, State of Delaware (Wilmington: The New Castle County Recorder of Deeds, July 21, 1813), N6, pp. 506ff.; Ramsey, Father Spencer, Our Founder, p. 7; and Russell, History of the African Union Methodist Protestant Church, p. 9.

36. Articles of Association of the Union Church of African Members (Wilmington, 1813), pp. 1-6; Incorporation in the Office of Recording Deeds, New Castle, Del., Book M, Vol. III, p. 470; and John A. Munroe, Colonial Delaware: A History (Millwood, N. Y.: Kto Press, 1959), p. 194; A Directory and Register for the Year 1814 ... of the Borough of Wilmington and Brandywine (n.p.: R. Porter, 1814), pp. 45-52.

37. Hoffecker, Wilmington, Delaware: Portrait of an Industrial City, pp. 75-76; and Lewis V. Baldwin, "The A. U. M. P. and U. A. M. E. Churches: An Unexplored Area of Black Methodism," Methodist History, Vol. XIX, No. 3 (April 1981), pp. 175-178.

38. The Discipline of the Union Church of Africans, 1841, pp. 7ff.; The Discipline of the African Union Church, 1852, pp. 8ff.; Peter Spencer, compiler, The African Union Hymn-Book, Collected from Different Authors (Wilmington: Porter & Naff, 1839), pp. 1ff.; and The Morning News, Wilmington, Del. (August 26, 1889), pp. 1 and 8.

39. The Discipline of the Union Church of Africans, 1841, pp. 80-84; The Discipline of the African Union Church, 1852, pp. 86-91; and The Morning News (August 27, 1883), p. 1.

40. The Morning News (August 26, 1889), pp. 7-8; and Colored American (October 21, 1837), p. 2.

41. Excerpts from the Discipline of the Union Church of African Members in Wilmington, State of Delaware, 1813, quoted in The Case of the Union Church of Africans, in Wilmington, Before the Superior Court of New Castle County, Comprising the Petition of Ellis Saunders for a Mandamus, The Return Thereto; Brief Notes of the Argument and Re-Argument of Counsel, and the Final Decision of the Court Awarding the Mandamus, 1852-53 (Wilmington: Henry Eckel, 1855), pp. 3-5.

42. Ibid.; and The Discipline of the African Union Church, 1852, pp. 52-64, 79-83, 96-100, 117, and 119-121. The sources are not clear as to when, where, and how Spencer and Anderson were ordained. The assumption is that they were. Their being "set apart" may well have reference to their ordination.

43. Articles of Association of the Union Church of African Members, 1813, pp. 1-2; and Incorporation in the Office for Recording Deeds, III, p. 470.

44. The Discipline of the African Union Church, 1852, pp. 98-100; and Matthew Simpson, ed., Cyclopaedia of Methodism Embracing Sketches of Its Rise, Progress and Present Condition, with Biographical Notices and Numerous Illustrations (Philadelphia: Everts & Stewart, 1878), pp. 876-877.

45. The Discipline of the African Union Church, 1852, pp. 84-85; and Simpson, ed., Cyclopaedia of Methodism, pp. 876-877.

46. The Discipline of the African Union Church, 1852, pp. 79-85; and The Case of the Union Church of Africans, 1852-53, pp. 6 and 16. This plan, adopted by the Presbyterian General Assembly and the Congregational General Association, was aimed at supplying the pulpits of pioneer congregations without a minister of their own denomination. After the American Revolution there began a considerable immigration into Western New York and the Old Northwest Territory. Many of those pioneers were of Presbyterian and Congregational backgrounds and lacked pastoral care. In view of this, and of the similarities between these denominations, the plan was approved and put into effect.

47. The Case of the Union Church of Africans, 1852-53, p. 16.

48. The Morning News (August 26, 1889), pp. 1 and 8.

49. Allen, The Life, Experience and Gospel Labors, p. 29; The Discipline of the Union Church of Africans, 1841, pp. 11-v; The Morning News (August 26, 1889), pp. 1 and 8; and Colored American (October 21, 1837), p. 2.

50. Colored American (May 20, 1837), p. 2.

51. Articles of Association of the Union Church of African Members, 1813, pp. 1-6; Carol V. R. George, Segregated Sabbaths: Richard Allen and the Rise of Independent Black Churches, 1760-1840 (New York and London: Oxford University Press, 1973), p. 67; and Colored American (May 20, 1837), p. 2.

52. Richardson, Dark Salvation, p. 302, note 45.

53. Gayraud S. Wilmore, Black Religion and Black Radicalism: An Examination of the Black Experience in Religion (New York: Doubleday, 1973), p. 115.

54. Colored American (October 21, 1837), p. 2.

55. Norwood, The Story of American Methodism, p. 171; and Richardson, Dark Salvation, p. 80.

56. Colored American (October 21, 1837), p. 2.

57. Norwood, The Story of American Methodism, pp. 171-174; and Richardson, Dark Salvation, pp. 80-84.

58. Levi J. Coppin, Unwritten History (Philadelphia: The A. M. E. Book Concern, 1919), pp. 264-265.

59. Charles H. Wesley, Richard Allen: Apostle of Freedom (Washington, D. C.: Associated Publishers, 1935), p. 151.

60. Milton C. Sernett, Black Religion and American Evangelicalism: White Protestants, Plantation Missions, and the Flowering of Negro Christianity, 1787-1865 (Metuchen, N. J.: Scarecrow Press, 1975), p. 123.

61. Richardson, Dark Salvation, p. 84.

62. The Morning News (August 26, 1889), pp. 1 and 7-8; and Norwood, The Story of American Methodism, p. 171.

63. Colored American (October 21, 1837), p. 2.

64. The Reverend Irene C. Dutton, a U. A. M. E. Church historian and pastor of the Mother U. A. M. E. Church in Wilmington, Delaware, contends that Spencer participated in "the election of Daniel Coker and Richard Allen to the posts of Bishop at the first convention (organic convention)-- April, 1816, three years after the founding of the Union Church of Africans." See Dutton, Our Church in Search of Itself: A Brief History (Wilmington: An unpublished paper presented at the 166th Annual Conference of the First and Fourth Districts of the U. A. M. E. Church, May 1-6, 1979), p. 3. The possibility that Spencer may have been involved in these activities deserves consideration, but no confirmation of this has been found.

65. Daniel A. Payne, History of the African Methodist Episcopal Church (Nashville: The A. M. E. Book Concern, 1891), p. 14.

66. Wesley, Richard Allen: Apostle of Freedom, pp. 152-153.

67. The Discipline of the African Union Church, 1852, p. 6.

68. Our Heritage: The History of the Union American Methodist Episcopal Church (Hackensack, N. J.: Custombook, 1973), pp. 12 and 34.

69. Ibid.; Articles of Association of the Union Church of African Members, 1813, pp. 5-6; and Colored American (October 21, 1837), p. 2.

70. Zebley, The Churches of Delaware, p. 172; Our Heritage, p. 20; and Norwood, The Story of American Methodism, p. 171.

71. Our Heritage, pp. 13-17; Conrad, History of the State of Delaware, II, p. 792; Scharf, History of Delaware, II, p. 730; Zebley, The Churches of Delaware, p. 104; The Discipline of the African Union Church, 1852, pp. 6-7; The Case of the Union Church of Africans, 1852-53, p. 5; and

Francis A. Cooch, Little Known History of Newark, Delaware and its Environs (Newark, Del.: The Press of Kells, 1936), p. 32.

72. Predow, A Brief History of the Spencer Movement, pp. 3-5.

73. Coppin, Unwritten History, pp. 264-265.

74. Predow, A Brief History of the Spencer Movement, pp. 2-4; and The Discipline of the Union American Methodist Episcopal Church (Wilmington: T. E. Bolden, printer, 1942), pp. 109-110.

75. Colored American (October 21, 1837), p. 2.

76. Elizabeth Montgomery, Wilmington: Reminiscences of Familiar Village Tales, Ancient and New (Cotton Port, La.: Polyanthos, 1971; originally published in 1851 by T. K. Collins, Jr., Philadelphia), p. 252.

77. Colored American (October 21, 1837), p. 2.

78. Colored American (May 20, 1837), p. 2; Colored American (October 21, 1837), p. 2; and Colored American (October 14, 1837), p. 2.

79. The Case of the Union Church of Africans, 1852-53, pp. 3ff.

80. See Wilson L. Bevan, ed., History of Delaware: Past and Present, 2 Vols. (New York: Lewis Historical Publishing, 1929), p. 740; Scharf, History of Delaware, II, p. 730; and Conrad, History of the State of Delaware, II, p. 792.

81. Predow, A Brief History of the Spencer Movement, pp. 3-5.

82. Articles of Association of the Union Church of African Members, 1813, pp. 1-6; Hanna, ed., Asbury Centennial, p. 178; and The Discipline of the American Union Church, 1852, pp. iii-v and 103-105.

83. Articles of Association of the Union Church of African Members, 1813, pp. 5-6; Ramsey, Father Spencer, Our Founder, p. 7; and Russell, History of the African Union Methodist Protestant Church, pp. 8-9.

84. The Discipline of the African Union Church, 1852, p. 100.

85. The Discipline of the Union Church of Africans, 1841, p. 67; Minutes of the Regular Monthly Meeting of the Elders of the African Union Church in Wilmington, Delaware, July 8, 1862 (Wilmington: unpublished accounts housed in the Historical Society of Delaware, 1862), pp. 1-2; Scharf, History of Delaware, I, pp. 214ff.; The Delaware Tribune, Wilmington, Del. (May 28, 1868), p. 3; and The Discipline of the African Union Church, 1852, pp. 100ff. Ferreby Draper was referred to at the time of her death in 1868 as "one of the early saints of the church." See The Morning News (August 26, 1889), pp. 1 and 8.

86. Constitution and By-Laws of the Grand Body of the Daughters of Conference of the A. U. F. C. M. P. Church (Wilmington: T. E. Bolden, printer, 1935), pp. 3-4.

87. The Discipline of the Union Church of Africans, 1841, pp. iii-v; The Discipline of the African Union Church, 1852, pp. iii-vi; Spencer, compiler, The African Union Hymn-Book, 1839, pp. i-iv; Colored American (October 21, 1837), p. 2; Ramsey, Father Spencer, Our Founder, pp. 9ff.; and Russell, History of the African Union Methodist Protestant Church, pp. 13-15.

88. W. L. Garrison, Thoughts on African Colonization (Boston: Garrison and Knapp, 1832), pp. 36-40; "The Wilmington Union Colonization Society Asks the General Assembly to Approve Its Objectives," Legislative Papers (Dover, Del.: Hall of Records, 1827); Carol E. Hoffecker, Delaware: A Bicentennial History (New York: W. W. Norton, 1977), pp. 98-99; and Anna T. Lincoln, Wilmington, Delaware: Three Centuries Under Four Flags, 1609-1937 (Rutland, Vt.: Tuttle, 1937), p. 150.

89. Horace Mann Bond, Education for Freedom: A History of Lincoln University, Pennsylvania (Oxford, Pa.: Lincoln University Press, 1976), pp. 126-129, 142, 197, 210, 225, and 238; and Carol E. Cotman, compiler, "Hosanna African Union Methodist Protestant Church," Link with Lincoln: Admissions Newsletter (Oxford, Pa.: Lincoln University Press, 1979), p. 2; and David McBride and Carol Oblinger, eds., Pennsylvania Oral History Newsletter, 2 Vols. (Harrisburg, Pa.: The Historical and Museum Commission, 1978), II, No. 2, pp. 8-9.

90. The Morning News (August 26, 1889), pp. 1 and 8. Delaware, one of the states occupying the borderline between the free and slave states, remained a slave state throughout the antebellum period.

91. Norwood, The Story of American Methodism, p. 171; Rogers, "The African Methodist Episcopal Church, A Study in Black Nationalism," pp. 17-43; Stuckey, ed., The Ideological Origins of Black Nationalism, pp. 1-29; and Hanna, ed., Asbury Centennial, p. 178.

92. The Discipline of the Union Church of Africans, 1841, pp. iii-v and 80ff.; and The Discipline of the African Union Church, 1852, pp. 104-105.

93. The establishment of black institutions or infrastructures for the liberation of people of African descent is a major theme in antebellum black literature such as David Walker's Appeal in Four Articles and Robert Alexander Young's Ethiopian Manifesto. Both of these pieces were issued in 1829.

94. Carter G. Woodson, "The Negro Church, An All-Comprehending Institution," The Negro History Bulletin, Vol. III, No. 1 (October, 1939), p. 7; and Sernett, Black Religion and American Evangelicalism, pp. 19-20.

95. Russell, History of the African Union Methodist Protestant Church, p. 11; and Colored American (October 21, 1837), p. 2.

96. Articles of Association of the Union Church of African Members, 1813, pp. 1-2.

97. See John M. Brown, "Richard Allen and His Co-adjutors," Repository of Religion and Literature, Vol. III, No. 1 (January 1861), p. 1. Brown was elected to the episcopacy of the A. M. E. Church in 1868. For a more recent account of Spencer's alleged reputation in these matters, see Sernett, Black Religion and American Evangelicalism, p. 145. Those who have made this claim regarding the early leaders of the Union Church of Africans seemed unmindful of the fact that white Methodists were also slow in responding to the need for a trained clergy, and so were the A. M. E. and A. M. E. Zion Churches. Only one theological school existed for the training of white preachers in the M. E. Church prior to 1850, and that institution, located in Concord, New

Hampshire, was not strategically situated to benefit the vast majority of preachers. Most institutions organized by the A. M. E. and A. M. E. Zion Churches for this purpose were post-Civil War developments. See Frederick A. Norwood, From Dawn to Midday at Garrett (Evanston, Ill.: Garrett-Evangelical Theological Seminary, 1978), pp. 5-6.

98. The Discipline of the Union Church of Africans, 1841, pp. 80ff.; and The Discipline of the African Union Church, 1852, pp. 104-105 and 115-117.

99. The Discipline of the Union Church of Africans, 1841, pp. 80ff.; The Discipline of the African Union Church, 1852, pp. 102-104; Ramsey, Father Spencer, Our Founder, pp. 11-13; and Russell, History of the African Union Methodist Protestant Church, pp. 13-15.

100. Colored American (February 18, 1837), p. 2; and William J. Walls, The African Methodist Episcopal Zion Church (Charlotte, N. C.: A. M. E. Zion Publishing House, 1974), p. 334.

101. Colored American (February 18, 1837), p. 2; and Walls, The African Methodist Episcopal Zion Church, pp. 334.

102. Articles of Association of the Union Church of African Members, 1813, pp. 1-6; The Discipline of the Union Church of Africans, 1841, pp. 80ff.; The Discipline of the African Union Church, 1852, pp. 84-85 and 102-107; and Ramsey, Father Spencer, Our Founder, pp. 11-13.

103. Predow, A Brief History of the Spencer Movement, pp. 3-5.

104. The Delaware Gazette (August 4, 1843), p. 2; and The Delaware State Journal (July 28, 1843), p. 3.

105. The Delaware State Journal (August 1, 1843), p. 3.

106. The Case of the Union Church of Africans, 1852-53, pp. 4-5; and Scharf, History of Delaware, II, p. 730.

107. The Case of the Union Church of Africans, 1852-53, Bevan, ed., History of Delaware, II, pp. 729-731; Conrad, History of the State of Delaware, II, pp. 790-792; and Scharf, History of Delaware, II, pp. 730-732.

Chapter III:

DIVISION IN THE UNION CHURCH OF AFRICANS:
THE UNION AMERICAN METHODIST
EPISCOPAL CHURCH

> Your petitioner showeth that by virtue of his
> office of elder minister, and according to the
> usages and discipline of said church, it is his
> duty and right to preach in the said Union
> Church in Wilmington, whenever he may see
> proper so to do, and to administer the ordi-
> nances and discipline thereof, and to exercise
> a pastoral charge over the same. Yet your
> petitioner humbly showeth that he has by the
> present Trustees of said church above named
> been forcibly excluded from said church, and
> debarred and prevented from performing the
> duties and exercising the rights above stated
> as pertaining to his said office, and that he
> is now so excluded, debarred and prevented.
> --Ellis Saunders[1]

All of the early African Methodist Churches demonstrated a
common tendency to contention, rivalry, and schism. Personality conflicts and irreconcilable differences within the
A. M. E. Church resulted in a split in 1840, producing a rival body known as the First Colored Methodist Protestant
Church. Even before the A. M. E. Zion Church was formally
organized in 1821, dissension entered the ranks of the Zionites, resulting in the organization of at least three rival
churches.[2] Early relations between the relatively autonomous congregations making up the Union Church of Africans
were constantly disturbed by conflicting interests, internal
bickering, and problems in communication. In view of such,
it is not surprising that a major dispute occurred within that
body between 1851 and 1856. The schism that eventually resulted, coming as it did shortly after the deaths of Peter
Spencer and William Anderson, attests further to long dormant problems and institutional weaknesses.

81

The Case Involving Saunders and Others

A number of explanations have been given for the great dispute which split the Union Church of Africans only eight years
after the demise of Spencer and Anderson. Some sources
contend, without being specific, that the church's educational
policy caused the dispute. Others have suggested that a controversy over paid or salaried ministers and disagreements
concerning lay representation at conferences were the main
issues involved. 3 John P. Predow, a retired bishop and educator in the Union American Methodist Episcopal Church, in-
sists that the schism took place because the members of the
Union Church of Africans could not agree on the appropriate
title for the spiritual heads of the body:

> One faction wanted their leader and presiding offi-
> cer to be named and called "President. " The oth-
> er group or faction wanted their leader and pre-
> siding officer to be named and called "Bishop. "
> The older members wanted a President; the younger
> members wanted to keep the original "Episcopal, "
> or "Episcopus" [Bishop]. The two factions could
> not agree as to the title of their leader and general
> officer; so the split came about. The faction that
> chose the title, "President, " to be their leader and
> presiding officer, moved to 819 French Street, Wil-
> mington, Delaware, and called themselves "The
> African Union Methodist Protestant Church. " The
> group that chose the title, "Episcopus, " or "Bish-
> op, " to be the name of their presiding officer,
> moved to 1206 French Street in Wilmington, and
> became "The Union American Methodist Episcopal
> Church. "4

The evidence contained in the most reliable sources
suggests that not one of the aforementioned concerns contributed directly to the dispute. The issue of what should
be the nature of basic and religious education in the Union
Church of Africans had been the source of some disagreement, but this issue had been largely forced into the background by this time. The issue regarding paid or salaried
ministers and that of lay representation at conferences had
been resolved for the most part. Bishop Predow's contention that the schism happened because of disagreements as to
the proper title of presiding officers is unfounded.

Apparently, bitter dissension entered the ranks of the

Union Church of Africans early in 1851 when elder minister Ellis Saunders insisted on the right to preach and administer the ordinances at the mother church in Wilmington whenever he pleased. He was convinced that this privilege was in accord with his authority as one who associated with Isaac Barney in presiding over all the congregations. [5] Saunders was right at this point. He received the support of the majority of the trustees at the mother church, among whom were Daniel B. Anderson, John M. Benton, George Brinkley, William Davis, William Ellias, Edmund Hayes, Peter Manlove, Abraham Robinson, Raymond Trusty, and Edward Williams. Most of the members of the church did not support Saunders and voted to expel from membership the small group of trustees who took sides with him. They believed that they had the right to hire and fire preachers at will, but this was not what the Discipline said. Their desire to choose their own preachers to preach for them ran into conflict with Saunders' attempt to use his authority in appointing whom he wanted to preach at the church. Neither side was willing to understand the other or to find an acceptable compromise. Saunders and the ousted trustees went to court to obtain a mandamus to restore their rights and privileges at the church. A long period of name-calling, frustrated hopes, and political maneuvering followed. [6]

The cases involving Saunders and the ousted trustees of the mother church were first argued before the Superior Court of Wilmington in the May term of 1852. Saunders' case proved to be the primary focus of the dispute. On May 2, Saunders presented his argument to the court in a carefully prepared statement. The statement made known the following events. Saunders had become a member of one of the congregations of the Union Church of Africans, a society formed at Christiana, Delaware, in 1815. In 1835 he was approved as a deacon by the elders at the Christiana church and was thereupon ordained to that office in accordance with the provisions of the Discipline by Peter Spencer. On April 25, 1846, he was nominated by the yearly conference in Wilmington as a candidate for the office of elder minister. On the following Sunday, April 26, 1846, Saunders preached a trial sermon before the elders and congregation of the mother church in Wilmington. The sermon was judged satisfactory, and the next day Saunders was ordained by Isaac Barney, the elder minister of the New York-New England congregations. [7] In setting forth his claim to the office of elder minister, Saunders advanced the following arguments before the court:

1. That the said Anderson, Spencer and Hill are deceased, that the said Gilmore has ceased to exercise the office of elder minister in said church, and that consequently the said Barney and your petitioner are the only surviving and acting elder ministers of the said African Union Church. That the said Barney, residing in the City of New York, assumed more particularly the charge of the Northern societies in the said church, and that the Southern societies, including the said original society in Wilmington, fell under the immediate charge and superintendance of your petitioner as elder minister as aforesaid, and still remain under such charge.

2. Your petitioner showeth that by virtue of his office of elder minister as aforesaid, and according to the usages and discipline of said church, it is his duty and right to preach in the said Union Church in Wilmington, whenever he may see proper so to do, and to administer the ordinances and discipline thereof, and to exercise a pastoral charge over the same. [8]

Saunders went on to indicate that he had been forcibly excluded from the mother church, and prevented from undertaking his duties by the following newly-elected trustees of that church: William Brown, Peter Chippey, Henry Richardson, William Black, Spencer Williams, Isaac Parker, and Levi Morris. He then requested the following of the court:

... wherefore having no other legal remedy in the premises, your petitioner humbly prays this Honorable Court to issue a writ of the said State, of mandamus, directed to the said "Union Church of Africans," commanding them to admit your petitioner to preach in said Union Church in Wilmington, whenever he may see proper so to do, and to administer the ordinances and discipline thereof, and to exercise a pastoral charge over the same, or to show cause to the contrary. [9]

Saunders' request before the court was angrily challenged by the defendants, the trustees of the mother church. They made the following return to the alternation writ of mandamus:

> That the plaint and matters and allegations con-
> tained in said petition are not the proper subject
> matter of a mandamus, because the office of a
> preacher or elder minister, or the right to exer-
> cise a pastoral charge in the said Union Church is
> not an office known to the law: that there are no
> fees or salary attached to it, and that the incor-
> poration of said Union Church is confined to the
> temporal concerns of said society or congregation,
> according to the provisions of the Act of the Gen-
> eral Assembly of the State of Delaware, "an act
> to enable the religious denomination in this State
> to appoint trustees, who shall be a body corporate
> for the purpose of taking care of the temporalities
> of their respective congregations. " Passed at
> Dover, February 3, 1787, under and by virtue of
> which act, said Union Church is alone incorporat-
> ed. [10]

In an adjoining statement presented before the court, the defendants not only questioned Saunders' right to use the pulpit at the mother church at will, but also denied that he was
ever "set apart" as an elder minister in the African Union
Church:

> And said Union Church further doth most humbly
> certify that the said Ellis Saunders was not and is
> not an elder minister in the said Union Church in
> Wilmington, nor is it his duty or right to preach
> in the said Union Church whenever he may see
> proper so to do, nor to administer the ordinances
> and discipline thereof, nor to exercise a pastoral
> charge over the same, (as by the within writ is
> within alleged) and that it is moreover expressly
> provided in the Articles of Association of said
> Union Church, in the within writ mentioned in the
> sixth article thereof in the words following, to wit:
> "And that no minister or teacher shall be privileged
> to preach or exhort in the said Union Church but
> with the consent of the trustees and a majority of
> the said incorporation, " which consent has not been
> given, but has been and is denied by the said
> Union Church at Wilmington, whensoever he may
> see proper so to do, or to administer the ordi-
> nances thereof, and exercise a pastoral charge
> over the same. [11]

One of Saunders' lawyers, M. L. Johnson, attacked the arguments set forth by the defendants. He noted that according to the second Act of Association, and the Act of 1787, the property of the Union Church of Africans was placed in the hands of the trustees "for the use of the ministers regularly ordained, and the members of this church." Therefore, Saunders, having gone through the proper process to become an elder minister, had the right to make use of the pulpit in that church. Mr. Johnson further contended that because Saunders had been denied that right, and because there was no specific legal remedy, it was incumbent upon the court to intervene in order to avoid a miscarriage of justice:

> The elder minister has therefore a right to the use of this pulpit, and without this right the objects of the association and subsequent incorporation are defeated, not only in reference to the minister, but to the membership. It is not merely a spiritual but a temporal right. The right to the pastoral charge and direction draws after it the right to the use of the church property, held by the trustees for this benefit. They refuse him the exercise of this right. He has no remedy--no action at law-- and there is a wrong without a remedy--a failure of justice entirely unless this court will compel these trustees to do him justice and restore him to his right. [12]

Continuing in that vein, Johnson attacked categorically the validity of the reasons given by the defendants to explain why Saunders had no right to perform the duties of an elder minister:

1. That the office of the petitioner is not an office known to the law. That means nothing in reference to the present argument unless it means that the office is not one which the law will protect; and that again begs the question.

2. Because there are no fees belonging to the office. That right does not depend on fees as such. There must be a temporal right--which there is here: The right to occupy the pulpit.

3. Because these trustees were created a corporation merely to take care of the temporalities

of the church. That is the very reason why they should be required to manage and dispose of it according to law and the objects of incorporation.

4. That no minister shall preach but with the consent of the majority of the trustees and congregation. This is not the meaning of the sixth article. It refers to the ministers of other churches, not to the elder ministers or superintendents. This last has been the construction from the beginning. The articles themselves make a distinction between minister and elder minister. The former, and not the latter, is meant by this sixth article. The minister is appointed by this majority; the elder minister by the eldership in conformity with the discipline. 13

Johnson's arguments were promptly responded to by John Wales, the brilliant lawyer for the defendants. Wales attempted to establish sufficient grounds of objection to the issuing of the writ to Saunders. He maintained that the trustees and members of the Union Church of Africans in Wilmington had conclusively and positively denied the allegation in the petition that Saunders was "the elder minister, pastor, or preacher of this church, duly appointed":

By the Articles of Association no one can be a minister without the consent of the trustees, and a majority of the corporation. The petition does not state such consent; but rather complains that it has been withheld. It appears from the Articles of Association and incorporation of this church that the congregation wisely intended to keep in their hands the choice of what preacher should instruct them in matters of religion. It is in the exercise of this power that they have declined to receive the pastoral services of this complainant; and it affords him no ground of relief. He has no right to be there without the consent of the trustees and congregation. 14

Wales continued in this line of argument by declaring that Saunders' complaint had to do precisely with "spiritual concerns," and, therefore, was not a matter to be decided on by the civil court:

> The matters here complained of are not the sub-
> jects of the civil jurisdiction of the court. The
> court can have nothing to do with the spiritual con-
> cerns of the church. The redress sought here has
> reference to the spiritual concerns of this church:
> to reinstate the complainant into the character and
> capacity of a minister and teacher of religion; a
> person seeking to obtrude himself upon a congrega-
> tion who are unwilling to hear him. [15]

The cases involving the ousted trustees were all
handled separately on May 17, 1852. The charge that they
had been unjustly denied the privileges of membership in
Wilmington provoked the following response from the trustees
of the mother church:

> In the case of Daniel B. Anderson and all the oth-
> er former trustees the return is the same as in
> the case of Ellis Saunders. The said church hath
> not, nor have the said trustees, removed, excluded,
> and debarred the said Daniel B. Anderson and oth-
> ers from the rights and privileges of membership
> in said church as alleged. And for these reasons
> we cannot restore or cause to be restored the said
> Daniel B. Anderson and others into the said place
> and function as members of the said Union Church
> of Africans with all the liberties, privileges, and
> advantages to that place and function belonging and
> appertaining. [16]

Being unwilling to pursue their cases beyond the May
term of 1852, Daniel B. Anderson, John Benton, George
Brinkley, William Davis, William Ellias, Edmund Hayes,
Peter Manlove, Abraham Robinson, Raymond Trusty, Edward
Williams, and a few others who were sympathetic to their
cause formed themselves into a new congregation. They
broke all ties with the mother church. They held worship
services for three years at the home of John Benton. Edward Williams emerged as the pastor of this small group.
On December 11, 1855, the group purchased a lot and built
a meeting house at Twelfth and French Streets in Wilmington.
It later became the mother church of the Union American
Methodist Episcopal denomination.

The Saunders case dragged on through the summer
and early fall of 1852 and there was no decision. At the
November term, another attorney became involved in the case

and argued Saunders' position with great skill. He called upon the court to consider the question as to whether or not Saunders, under the constitution of the church itself, had the right to be an elder minister of the Union Church of Africans. He suggested that the evidence in the petition established three points with clarity:

1. That there is under the constitution of the church such an office as the elder minister.

2. That Ellis Saunders has been duly chosen to and inducted into said office.

3. That this office draws with it the right to preach and teach in said church. 17

This lawyer, who was listed as Mr. Bates, focused his argument primarily on two concerns. First, he insisted that the defendants, by strongly implying that the function of the office of the elder minister rested on the consent of the trustees and congregation, were introducing a new rule of election which had never previously been a policy in the Union Church of Africans:

> It sets up a different rule of election, which does not even in terms apply to this office of elder minister, and which, allowing for the apparent looseness of expression in all these articles, is easily susceptible of an explanation which applies it to other preachers, and not to the elder ministers. In the second article the use of the church is carefully preserved to the ministers duly licensed and ordained according to the constitution and discipline of the church. The contemporaneous exposition of this constitution shows that no such notion ever existed as that the elder ministers were subject from Sabbath to Sabbath to Sabbath to the consent of the trustees. The very first step was to vest the whole power of election in five ruling elders, who chose Anderson and Spencer the first elder ministers: all who have succeeded them have been elected the same way. 18

Secondly, Bates insisted that Wales, the attorney for the defendants, was wrong in saying that the Saunders case did not come under the jurisdiction of the civil court:

This is a civil right. Existing under the provisions of our Act of Assembly of 1787, a right which, though it relates to spiritual matters, has civil relations. The trustees hold the property "to and for the use of their society or congregation;" this house for the objects for which it was built, as a place of public worship; where ministers duly authorized by the church should preach; and where the members of the association could have such preaching. A right therefore connected with an office belonging to the church, to be exercised by the use of the church, is a right which the trustees are bound to permit, and their refusal to do so deprives the person authorized so to exercise his office of a civil right--one that this court will enforce. The right of Ellis Saunders, holding the office of elder minister, to use that church as a place for preaching the Gospel, is a civil right, protected by the Act of Assembly, and capable of enforcement by the mandamus of this court, obliging the trustees to do that which they hold the temporalities of the church to secure. Wherever there is a duty imposed by law, and individual rights are involved in it, there is a remedy. [19]

Toward the end of the November term, the court announced its decision upon one branch of the case, refusing the mandamus, but expressing the hope that "compromise and conciliation among the members of this religious society might occur through further negotiations. "[20] A year passed and there was still no compromise between the parties involved. The court eventually ordered a re-argument.

The Saunders Case Re-argued

At the November term, 1853, the Saunders case was re-argued by the same counsel. Questions and debate as to the legal merits of the case, and as to the sufficiency of the return to the first mandamus, continued on a higher level. The opening remarks were made by Mr. Johnson, one of the attorneys representing Saunders. He denied once again that the consent of the congregation and trustees was necessary to a valid ordination of an elder minister. While congregational consent was practicable in reference to subordinate officers such as deacons and licensed preachers, it was destructive, continued Johnson, when applied to the elder minister, "who is the Bishop of the church."[21] He reiterated a point made during the previous court term by Mr. Bates, his associate in the case, declaring, "Until this case, the congregation never exercised or claimed to have any control of the election and appointment of an elder minister."[22]

After some deliberation, a reply was offered by John Wales, the attorney for the defendants. He restated an argument made earlier, contending that the case was not a matter of civil rights, "but of a religious privilege, a matter of church discipline of which this court can know nothing and claim nothing."[23] Mr. Bates promptly expressed disagreement. The first session of the court ended on that note.

Mr. Bates resumed his argument on December 13, after a repose of several days. Citing a legal precedent set in similar cases in England and America, he argued that "whenever there is a right to exercise any office, franchise or functions, the exercise of which concerns the public, the court will interfere to assure that it is protected." Bates suggested that this principle definitely applied to the Saunders case, a case which, though related to an ecclesiastical office, was "a civil right both to the minister and to the members of the Union Church of Africans."[24] This was the final argument offered prior to the rendering of a decision in the case.

The long-pending church controversy resulted in a decision in mid-December 1853, which marked the end of the November term. The three judges involved delivered separate opinions. Judge Harrington, the first to deliver an opinion, prefaced his decision by establishing the right of the court to intervene in the Saunders case, a right which had been consistently denied by the attorney for the defendants:

> I have no doubt of the jurisdiction of the court to restore by mandamus a minister illegally excluded from a pulpit, which he has the right to occupy. The application of this writ to that extent was affirmed by Lord Mansfield, in Rex vs Barker 3 Burr 12-66, the principle of which decision has been since applied in a multitude of cases in England and in the United States. "Where there is a right to execute an office, perform a service, or exercise a franchise (more specifically if it be in a matter of public concern, or attended with profit),

> and a person is kept out of possession, or dispos-
> sessed of such right, and has no other specific
> legal remedy, this court ought to assist by man-
> damus upon reasons of justice, and upon reasons
> of public policy, to preserve peace, order, and
> good government. [25]

Judge Harrington went on to point out that it was difficult to render a decision in the case primarily because Saunders' claim
to be the elder minister "in charge of this congregation could
not be sustained upon the face of the very imperfect and con-
fused Articles of Association and printed Book of Discipline
alone." Nevertheless, a majority of the court rendered a
decision upon the whole case, awarding the Writ of Peremptory Mandamus "in accordance with the prayer of the complainant, commanding the trustees to restore Saunders to his
office of elder minister in the said church at Wilmington,
from which he had been illegally excluded." Judge Harrington and Chief Justice Booth agreed on the decision and Judge
Wootten dissented. [26]

Based on the final decision of the Superior Court, it
appeared that Saunders had won in his legal fight against the
mother church. But the church showed no inclination to accept him after the decision was rendered on his behalf.
The case was taken before the Court of Errors and Appeals
in Wilmington. At the end of its June term, 1855, this
court rejected the decision of the Superior Court, declaring,
"A Writ of Peremptory Mandamus in this case is hereby in
all things reversed, annulled, and held for nothing." Chief
Justice Johns rendered the final decision on October 26,
1855, charging that "where there is no legal right there is
no legal remedy, and that the question in dispute is for an
ecclesiastical body to settle."[27] The long and bitter court
battle had now ended, but personal antagonisms and a stubborn unwillingness to compromise remained and opened the
way toward schism.

The Union American Methodist Episcopal Church

Prospects for a united African Union Methodism faded when
Ellis Saunders and Isaac Barney led thirty congregations out
of the Union Church of Africans, leaving only the parent
church in Wilmington. When the congregations withdrew,
they took all of their properties and finances with them.
This did not pose a legal problem because the weak connec-

tional system gave local trustees in each congregation the right to affiliate with the body of their choice. By 1856 the thirty congregations under Barney and Saunders had joined the small congregation of former trustees and members who had broken with the Union Church of Africans in Wilmington in 1852. These congregations chose to continue as the African Union Church. In time, at least six of these congregations returned to the parent body, which also continued as the African Union Church until its merger with the First Colored Methodist Protestant Church in 1866. Relations between the rival bodies were embittered by much name-calling and unscrupulous competition in the years that followed. There were even disputes over who were the rightful heirs of Peter Spencer, thereby making it more difficult for the churches to reunite or to cooperate in a friendly manner. [28]

The congregations that organized under Barney and Saunders did not then break with the Spencer tradition. Their church remained in effect a Methodist Church with articles of religion, general rules, discipline and polity which conformed to the Spencer model. Constitutional conventions and general conferences were adopted to appoint presiding officers, to fix the limits of districts, to hear and decide on appeals, and to make necessary changes in doctrine and discipline. [29] In January 1865 a special convention of all the congregations was called in Wilmington, and the name Union American Methodist Episcopal Church in the United States of America and Elsewhere was chosen for the body. [30] This decision was made largely because of the need to avoid the confusion caused by the presence of two bodies which claimed to be the true African Union Church. The leaders of the U. A. M. E. Church dropped the name "African," feeling that it was no longer fitting for them as black Americans. The rival body, which was the smaller of the two, continued as the African Union Church until 1866, when it merged with several congregations of the First Colored Methodist Protestant Church.

The Union American Methodist Episcopal Church, having common roots in the Union Church of Africans, exemplified the same unique characteristics embodied in that body. It continued a strong tradition of lay involvement, emphasizing that all should have a voice in the spiritual and temporal affairs of the church: "It is a fundamental principle in our church government that all power is inherent in the people. It is their prerogative to exercise it directly or indirectly. "[31]

The acceptance of women in ministry also continued. Although women never held positions as elder ministers, general superintendents, or bishops, they were accepted as licensed preachers. The position of the U. A. M. E. Church concerning this issue was made abundantly clear in the 1892 edition of its Book of Discipline:

> All female members of the Union American M. E. Connection (or any individual church) that are, or may be wrought upon to preach the Word of God, may be dealt with according to the rules of our Book of Discipline; namely, application may be made to the Board of Stewards. The Pastor in charge, with the Stewards, shall at a specified time, examine the applicant without prejudice or partiality. If in their judgment she be a proper person, a time shall be designated for a trial sermon before the membership and officials of said church. A two-thirds vote of the membership and officials present on the occasion of the trial sermon shall determine whether or not she shall be accorded the privilege of exercising her gifts and graces in the church of which she is a member; and elsewhere at such times as the pastor and officials may deem expedient, so long as her life and doctrine accord with the Christian profession. [32]

Women who were accepted as licensed preachers were subject to the same restrictions as men who served in that capacity. Each year they had to receive special recommendations from their pastors-in-charge in order to remain active. They could not hold any other form of license, were not to be considered members of any quarterly conference, and were prohibited from being a part of the official board of the church. Women who assumed pastoral charge of churches were automatically considered members of the quarterly conferences and the official board of the church. [33]

Of equal importance was the firm stand the U. A. M. E. Church took against slavery and racism. In its doctrine it recognized the humanity of all persons, and affirmed the duty of all to practice community and love with one another. Thus slaveholders and others associated with this immoral practice were excluded from membership in the church.

Additionally, the church was an institutional symbol of black power and black nationalism from its origin. Its

Book of Discipline stressed the significance of identity and unity among its black constituents and called upon them to take leading roles in establishing their own homes, churches, schools, and other institutions. 34   Thus, the U. A. M. E. Church was similar to the early A. M. E. , A. M. E. Zion, and African Union Churches in that its activities went beyond the strictly ecclesiastical to embrace the economic, intellectual, and political areas of black life.

NOTES

1.   Quoted in The Case of the Union Church of Africans, in Wilmington, Before the Superior Court for New Castle County, Comprising the Petition of Ellis Saunders for a Mandamus, the Return Thereto; Brief Notes of the Argument and Re-Argument of Counsel, and the Final Decision of the Court Awarding the Mandamus, 1852-53 (Wilmington: Henry Eckel, printer, 1855), p. 7.   The names Saunders and Sanders have been used in reference to the plaintiff in this case.   The name Saunders appears on the plaintiff's will record.   See The Personal Will Record of Ellis Saunders, Will Record X (Wilmington: Register of Wills, New Castle County, 1859), I, p. 240.

2.   Frederick A. Norwood, The Story of American Methodism: A History of the United Methodists and Their Relations (Nashville and New York: Abingdon Press, 1974), pp. 171-174; and Carter G. Woodson, The History of the Negro Church (Washington, D. C. :   The Associated Publishers, 1921), pp. 66-73.

3.   Irene C. Dutton, Our Church in Search of Itself: A Brief History (Wilmington: An unpublished paper presented at the 166th Annual Conference of the First and Fourth Districts of the U. A. M. E. Church, May 1-6, 1979), pp. 3-4.

4.   John P. Predow, A Brief History of the Spencer Movement (Wilmington: unpublished paper, the Predow Collection, the Boulden Academy and Seminary, 1979), p. 2; and Benjamin Arnett, ed. , The Budget: Containing the Annual Reports of the General Officers of the African M. E. Church (Xenia, Ohio: Torchlight Printing, 1904), pp. 232ff.

5.   The Case of the Union Church of Africans, 1852-53, pp. 1-24; The Discipline of the African Union Church in

the United States of America, Third Edition Enlarged (Wilmington: Porter & Eckel, 1852), pp. 1ff.; and Daniel B. Anderson, et al. vs the Union Church of Africans (Dover: Division of Historical and Cultural Affairs, Department of State, Hall of Records, 1852), pp. 1-4.

6.   The Case of the Union Church of Africans, 1852-53, pp. 1-7; Daniel B. Anderson, et al. vs the Union Church of Africans, pp. 1-4; and Thomas Scharf, History of Delaware, 1609-1888, 2 Vols. (Philadelphia: L. J. Richards, 1888), II, pp. 729ff.

7.   The Case of the Union Church of Africans, 1852-53, pp. 4-7.

8.   Ibid.

9.   Ibid.

10.   Ibid., pp. 7-8.

11.   Ibid., p. 9.

12.   Ibid., pp. 8-9.

13.   Ibid., pp. 9-10.

14.   Ibid., pp. 10-11.

15.   Ibid., p. 10.

16.   Daniel B. Anderson, et al. vs the Union Church of Africans, p. 4.

17.   The Case of the Union Church of Africans, 1852-53, p. 11.

18.   Ibid., p. 12.

19.   Ibid., pp. 12-13.

20.   Ibid., pp. 12 and 21.

21.   Ibid., pp. 13-14.

22.   Ibid.

23. Ibid., pp. 14-15.

24. Ibid., pp. 19-20.

25. Ibid., p. 21.

26. Ibid., pp. 3 and 21-24.

27. The Union Church of Africans vs Ellis Saunders in the Court of Errors and Appeals (Dover: The Division of Historical and Cultural Affairs, Department of State, Hall of Records, 1855), pp. 100-138; and Scharf, History of Delaware, II, p. 730.

28. Deed Record to the Property of the Union Church of Wilmington, A Religious Corporation of the State of Delaware (Wilmington: The New Castle County Recorder of Deeds, December 11, 1855), X-6, pp. 96-99; and Scharf, History of Delaware, II, p. 730.

29. Our Heritage: The History of the Union American Methodist Episcopal Church (Hackensack, N. J.: Custombook, 1973), pp. 3-39; and The Discipline of the Union American M. E. Church, in the United States of America and Elsewhere, Sixth Edition Revised (Wilmington: Henry Eckel, printer, 1872), pp. 12ff.

30. Written Indenture to Be the Act and Deed of the Union Church of Wilmington (Wilmington: The New Castle County Recorder of Deeds, October 14, 1867), N-8, p. 319.

31. The Discipline of the Union American M. E. Church, 1872, p. 6.

32. The Discipline of the Union American Methodist Episcopal Church in the United States of America, Province of Ontario, and Elsewhere, Tenth Edition (Wilmington: Hubert A. Roop, printer, 1892), pp. 157-158.

33. Ibid.

34. Ibid., pp. 135-144.

Chapter IV:

THE CIVIL WAR AND RECONSTRUCTION:
THE SPENCER CHURCHES IN
AN ERA OF CRISIS

> Let each and every branch of the church en-
> ter at once earnestly in the work, and vie
> with every other, to prove which will be most
> effective in making this system a complete suc-
> cess. By so doing the Lord will bless the ef-
> fort, victory crown the labor, and the Church
> of Christ be spread abroad.
>   --Edward Williams[1]

The signing of the Emancipation Proclamation by President
Abraham Lincoln in 1863 and the climax of the Civil War
two years later produced radical social changes among black
Americans. Homeless, penniless, uncertain, and illiterate,
some four million freedmen and women in the South were
sent out to face a hostile white world. Black churches, the
only institutions owned by black people on a wide scale,
were compelled to confront this catastrophic social crisis
with a broader sense of ministry and mission. This challenge was met in several ways. First, there was a strong
effort on the part of black churches, primarily of Baptist
and Methodist persuasions, to attract thousands of freed
blacks who had previously been members of white churches.
Thus, the establishment, growth, and expansion of black ecclesiastical institutions continued to be a mission priority.
Second, black churches assumed postures as benevolent or
beneficial societies, concerned with the poor, the handicapped,
the sick, the widowed, the orphaned, and the imprisoned.
Finally, they moved to organize and finance secondary
schools, academies, and colleges. The tremendous struggle
to wrest meaning and significance out of the black experience became less onerous because of such activities. [2]

The African Union First Colored
Methodist Protestant Church

The Spencer Churches were weak and demoralized when the
Civil War began. The split involving Barney, Saunders, and
others had proven to be a serious blow to an already weak
and unstable African Union Methodism. After the split, the
smaller African Union Church continued to experience problems which threatened its existence as a unified body. In
December 1859 internal bickering surfaced and almost split
the congregations in New York and Providence, Rhode Island.
William Coursey, who was the pastor of these congregations,
was charged with "preaching to make divisions in the church"
by the ruling elders. To demonstrate his displeasure with
the charges, Coursey refused to attend trial to answer the
charges against him. In accordance with the laws of the
church's Discipline, he was silenced from preaching until the
annual conference in April 1860. [3] After refusing to clear
himself at the conference, he was simply replaced. Had it
not been for the common sense approach of leaders like Edward Chippey and Isaac Parker, who took the lead in settling
the matter, another schism would have most likely occurred
within the church. [4]

The schism involving Barney and Saunders, coupled
with the dispute concerning Coursey, simply revealed long
dormant problems and institutional weaknesses which had long
beset the Spencer Churches. The tremendous struggle to
achieve stability, growth, and expansion out of institutional
chaos rested largely on the shoulders of a few capable leaders in the churches. As shall be revealed later, the congregations under Barney and Saunders achieved some stability, growth, and expansion with the passing of time. The
congregations that rejoined the parent body took steps after the Civil War to regain strength as a regional denomination. In September 1865 they approved a plan to merge with
a number of congregations of the First Colored Methodist
Protestant Church. [5] Edward Chippey, Isaac Parker, Absalom Blackson, Robert H. Lewis, Isaac Foster, and Peter
S. Chippey (Edward's brother) were chosen to serve as
delegates at a conference with representatives of the First
Colored Methodist Protestant Church in Baltimore in November 1865. After several days in session, a platform for the
merger was adopted. To consummate the union, a general
conference was planned for August 1866 in Wilmington. At
the appointed time, representatives from both churches met
and officialized the union. The name adopted for the re-

sulting body was the African Union First Colored Methodist
Protestant Church of America or Elsewhere, ordinarily called
the African Union Methodist Protestant Church. 6

The First Colored Methodist Protestant Church was
less than three decades old when the merger took place.
The Church had begun as early as 1840 when members of
A. M. E. congregations in Maryland and Pennsylvania broke
away because of differences regarding church polity.   Convinced that the episcopal structure on which the A. M. E. 's
operated was inimical to their best interests, they organized
a church with a more democratic or representative form of
government.   The group met in Elkton, Cecil County, Maryland, and formally organized the First Colored Methodist
Protestant Church.   The founders of the church adopted the
articles of religion, general rules, and discipline of the
Methodist Episcopal Church, but chose to organize on essentially the same principles as those on which Peter Spencer's Union Church of Africans was organized in 1813, and
on which the predominantly white Methodist Protestant Church
was founded in 1830. 7   The church's structure included the
following: 1) no episcopacy, their ministers being simply
elders; 2) lay representation in all conferences and meetings; and 3) the representation of local preachers at general
conferences. 8   The remarkable similarities which the church
shared with the African Union Church made union possible
between the two bodies.

Immediately after the merger, a form of church
government was adopted.   The ministerial hierarchy of the
church was to include presidents, vice-presidents, elders,
deacons, and licensed preachers and exhorters.   Presidents,
who were equal in rank to Methodist Episcopal bishops, were
installed rather than consecrated.   The annual conferences
were invested with the power of electing presidents, who
were expected to serve four-year terms.   They were eligible
for re-election.   Candidates for the presidency had to be
elders, citizens of the United States, and members of the
A. U. M. P. Church and of an annual conference for five years.
They had to submit to a thorough examination by a committee of five, and were expected to demonstrate competency in
theology, U. S. Government; church law and doctrine, psy-
chology, grammar, and reading.   This says something about
the level of importance A. U. M. P. 's attached to an educated
leadership during this time.   In addition, presidential candidates had to show that they were of sound moral character.
Once installed, they had the responsibility of presiding over

districts, of receiving and settling complaints and charges against preachers, of transferring preachers from one district to another, of making appointments at various churches in their designated districts, of organizing and receiving new churches into the connection, and of settling difficulties which arose in districts among churches, circuits, or stations. A General President was appointed every four years to preside over presidents at general conferences and general board meetings. [9]

Vice-presidents were elected by annual conferences to assist presidents and to take charge of districts in case of their death, resignation, or disqualification in managing the affairs of districts. Next in line to vice-presidents were elders, who were ordained and given the authority to preach and to administer the ordinances. Deacons, likewise ordained, were invested with the privilege of preaching and of giving assistance to elders. Licensed preachers, whose licenses had to be renewed annually, simply had the right to preach. Exhorters were those who often preached without a license. [10]

The newly formed body retained many of the elements of the Wesleyan and Methodist tradition. The articles of religion, general rules, and discipline of the M. E. Church were included in a slightly altered form. The itinerancy was adopted, and ministers were to be paid such salaries as agreed upon by the members of the congregations they served. This represented a move away from the Spencer style of organization. Also adopted were Episcopal Methodism's system of classes and class leaders, its methods and modes of trustee election, and its multiple conference system which included annual, district, quarterly, and general conferences. Prior to the merger, general conferences as understood in the traditional Methodist sense were not held by the African Union Church. [11]

The general conference made provisions at the outset to insure the growth and expansion of the A. U. M. P. Church. Edward Chippey, Moses Chippey, Gaylord V. Peterson, Daniel Russell, Sr., Benjamin Scott, and other leading figures in the church were convinced that three steps had to be taken if such growth and expansion were to take place. First, there had to be a sufficient number of dedicated foreign and home missionaries, or church extension workers as they were called. Second, funds had to be created to support home and foreign mission programs. Finally, there had to be safeguards against schisms. Beginning in 1866, foreign missionaries were chosen from among the delegates of the general conference, and home missionaries were chosen and made subject to the nearest quarterly conference. Regulations were adopted requiring all congregations to make financial contributions quarterly to home and foreign missionary efforts. A Church Extension Fund was started in 1878 to aid struggling congregations and to assist in the establishment of new churches and missions. In addition, a provision was included in the church's Discipline which called for the expulsion of any clergy or lay person found guilty of conspiring to cause splits in the denomination. This proved to be a feeble attempt to strengthen connectional authority and to avoid schisms of the kind which occurred between 1851 and 1856. [12]

Despite such provisions, the growth and expansion of the A. U. M. P. Church during the four decades after the Civil War were far less than impressive. The church's membership increased from about 1,500 in 1865 to around 4,000 by 1900. [13] Its slow growth is especially apparent when measured in comparison with the mushrooming of the African Methodist Episcopal Church, the African Methodist Episcopal Zion Church, and the Colored Methodist Episcopal Church. The membership of the A. M. E. Church grew from some 35,000 in 1865 to a half million in 1900. During that same period, the A. M. E. Zion Church increased from around 14,000 to approximately 300,000 members. The C. M. E. Church, which emerged out of the predominantly white M. E. Church, South in 1870, reported a membership of around 150,000 in 1900. Apparently, these bodies had a stronger and more vigorous itinerant ministry than the A. U. M. P. Church, and they made a greater effort to reach the thousands of newly-freed blacks in the South who had broken ties with white churches. [14]

The A. U. M. P. denomination experienced its greatest growth during the latter nineteenth century in the Middle District, which embraced Delaware, Maryland, Pennsylvania, and parts of New Jersey and New York. This was due largely to the efforts of Edward Chippey, who was most likely the son of Moses Chippey, one of Peter Spencer's earliest followers and most active preachers. Born in Wilmington, Delaware, in 1825, young Chippey had joined the Union Church of Africans under Spencer. In 1861 he received deacon's orders and was "set apart" as an elder minister one year later. [15] He was one of three men elected to the

Edward H. Chippey (from History of the African Union Methodist Protestant Church, by Daniel J. Russell, Jr.).

presidency of the newly-organized A. U. M. P. Church in 1866.
After being placed in charge of the Middle District, Chippey
soon emerged as the most widely known figure and the most
successful church extension worker in his denomination. [16]
In 1870 he started a small mission in Wilmington which developed into the St. Peter A. U. M. P. Church. He had a
platform erected in a cemetery on Union Street and there
conducted the first worship service. A building was soon
constructed and dedicated. In 1873 he organized another
small mission at the home of Stephen Welsh in Wilmington.
This mission, which became the St. James A. U. M. P. Church,
was conducted in various homes for a few years before a
church edifice was completed. In 1874 Chippey started still
another small mission in South Wilmington which evolved into the St. Paul A. U. M. P. Church. [17] He was also responsible for the rise of small missions and congregations in
parts of New Jersey, New York, and Pennsylvania. In
tribute to his work, the A. U. M. P. Church of Hockessin,
Delaware, organized in 1886, was renamed the Chippey Chapel A. U. M. P. Church in 1897. This church still stands as
a memorial to a long line of Chippeys who were active in
the A. U. M. P. denomination between 1813 and 1900, the most
notable among whom were Moses Chippey, Edward H. Chippey, Peter S. Chippey, Jonathan Chippey, Anna M. Chippey,
and Sarah E. Chippey. [18]

The other two districts in the A. U. M. P. denomination, known specifically as the Eastern District and the
Maryland or Southern District, reported very few gains in
terms of churches during the four decades after the Civil
War. Five congregations were started in New York under
the Eastern District. Congregations were also formed in
Norfolk, Virginia, and Washington, D. C., under the Maryland or Southern District. [19] The St. John A. U. M. P. Church
of Chatham, Ontario, Canada was also built, representing
the first attempt on the part of A. U. M. P.'s to establish
churches outside of the boundaries of the United States. Despite such gains, the A. U. M. P. denomination consisted of
fewer than a hundred churches and small missions in 1900. [20]

Meager gains of this nature illustrated the A. U. M. P.
Church's peculiar pattern of growth and expansion. Regionally, the development of the church was spotty. Most congregations were concentrated in the states of Delaware, Maryland, New Jersey, and Pennsylvania. Outside of these states
the movement was irregular and sporadic, producing only one
congregation in each of the following: Connecticut, Michigan,

Rhode Island, Virginia, Washington, D. C., and Chatham, Ontario, Canada. Only five congregations existed in New York. Yet most A. U. M. P. leaders were convinced that their church constituted a strong regional denomination. 21

This pattern of slow growth and expansion resulted from a number of factors, the more important among which where the dearth of vigorous leadership, problems of organization caused primarily by the constant reorganization and reshuffling of districts, a scarcity of resources, and the absence of a sufficiently strong and active itinerant ministry. These explain why no serious effort was made by the church to attract the thousands of freed men and women in the South. Even if a serious effort had been made to do so, it doubtlessly would have met with little success, because the A. U. M. P. Church was simply too small and weak institutionally to compete with the A. M. E., the A. M. E. Zion, and the C. M. E. Churches for this great harvest of black souls.

The A. U. M. P. Church continued to reflect the distinctive features of the Spencer tradition; namely, strong lay participation, the active involvement of women, and the support of projects and institutions for the economic, political, and educational development of black people. In this manner the church continued to find a special or unique expression.

Of particular significance was the role played by women in the church. A number of conference auxiliaries were organized by females to assist in missionary activity and church building and maintenance. In November 1867 a group of women under the leadership of Araminta Jenkins reactivated the Grand Body of the Daughters of Conference, which had been founded in 1861, but was inactive for a time after the merger between the African Union and First Colored Methodist Protestant Churches. 22 "Mother" Katie Hopkins, Lena Richardson, and Emma Skinner met in Chester, Pennsylvania, in 1897 and formed the Home Mite Missionary Society of the A. U. M. P. Church. This conference auxiliary was established to undertake fund-raising activities, to take part in conference decisions concerning home and foreign mission work, and to enter the mission fields in an effort to reach the unsaved. 23 At another level women were active in benevolent societies associated with the A. U. M. P. denomination, such as "The Christian Endeavor Society" and "The Helping Hand Crusade." These societies assisted the needy in times of sickness and death. 24 At still another level women sought recognition as preachers and pastors. Martha Abrams applied for a license to preach at the quarterly conference in Wilmington in November 1885, but there is no record to indicate that her wish was granted. But the mere fact that the conference was willing to seriously consider her request suggests that the A. U. M. P. Church was more progressive than other black churches in its policy toward women who felt the divine call to preach. 25 Around the same time, a dynamic young black woman named Lydia Archie was granted a license to preach. During the final two decades of the century, she was one of the most active preachers in the A. U. M. P. Church, receiving recognition in such reputable Wilmington newspapers as The Evening Journal. 26 She was later ordained and given pastoral charge of a congregation in Chadds Ford, Pennsylvania. 27

Another significant aspect of the life of the A. U. M. P. Church was its contributions to the struggle for black liberation and survival. A number of benevolent societies, such as "The Christian Endeavor Society" and "The Helping Hand Crusade," functioned in connection with the church to assist poor blacks in the 1890s. They were supported by the pennies which the congregations could collect. It is extremely difficult to determine how much these societies contributed to the elevation of freedmen and women in the South. It appears that they were aimed primarily at assisting black people, many of whom had been slaves, who lived in areas where A. U. M. P. congregations existed. Members of the church were encouraged not only to give generously through these societies in support of black causes, but also to pool their economic resources and buy buildings and land, and to advise other blacks concerning the necessity of owning property. Land ownership was considered the first step along the road to freedom and independence. This emphasis on self-help and institution-building can be seen as an expression of black power or black nationalism.

The A. U. M. P. Church, unlike the larger and more popular branches of African Methodism, did not accomplish very much in the way of education for black people. By 1900 the A. M. E. 's were sustaining thirty-two secondary schools and colleges, the A. M. E. Zion Church was underwriting eight secondary schools and colleges, and the C. M. E. Church was supporting five secondary schools and colleges. The size and relative poverty of the A. U. M. P. Church made it almost impossible for it to move with great success and authority in this area. A few educational programs were

Lydia Archie, the oldest ordained female preacher in the
A. U. M. P. Church in 1920 (from History of the African
Union Methodist Protestant Church, by Daniel J. Russell,
Jr.).

Gaylord V. Peterson, one of the few well-educated leaders
in the A. U. M. P. Church in the late nineteenth century (from
History of the African Union Methodist Protestant Church, by
Daniel J. Russell, Jr.).

conducted through the church, but the emphasis was placed
primarily on religious teachings and moral training.   Edward Chippey, Gaylord V. Peterson, and a few other leaders
in the church consistently made an issue of the need for the
training of black people in such basic subjects as reading
and writing.   Chippey had been a strong supporter of the
African School Society in Wilmington in the 1850s.   When he
founded the St. James A. U. M. P. Church in 1873, he started
a Sunday School which later became one of the first public
schools for black children in the state of Delaware. 28 He
joined a number of black and white protest groups in attacking not only education proscription, but also disfranchisement
and the economic and theological roots of white racism.
Chippey, Hooper Jolly of Ezion M. E. Church, and Edward
Williams, who emerged as a bishop in the U. A. M. E. Church,
often associated with each other in supporting activities designed to elevate blacks and to improve race relations.   Levi
J. Coppin, the highly regarded bishop of the A. M. E. Church,
became well acquainted with all three men during his stay in
Wilmington.   He described them as "men who enjoyed the
confidence of the community, " and "who were above reproach
in character and above average in ability":

> It was my good fortune to know these men personal-
> ly, to enjoy their confidence and respect; to be en-
> couraged by them as a "likely" young man; to be
> sought and brought forward to work with them in
> civic, religious, and political activities.   It was
> my better fortune to have been influenced by their
> lives.   They were men of thought and vision as
> well as character.   Solid men, who could be de-
> pended upon to advocate a cause because it was
> good and worthy, and not on account of what they
> selfishly hoped to get out of it.   They were big
> men to me then, but much bigger now, as from
> this distance I look back upon them. 29

During this period, the A. U. M. P. 's became increasingly aware of the need for better trained ministers to provide leadership for the church and the race.   In 1894, an
educational bureau, consisting of five elders and five laymen, was created in each of the annual conferences to aid
young men in entering a Methodist theological seminary to
pursue and complete a thorough course of study.   Once accepted into a theological school, they were expected to study
Waddington's Church History, Watson's Theological Institutes,
Kidder's Homiletics, and Wesley's Plain Accounts of Christian

Levi J. Coppin, the A. M. E. bishop who was strongly influenced by Edward H. Chippey and other leading figures in the Spencer Churches (from Unwritten History, by Levi J. Coppin).

Perfection. [30] This course of study received strong support
from most of the leading ministers in the church. One of
its principal advocates was Gaylord V. Peterson, D. D. ,
Ph. D. , who was affectionately called "The Great Theologian"
of the A. U. M. P. Church by many within his denomination
who had a high regard for his knowledge of biblical literature
and church history. [31] Promising young ministers like Isaac
B. Cooper and Daniel J. Russell, Jr. , the son of Daniel J.
Russell, Sr. , one of Peter Spencer's early associate ministers, benefited immensely from this course of study. Although few ministers in the denomination actually took advantage of it, the fact that such a course of study was encouraged and officially adopted suggest that A. U. M. P. 's
were willing to come to terms with a trained clergy.

The Union American Methodist
Episcopal Church

The body which became the U. A. M. E. Church was about
thrice the size of the African Union Church when the Civil
War began. Soon after the war ended, both Isaac Barney
and Ellis Saunders passed on, thus making way for the
emergence of John C. Ramsey, Edward Williams, Richard
Wilson, and William Hutchins as elder ministers. These
men had been ardent supporters of Barney and Saunders, but
they had their own ideas about how to make their church a
strong, relevant institution. [32] In 1871 they moved to trans-
late those ideas into action by modifying the structure of
their denomination. The itinerant ministry was officially
adopted, limiting the pastoral term to two years and allowing
compensation. The offices of elder, deacon, and licensed
preacher were upheld, but the title "elder minister" was
dropped and replaced by the title "General Superintendent. "
The office of "Sub-Superintendent" was created for assistants
to the General Superintendents. The General Superintendents,
who were elected by the general conference, were expected
to serve four years, after which they were eligible for re-
election. Sub-Superintendents, having the same privilege,
were also elected by the general conference. [33]

Other changes were made in the doctrine and polity
of the church. The Book of Discipline of the M. E. Church
was maintained, but only 18 of its 25 articles of religion
were adopted. The articles left out were primarily doctrinal,
covering such subjects as purgatory, communion in both kinds,
speaking in tongues, the marriage of ministers, and the rites

and ceremonies of the church. In addition, a provision was included in the church's Discipline for a general convention as a constitutional lawmaking body, to be summoned only when there was under consideration a change in name and polity. [34]

At their general conference in West Chester, Pennsylvania, in October 1886, U. A. M. E.'s seriously considered adopting the episcopal structure in order to be more in line with the Wesleyan and Methodist tradition. The change to the episcopal form of polity was made official at the next general conference, which was held in New York in October 1890. Included in the new structure were bishops, elders, deacons, preachers, and exhorters. [35] For the first time the general organization of the church, which had carried the name "episcopal" in its title since 1865, actually conformed to the polity of episcopal Methodism.

The growth and expansion of the U. A. M. E. Church between 1865 and 1900, like that of the A. U. M. P. Church, were exceedingly slow. A few congregations and small missions were started in Connecticut, Delaware, Maryland, Massachusetts, New Jersey, New York, Pennsylvania, and Rhode Island. The U. A. M. E.'s did develop with slightly better success than the A. U. M. P.'s in the South and Midwest, establishing one congregation in each of the states of Alabama, Arkansas, Mississippi, Michigan, and Ohio. At least four churches were organized in the Province of Ontario in Canada. When the century came to an end, however, the U. A. M. E. denomination embraced fewer than a hundred congregations and small missions. [36]

During most of this time the church operated within the confines of four districts. Churches located in Delaware, Maryland, and Pennsylvania were placed under the First Episcopal District. The Second Episcopal District was set up to embrace congregations in New Jersey, New York, Connecticut, and Rhode Island. Congregations in Michigan, Ohio, and the Province of Ontario in Canada made up the Third Episcopal District. The Fourth Episcopal District, also called the Southern District, included congregations in Alabama, Arkansas, and Mississippi. These districts were frequently reorganized and reshuffled, making for a confusing and unstable situation. [37]

Certain U. A. M. E. preachers expressed concern that little was being done to expand the church beyond a mere regional existence. In April 1895 H. R. Edwards of New York reminded the conference delegates of the First Episcopal District that "The U. A. M. E. Church does not belong to Delaware, Pennsylvania, New York, or any other state. We have the world for our field and we should strive to reach it all."38 But after all was said and done, slow growth continued and the U. A. M. E. Church appeared destined to be a regional one. This pattern of slow growth and expansion was caused by the same factors which confined the A. U. M. P. Church to a regional existence; namely, a dearth of vigorous leadership, a scarcity of resources, the lack of a sufficiently strong and vigorous itinerant ministry, and problems of organization resulting largely from the frequent reorganization and reshuffling of districts along geographical lines.

Despite having meager financial resources at their disposal, U. A. M. E. 's gave endorsement and support to efforts aimed at improving the quality of life among black people. Conference auxiliaries such as Church Extension, the Episcopal Fund, and the Stewards and Stewardesses extended their efforts beyond church growth and expansion to assist the destitute. Branches of "The Christian Endeavor Society" and "The Helping Hand Crusade" functioned in connection with local congregations and the various conferences to help the needy in times of sickness and death, and to give support to the handicapped, the imprisoned, the widowed, the orphaned, and to some freedmen and women in the South where U. A. M. E. congregations existed. Women formed the backbone of these societies. The Peter Spencer United Daughters of Conference and the Women's Home Mite Missionary Society, organized and controlled by women, also contributed to this effort. Speaking before the delegates of the Delaware Conference on May 1, 1876, George W. Bailey, one of the general superintendents of the U. A. M. E. Church, praised the work of the Peter Spencer United Daughters of Conference, noting that "much good had been accomplished by the Society."39

The record compiled by the U. A. M. E. Church in the area of education was not much better than that compiled by the A. U. M. P. Church. The Mother U. A. M. E. Church and other churches in the connection functioned as schools designed to teach black children and adults reading and writing. The church's concern for the education of black children was given powerful expression at its general convention in 1871:

In order to benefit the rising generation, it is the

duty of the official board in each Church or Society in the connexion to use all their influence in
encouraging education. It is their duty to request
the parents of children to send their children to
school daily, where they have an opportunity; and
especially where there are public schools, they
should see that all the children who are old enough
to be in school are at school. It is their duty,
also frequently to have lectures delivered to the
children of their charge, in such plain, simple,
and comprehensive manner as will suit their understanding. 40

Day schools were supported by the church, and committees on education were appointed from time to time to investigate the educational progress of both children and adults.
The Peter Spencer Fund and other sources of financial support were created by the annual and general conferences.
Some of these resources were used to support religious education through the church's Sunday School movement. Soon
after the Civil War the following recommendation was made:

It shall be the duty of every Minister, Deacon,
Steward and Preacher in charge of a Society or
Congregation to organize Sabbath Schools, wherever
it can possibly be done, and at all times to en-
courage and support that institution. Let him
preach, or cause to be preached, special sermons
to the youth of his charge. 41

By 1876 the U. A. M. E. Church, considering its small
size, had achieved some success in this area. The Delaware and Pennsylvania Conferences reported a total of 2,180
Sunday School scholars; The New England Conference recorded 200; the New Jersey Conference listed 103; the Canada
West Conference reported 50; and the Arkansas Conference
recorded no Sunday School scholars. 42 By 1890 a Committee on Sunday Schools had been formed to monitor the educational activities of Sunday Schools. By the end of the century, a Committee on Mission Schools was operating in conjunction with the conferences to support the work of both
public schools and Sunday Schools. The church's Sunday
School movement emerged as its single most important ve-
hicle for black education. 43

The tremendous importance attached to Sunday Schools
was born of a belief that moral and/or religious training

was absolutely essential for developing human beings who were ethical, honest, and hard-working. The U. A. M. E. 's were as convinced of this as were the A. U. M. P. 's. Thus, through religious training they set out to strengthen family life and to censure sexual behavior they considered immoral and unconventional. Piety and marriage fidelity were encouraged. Temperance was strongly emphasized because the drinking and selling of alcoholic beverages were considered alien to Christian principles and detrimental to the welfare of black people who were already struggling against the forces of a racist, oppressive society.[44]

John C. Ramsey, the highly-regarded U. A. M. E. bishop (from Our Heritage: The History of the Union American Methodist Episcopal Church).

The church produced a few able leaders, among them John C. Ramsey, Edward Williams, Richard Wilson, J. T. Morgan, William Hutchins, Benjamin Jefferson, Solomon Hutchins, James C. Wilmore, James L. Cook, and Benjamin T. Ruley. All of these men rose to the episcopal office in the late nineteenth century. Of particular importance were Edward Williams and John C. Ramsey. Williams, who had been one of the plaintiffs involved in the case of Ellis Saunders and the Union Church of Africans in the period 1852-55, was for almost four decades one of the leading spokesmen for black people in Wilmington, Delaware. After serving as an early pastor of the Mother U. A. M. E. Church, he emerged to become one of the first elder ministers of his denomination. He also served as a general superintendent and as a bishop before his death toward the end of the century.[45] A distinguished looking gentleman, Ramsey was also well-known for his activities as a leader, a powerful preacher, and a gifted church builder. His influence was

evident in the U. A. M. E. Church long after he had passed
on. [46]

U. A. M. E. 's agreed that a major educational program
was necessary to develop such leadership for the church and
the race in the future.   By 1890, a Committee on Ministerial
Studies had been formed to plan courses of study for young
ministers.   The third Sunday in November of each year was
officially designated "Educational Day" to accept offerings for
the benefit of ministerial training.   In 1897 Bishop Benjamin
T. Ruley appointed an Education Committee to work in conjunction with the Committee on Ministerial Studies. [47]   The
success of such committees was seriously restricted because
of a scarcity of financial recourses, but their mere existence
testified to the fact that the U. A. M. E. Church was willing
to deal with an educated ministry.   Perhaps references to
two preacher-intellectuals in the church are in order for the
sake of countering the widely held notion that the Spencer
Churches were opposed to a trained clergy.   The first such
person to be mentioned in this regard is Lorenzo Dow Blackson, who was named for the great Methodist traveling preacher, Lorenzo Dow, who felt a divine impression to go to Ire-
land to proclaim the gospel in the early 1800s.   Blackson
was one of the most talented black intellectuals of the late
nineteenth century--one who could be compared in some ways
to Daniel A. Payne of the African Methodist Episcopal Church.
Born in Christiana, Delaware, in 1817, he joined the Union
Church of Africans at the age of sixteen.   He accepted the
call to the ministry and went on trial in 1839 under Peter
Spencer, of whom he spoke very highly in later years. [48]
When the great split occurred in the period 1851-56, he was
among those who followed Isaac Barney and Ellis Saunders.
In 1867 Blackson published a rare book entitled, The Rise
and Progress of the Kingdoms of Light and Darkness, or the
Reign of Kings Alpha and Abadon.   Levi J. Coppin of the
African Methodist Episcopal Church described the source as
"a counterpart of the 'Pilgrims' Progress, ' written in exactly the same style, poetry, and all. " Coppin went on to
record the following concerning the book and its author:

> He could sustain himself in an argument upon the
> doctrine he preached.   After preaching fifty years
> he was active; still writing and preaching.   I be-
> lieve that if the book should be published, the
> scholars and churchmen of the present day would
> discover its true value as the men of his day did
> not. [49]

Lorenzo Dow Blackson, the educator and preacher (from The Rise and Progress of the Kingdoms of Light and Darkness, by Lorenzo Dow Blackson).

Toward the end of the nineteenth century, Blackson broke with the U. A. M. E.'s and joined the A. M. E. Zion Church. He had been discouraged by the slow development of the U. A. M. E. denomination. He died as a preacher in the A. M. E. Zion Church. 50

The second figure to be mentioned in this connection is Jacob F. Ramsey, who was born the son of Bishop John C. Ramsey in Woodstown, New Jersey, in 1851. As a child he received special instruction from a private teacher in Philadelphia. After entering the ministry, Ramsey attended

Jacob F. Ramsey, the U. A. M. E. historian (from Father Spencer, Our Founder: His Work for the Church and Race, by Jacob F. Ramsey).

the Divinity School at West Philadelphia. His ability as a
thinker and debater was well-established during the flourish-
ing years of literary societies in Philadelphia. After ten
years of pastoring in West Chester and Philadelphia, he ran
for bishop and was elected at the general conference in Wilmington, Delaware, in October 1902. Described as "a forci-
ble and eloquent speaker" like his father, Ramsey was re-
peatedly called upon to deliver his famous lectures, entitled
"The Mighty Dollar," "Luck or Pluck," and "The Forces to
Win." As one who was very close to several preachers who
knew Peter Spencer and William Anderson, he was fortunate
to complete one of the earliest accounts of the development
of the Spencer movement. He also became the author of
Ramsey's Digest of the Union A. M. E. Church Laws and several other special papers on the history and doctrine of his
denomination. 51

Because of leaders like Ramsey, who had a great degree of black consciousness, the U. A. M. E. Church never
wavered in its stress on black self-help and race pride.
All in the church were constantly urged to deal fairly with
members of their race, and to support them in business ventures. Economic cooperation was vigorously preached, and
so was the need for black people to pool their finances to
buy buildings and property. 52 These expressions of black
power or nationalism, born of the conviction that black people had to take primary responsibility for their own liberation, remained one of the unique aspects of the life of the
U. A. M. E. Church and of African Union Methodism generally.
The following chapter sheds further light on how the Spencer
Churches found a special or unique expression prior to the
twentieth century.

NOTES

1. Quoted in The Discipline of the Union American
M. E. Church in the United States of America and Elsewhere,
Sixth Edition Revised (Wilmington: Henry Eckel, printer,
1872), p. 8.

2. August Meier and Elliot Rudwick, From Plantation to Ghetto (New York: Hill & Wang, 1970), pp. 158-159;
and Carter G. Woodson, The History of the Negro Church
(Washington, D. C.: The Associated Publishers, 1921), Chapters IX-X.

3. A Letter from the Elders of the African Union Church, New York City, to the Elders of the Mother African Union Church, Wilmington, Del., December 17, 1859.

4. Minutes of a Meeting of the Elders of the African Union Church, Wilmington, Delaware, April 10, 1860 (Wilmington: unpublished accounts housed in the Historical Society of Delaware, 1860), pp. 1-2.

5. Minutes of a Call Meeting of the Official Board of the African Union Church, Wilmington, Delaware, September 26, 1865 (Wilmington: unpublished accounts housed in the Historical Society of Delaware, 1865), pp. 1-2; and Minutes of a Call Meeting of the Congregation of the African Union Church, Wilmington, Delaware, October 4, 1865 (Wilmington: unpublished accounts housed in the Historical Society of Delaware, 1865), pp. 1-2.

6. The Doctrine and Discipline of the African Union First Colored Methodist Protestant Church of the United States of America or Elsewhere, First Edition (Wilmington: Henry Eckel, printer, 1867), pp. 8-11; Daniel J. Russell, Jr., History of the African Union Methodist Protestant Church (Philadelphia: The Union Star and Job, 1920), p. 20; and "The African Union Methodist Protestant Church," The United States Department of Commerce, Bureau of Census, Religious Bodies: Statistics, History, Doctrine, Organization, and Work, 1926 (Washington, D.C.: The U.S. Government Printing Office, 1929), pp. 1015-1025.

7. "The African Union Methodist Protestant Church," The United States Department of Commerce, Bureau of Census, Religious Bodies, pp. 1015-1025; and Lars P. Qualben, A History of the Christian Church (New York: Thomas Nelson, 1942), p. 541.

8. Qualben, A History of the Christian Church, p. 541; and The Doctrine and Discipline of the African Union First Colored Methodist Protestant Church, 1867, pp. 8-11.

9. The Doctrine and Discipline of the African Union First Colored Methodist Protestant Church, 1867, pp. 23-32.

10. Ibid., pp. 33ff.

11. Ibid., pp. 7ff.

12.   Ibid., pp. 35-38 and 120ff.; and The Doctrine and Discipline of the African Union First Colored Methodist Protestant Church of the United States of America or Elsewhere, Sixth Edition Revised (Wilmington: H. A. Roop, printer, 1895), pp. 143-144.

13.   Benjamin W. Arnett, ed., The Budget: Containing the Annual Reports of the General Officers of the African M. E. Church (Philadelphia, 1904), p. 235; and Minutes of a Quarterly Conference of the A. U. F. C. M. P. Church, Wilmington, Delaware, December 1, 1866 (Wilmington: unpublished accounts housed in the Historical Society of Delaware, 1866), pp. 1-2.

14.   Frederick A. Norwood, The Story of American Methodism: A History of the United Methodists and Their Relations (New York and Nashville: Abingdon Press, 1974), Chapter XXIV.

15.   The Personal Will Record of Edward H. Chippey, Will Record W-2 (Wilmington: Register of Wills, New Castle County, 1900), pp. 512-513; The Sunday Morning Star, Wilmington, Del. (August 12, 1900), p. 6; Minutes of a Quarterly Conference of the African Union Church, Wilmington, Delaware, March 9, 1861 (Wilmington: unpublished accounts housed in the Historical Society of Delaware, 1861), pp. 1-2; Minutes of a Quarterly Meeting of the Official Board of Elders of the African Union Church, Wilmington, Delaware, March 15, 1862 (Wilmington: unpublished accounts housed in the Historical Society of Delaware, 1862), p. 1; and Minutes of a Special Meeting of the Elders of the African Union Church, Wilmington, Delaware, April 24, 1862 (Wilmington: unpublished accounts housed in the Historical Society of Delaware, 1862), pp. 1-2.

16.   Minutes of a Quarterly Conference of the A. U. F. C. M. P. Church, Wilmington, Delaware, August 24, 1867 (Wilmington: unpublished accounts housed in the Historical Society of Delaware, 1867), p. 1; and Minutes of a Quarterly Conference of the A. U. F. C. M. P. Church, Wilmington, Delaware, August 29, 1868 (Wilmington: unpublished accounts housed in the Historical Society of Delaware, 1868), pp. 1-2.

17.   Henry C. Conrad, History of the State of Delaware: From Its Earliest Settlements to the Year 1907, 3 Vols. (Wilmington: the author, 1908), II, p. 793; Thomas

Scharf, History of Delaware, 1609-1888, 2 Vols. (Philadelphia: L. J. Richards, 1888), II, pp. 730-732; and Frank
R. Zebley, The Churches of Delaware (Wilmington: the author, 1947), pp. 104, 106, 109, 149, and 181.

18. Scharf, History of Delaware, II, p. 730-732;
and Zebley, The Churches of Delaware, pp. 104ff.

19. The Doctrine and Discipline of the African Union
First Colored Methodist Protestant Church of the United
States of America or Elsewhere (Wilmington: Henry Eckel,
printer, 1871), pp. 5ff.; Russell, History of the African
Union Methodist Protestant Church, p. 34; and "The History
of Wickham A. U. M. P. Church," in The 125th Anniversary
Booklet, Port Jervis, New York, May 2, 1976 (Port Jervis,
N. Y.: The Imperial Press, 1976), p. 5.

20. Russell, History of the African Union Methodist
Protestant Church, p. 57; and Arnett, ed., The Budget:
Containing the Annual Reports of the General Officers of the
African M. E. Church, 1904, p. 235.

21. The Doctrine and Discipline of the African Union
First Colored Methodist Protestant Church, 1871, pp. 5ff.;
Russell, History of the African Union Methodist Protestant
Church, pp. 34, 57-58, and 63; and "The History of Wickham
A. U. M. P. Church," in The 125th Anniversary Booklet, May
2, 1976, p. 5.

22. The Constitution and By-Laws of the Grand Body
of the Daughters of Conference of the A. U. F. C. M. P. Church
(Wilmington: T. E. Bolden, printer, 1935), pp. 3ff.; and
Minutes of the Quarterly Conference of the African Union
First Colored Methodist Protestant Church, Wilmington, Delaware, November 30, 1867 (Wilmington: unpublished accounts
housed in the Historical Society of Delaware, 1867), pp. 1-
2.

23. The Constitution and By-Laws of the Women's
Home Mite Missionary Society of the African Union First
Colored Methodist Protestant Church (Wilmington: T. E.
Bolden, printer, n. d.), pp. 4ff.; Minutes of the 129th An-
nual Conference of the African Union First Colored Methodist
Protestant Church, Washington, D. C., May 20-25, 1942
(Wilmington: T. E. Bolden, printer, 1942), pp. 27-28; and
Russell, History of the African Union Methodist Protestant
Church, pp. 22-23.

24. History of Wilmington: The Commercial, Social, and Religious Growth of the City During the Past Century (Wilmington: F. T. Smiley, 1894), p. 153.

25. Minutes of the Quarterly Conference of the African Union Methodist Protestant Church, Wilmington, Delaware, November 27, 1885 (Wilmington: unpublished accounts housed in the Historical Society of Delaware, 1885), pp. 1-2.

26. The Evening Journal, Wilmington, Del. (August 25, 1890), p. 3; and Russell, History of the African Union Methodist Protestant Church, p. 51.

27. Russell, History of the African Union Methodist Protestant Church, p. 51.

28. Conrad, History of the State of Delaware, II, p. 793; and The Doctrine and Discipline of the African Union First Colored Methodist Protestant Church, 1871, pp. 26-27 and 102-105.

29. Levi J. Coppin, Unwritten History (Philadelphia: The A. M. E. Book Concern, 1919), pp. 189-190.

30. The Doctrine and Discipline of the African Union First Colored Methodist Protestant Church, 1895, pp. 147-148 and 156-157.

31. Russell, History of the African Union Methodist Protestant Church, p. 28.

32. The Discipline of the Union American M. E. Church, 1872, pp. 8-11 and 55; Jacob F. Ramsey, Father Spencer, Our Founder: His Work for the Church and Race (Camden, N. J.: The General Conference of the U. A. M. E. Church, 1914), pp. 10-11; Matthew Simpson, ed., Cyclopaedia of Methodism Embracing Sketches of the Rise, Progress, and Present Condition, with Biographical Notices and Numerous Illustrations (Philadelphia: Everts & Stewart, 1878), p. 877; and "The African Union Conference at Wilmington, Delaware, August 25, 1864," A Letter in the Christian Recorder of the African Methodist Episcopal Church (September 3, 1864), pp. 2-3.

33. Ramsey, Father Spencer, Our Founder, pp. 10-11; and Simpson, ed., Cyclopaedia of Methodism, pp. 876-877.

34.   The Discipline of the Union American M. E. Church, 1872, pp. 8-51; and Simpson, ed. , Cyclopaedia of Methodism, p. 877.

35.   The Discipline of the Union American Methodist Episcopal Church in the United States of America, the Province of Canada, and Elsewhere (Wilmington: Hubert A. Roop, printer, 1892), pp. 111 and 170-171.

36.   Our Heritage: The History of the Union American Methodist Episcopal Church (Hackensack, N. J. :   Custombook, 1973), pp. 1-40; Every Evening, Wilmington, Del. (April 28, 1890), p. 1; Zebley, The Churches of Delaware, pp. 238ff. ; The Discipline of the Union American Methodist Episcopal Church, 1892, p. 9; and Arnett, ed. , The Budget: Containing the Annual Reports of the General Officers of the African M. E. Church, 1904, p. 231.   Arnett's statistics on the U. A. M. E. Church for the year 1904, which list 205 churches and only 1, 650 members, are far from accurate.

37.   The Discipline of the Union American Methodist Episcopal Church, 1892, pp. 9 and 11-12; and Every Evening (April 28, 1890), p. 1.

38.   The Morning News, Wilmington, Del. (April 27, 1895), p. 1.

39.   Every Evening (May 1, 1876), p. 3.

40.   Scharf, History of Delaware, II, p. 731; The Discipline of the Union American Methodist Episcopal Church, 1872, pp. 65-66; and The Discipline of the Union American Methodist Episcopal Church, 1892, p. 116.

41.   The Discipline of the Union American M. E. Church, 1872, p. 66.

42.   Simpson, ed. , Cyclopaedia of Methodism, p. 877.

43.   The Discipline of the Union American Methodist Episcopal Church, 1892, p. 114.

44.   The Discipline of the Union American M. E. Church, 1872, pp. 122-123; The Discipline of the Union American Methodist Episcopal Church, 1892, pp. 108 and 114; and The Morning News (April 21, 1897), pp. 1ff.

45. Ramsey, Father Spencer, Our Founder, pp. 10-11; Coppin, Unwritten History, pp. 189-190; and The Discipline of the Union American Methodist Episcopal Church, Thirty-first Edition (Chester, Pa.: The General Conference of the Union American Methodist Episcopal Church, 1976), p. 4.

46. Ramsey, Father Spencer, Our Founder, pp. 1-2; Our Heritage, p. 2; and The Discipline of the Union American Methodist Episcopal Church, 1976, p. 4.

47. The Discipline of the Union American Methodist Episcopal Church, 1892, pp. 108, 114, and 166; and The Morning News (April 21, 1897), pp. 1ff.

48. Lorenzo Dow Blackson, The Rise and Progress of the Kingdoms of Light and Darkness, or the Reign of Kings Alpha and Abadon (Philadelphia: J. Nicholas, printer, 1867), pp. 3, 7, and 170.

49. Coppin, Unwritten History, pp. 264-265.

50. Ibid.

51. Ramsey, Father Spencer, Our Founder, pp. 1-2.

52. The Discipline of the Union American M. E. Church, 1872, pp. 7, 122-123, and 134-135; and The Discipline of the Union American Methodist Episcopal Church, 1892, pp. 7-8 and 134-140.

Chapter V:

FESTIVITY AND CELEBRATION: EARLY AFRICAN
UNION METHODISM AND THE SHAPING OF
A WORSHIP TRADITION

> These meetings are the interesting features of
> the colored peoples' religious services. They
> generally end in a shout. They consist of a
> grouping of men in an open space in front of
> the preacher's stand, with a bench for a peni-
> tent's altar in the midst of the group. A con-
> gregation of all ages and conditions crowding
> as near as possible and all listening as if they
> expected some remarkable occurrence, make
> up the actors.
> > --An unnamed nineteenth-century
> > Wilmington newspaper reporter[1]

Any attempt to understand fully the character and development of the A. U. M. P. and U. A. M. E. Churches must take
into account that marvelous expression of both culture and
worship known as Big August Quarterly. This religious festival not only has the distinction of being Wilmington, Delaware's oldest folk festival and black America's first major
religious festival, but also is the most unique and significant
feature of African Union Methodism. [2] It is symbolic of the
fact that those of African descent are essentially festive and
feeling-oriented people who are given to expressive celebration. [3]

Big August Quarterly has been variously referred to
as Big Quarterly, August Quarterly, the Big Quarterly Meeting, and the Annual Big Meeting Day. It was inaugurated by
Peter Spencer in connection with the Union Church of Africans in 1814, one year after the church was formally organized. Big Quarterly was the one quarterly meeting held
annually at which time a general reunion and religious revival occurred at the mother church on French Street in Wil-

mington. Spencer apparently adopted the idea for such a
meeting from the Quakers, who were then one of the most
numerous societies in Wilmington, and who were well known
for their big annual meetings. [4] He chose late summer, specifically the last Sunday in August, as the most opportune
time for Big Quarterly. By this time, most of the grain had
been harvested, fruits were ripening, subsistence was cheap-
er, and many black workers--slave and free--could take the
weekend off to join the feasting, the social intercourse, and
the religious celebration which became characteristic of the
festival. [5]

Big Quarterly's Pilgrims

A number of black people on the Eastern Shore of Maryland
and Virginia, of Delaware and southeastern Pennsylvania,
figured prominently in the development of the Big Quarterly
festival. The small band of free blacks who organized the
Union Church of Africans actually adopted the festival as a
sort of independence day to celebrate the religious freedom
they had attained by breaking with the white Methodist Episcopal structure. It was to be principally a religious festival,
and the Mother Union Church of Africans was to be the religious nucleus and mainstay of the observance. [6]

Some of the black people who established Big Quarterly were slaves, many of whom were not long removed from
Africa. It became a custom for some of the slavemasters
in Maryland, Virginia, and lower Delaware to allow their
slaves to go to Wilmington for this glorious holiday. [7] Strong
precautionary measures were taken to prevent bondsmen from
escaping since Philadelphia, known as free territory, was
situated within a hundred miles of Wilmington. Slaves who
attended Big Quarterly had to carry passes or identification
papers and were accompanied in some instances by their
masters or by loyal black slave drivers. Sheriffs, constables,
and U. S. Marshalls were known to be present in considerable
numbers at Big Quarterly meetings. Security was often
strengthened by the presence of active slave catchers who,
as early as 1816, were established from Philadelphia through
Delaware and in every Eastern Shore county in Maryland,
particularly from Queene Anne's and Caroline Counties, to
New Market in Dorchester. All of these factors apparently
combined to give slaveholders the confidence they needed not
only to permit their slaves to attend Big Quarterly celebrations, but also to mingle with some degree of freedom with
free blacks who appeared. [8]

Of equal importance was the role assumed by women in the establishment of Big Quarterly, especially those women who were a part of the Union Church of Africans. Women not only formed much of the audience at these festivals, but were largely responsible for making the major preparations for them. Weeks in advance of the gatherings, they mapped plans, conducted fund-raising activities, and held prayer meetings to prepare themselves spiritually for the "big day." They alone undertook the burdensome task of preparing the large quantities of cabbage, collard greens, chickens, roasted-ears, spare-ribs, and other so-called "soul foods" consumed at Big Quarterlies. Much of the spirit and excitement of these camp-meeting-style gatherings in the pre-Civil War years was generated by women like "Mother" Ferreby Draper, Araminta Jenkins, and Annes Spencer, the wife of Peter Spencer. They involved themselves freely and collectively in the preaching, singing, shouting, feasting, and storytelling which marked the occasions, thereby playing a vital part in bequeathing a rich legacy of black custom, folklore, and tradition. 9

Before the facilities of quick transportation were supplied by the railroads and steamboats, the pilgrimage was the matter of a week's visit. Many of the pilgrims walked long distances and arrived in Wilmington on Saturday night, foot sore and dusty. Others came in hay wagons, in ox-carts, and on muleback. 10 Slave men appeared in long linen dusters and other articles of clothing borrowed from their masters or obtained on the orders of their masters. Women came in satins and homespuns, calicoes and velvets, and in the cast-off finery of their white mistresses. Young boys clad in plain clothes and staggering under the weight of water-melons were a common sight. 11 Beginning in the 1840s, Wilmington newspapers carried descriptive accounts of those who frequented the festivals in the antebellum period. The Delaware State Journal provided the following information concerning those who showed up for the 1845 Big Quarterly:

> Colored folks--Our town, on Sunday last was pretty well filled by "colored folks," who came to attend a religious meeting, called, generally, "the Big Quarterly." All sizes, of both sexes, and all ages, and we might say all colors, for there was a sample from the jetty African to the almost white-faced mulatto were present. The aged came with their gray heads and bowed forms, and little infant children were carried in the arms--some

chuckling forth their pleasure, others squalling out
their dissatisfaction. Some were clad in plain
habiliments, others, both male and female, reached
at the bon ton, and moustaches and imperials,
bowed and smiled complacently at the side of full
skirts and flounces. Many of these persons came
from a great distance, and it is believed that
Philadelphia furnished about 1, 000. The whole
company were well-dressed, and with few exceptions, as far as we can learn, conducted themselves in an orderly manner. The services at the
"Union" Church were performed with proper decorum and gravity. 12

According to Wilmington's Blue Hen's Chicken, the 1848 Big
Quarterly attracted an equally impressive crowd:

Colored Quarterly meeting--The colored people of
Spencer's Brick Church held a Quarterly meeting
on Sunday last. The number in attendance was
very large. They were generally healthy, fine
looking, very orderly men and women; and in dress
and appearance, many of them might favorably
compare with the whites. No similar number of
white people it is presumed, could have behaved
with more decorum. 13

The Delaware Gazette reported that the 1849 celebration drew
one of the largest crowds of the pre-Civil War period:

Big Quarterly--Our city was unusually crowded on
Saturday and Sunday last, by the colored brethren
from all parts of the country, in attendance upon
their annual Big Quarterly meeting. We think that
such a collection of them has seldom been witnessed. 14

The levels of attendance and enthusiasm at Big Quarterlies during the 1850s and 1860s diminished sharply for a
number of reasons. The great dispute which split the Union
Church of Africans into various factions between 1851 and
1856 was a contributing factor. For a time during the Civil
War the festival was not held for obvious reasons. 15

During the latter nineteenth century, such Wilmington
newspapers as Every Evening, The Evening Journal, The
Morning News, and The Sunday Morning Star were particularly

assertive in charging that attendance and excitement at Big
Quarterly celebrations were rapidly waning. [16] But such accounts were grossly inconsistent. While claiming that the
festival was declining, they afforded evidence to the contrary.
The 1865 meeting, the first held after the Civil War, was
not only very animated and spirited, but was attended by a
very large crowd:

> Big Quarterly last Sunday was "big" with the col-
> ored folks in this city. A large steamboat load
> arrived in the morning and an extra train of cars
> from Philadelphia. But hundreds had preceded
> them the evening before, and some parts of the
> town were literally crowded with them on Sunday
> afternoon. A large number flocked in from the
> country in carriages also. [17]

An "unusually large number of colored people" were present
at the 1866 event, and as many as five thousand visitors
were in Wilmington for the observance in 1867. [18] These
were the first Big Quarterlies held after the African Union
and First Colored Methodist Protestant Churches merged to
form the African Union Methodist Protestant Church. The
final three decades of the century evidently witnessed a significant increase in the number of celebrants who appeared.
The 1871 and 1876 celebrations attracted an enormous crowd
of both blacks and whites. [19] In describing the pilgrims of
the 1878 Big Quarterly, an editor of Every Evening declared,
"Never in the memory of the oldest inhabitant has the colored individual been around so numerously as he was yester-
day, " and continued,

> It was a heterogenous crowd of young and old, big
> and little, male and female, lame and lazy, mar-
> ried and single, gentle and simple individuals of
> African descent; of all shades of color from the
> barely noticeable tinge of the octoroon down to the
> thick lips, flat nose and stovepipe hue of the full-
> bloodied descendant of the old Congo Kings, disem-
> barked from the incoming railway trains and
> swarmed over the streets and pavements around
> the depot as thick as mosquitoes at Bombay Hook. [20]

Some of the members of the A. U. M. P. Church reported that
twenty thousand were on French Street for the fiesta in
1879. [21] This was probably the largest crowd to attend in
the nineteenth century. Thirteen thousand came via boat,

train, and on muleback to take part in the ceremonies and festivities in 1883. Between 1885 and 1890, an average of about seven thousand attended the festival annually. 22 "An army of fully ten thousand" appeared for the celebration in 1892, and the final meeting of the century was described as "successfully celebrated. "23 Such accounts bear out Alice Dunbar-Nelson's contention that "Big Quarterly was re-established with even more fervor and brilliance immediately after emancipation. "24

    The foregoing is not to suggest that Big Quarterly did not change in appearance at all after the Civil War. The Civil War and emancipation, which were attended by visible changes in the social and political condition of black people, slightly altered the image of the festival. Blacks could now participate in Big Quarterlies without having to carry passes and identification papers and free of the almost ubiquitous presence of constables, slavemasters, overseers, spies, slave catchers, sheriffs, and U. S. Marshalls. Also symbolic of this new era in the history of Big Quarterly was the growing number of intellectually inclined blacks who, turned off by the emotional religion associated with the festival, began to attack it as the stereotypical and out-dated remains of slave customs. One such black, who declined to give his name, called for the abolishment of Big Quarterly:

> These special meetings are no longer necessary either religiously or socially. The colored people have all the advantages for social intercourse and religious fellowship that other people enjoy. Spiritually, they hurt more than they help us. 25

    Some blacks of the intellectual type, who apparently failed to grasp the cultural significance of Big Quarterly, ceased to support the festival. An issue of The Evening Journal, dated August 26, 1895, took special note of this:

> Education has tended to keep the intelligent colored persons from attending, the festival being practically meaningless. It is now attended by Negroes of average condition and intellect, divided into two classes, of those who enjoy the religious services and those who delight in the worldly pleasures of the occasion. But it is still Big Quarterly and is always a great event for the colored people of Wilmington and the Peninsula. 26

Despite a growing chorus of voices in opposition to the festival, it continued to grow in popularity and remained an occasion for celebration, feasting, music, family reunions, spiritual revival, and historical remembrance.

The Worship Tradition

One of the most colorful aspects of the Big Quarterly festival was the worship tradition shaped in connection with it. That tradition was distinctly Afro-American in that it owed much to the African background and was born and nourished in the context of the black struggle for freedom, justice, and human dignity.

Worship exercises at Big Quarterlies during the nineteenth century generally followed a set pattern, beginning with the early Sunday morning love feast, and ending with the shout or the ring dance. The love feast was always celebrated in the traditional Methodist fashion. The celebrants would gather at the Mother A. U. M. P. Church as early as 6 a.m. to share in the breaking of bread and the drinking of water. It was a communal experience through which an abused people encountered God's presence in the Holy Spirit, and the mood never ceased to be serious and highly emotional. Public acknowledgments of divine goodness, mercies, and deliverance would be offered by both ministers and lay persons. The opening remarks at the 1884 Big Quarterly by P. S. Williams, the assistant pastor at the mother church, were typical:

> Brethren, the Lord has been merciful to us in sparing so many for this occasion. A goodly number of those who once gathered with us now sleep beneath our feet, and we should be more than thankful for his mercy to us. [27]

This part of the services commonly ended on a note of praise and thanksgiving. The worshipers would embrace one another, shout, and sing songs considered fitting for the occasion. The songs most frequently heard included:

> One more time, Lord,
>   One more time,
> Lord, I'm glad to be
>   in the service,
>   One more time.

and:

> And are we yet alive,
> To see each other's face. 28

The Big Quarterly style of worship was characterized by six major components: preaching, singing, the frenzy, prayer, testimony, and faith-healing. Each of these components must be considered individually if one is to understand clearly their importance in the context of this black worship tradition.

From the time of Peter Spencer and William Anderson, the sermon was the central feature of worship at Big Quarterly celebrations. Oftentimes several sermons were delivered simultaneously in the Mother A. U. M. P. Church, in tents set up alongside the church, and in other black churches in the vicinity of French Street. 29 Fortunately, nineteenth-century Wilmington newspapers tell us a great deal about the content, style, and delivery of sermons preached at Big Quarterlies during that period. Some of the sermons delivered were of a consolatory kind, having the effect of comforting people who were afflicted daily by the powerful forces of racism and oppression. Others were of a prophetic nature in that the preachers proclaimed with passion God's judgment upon the wicked and urged sinners to repent. The metaphors used in such sermons were usually very captivating. An important illustration is provided in a sermon preached from Ezekiel 37:3 at the 1883 Big Quarterly by the Reverend R. W. Scott:

> After alluding to Ezekiel and his prophecies, which are noted for their majestic splendor and highly figurative style, Mr. Scott said the world is one vast graveyard, one extensive charnel house, and the valley of dry bones is a fit emblem of its condition. Referring to the instruction given to prophecy, the speaker said the probability of the dead hearing was a question with some. They said preaching would be in vain. The dead, however, did hear. The dry bones heard the word. When they heard it they grew excited. Their stillness was disturbed. There was a great shaking. They were brought together by the word of God. So are men. They were clothed with sinews and flesh. The bones no longer rattled. They lived. The winds blew, which is intended to say the spirit of

the Lord moved upon them. They appeared in an
exceeding great army. While sinners are willing
to be still in the valley and charnel house, there
are sinners disturbed. While sinners were dead
they were naked. When they were brought from
the valley they were clothed with the grace of God.
You whose bones are no longer dry shall come forward in the morning of the resurrection with palms
in your hands, crowns on your heads, robed in
raiments of glory, and will march to the throne of
God. [30]

The editor of The Evening Journal reported on another sermon delivered at Big Quarterly in 1890 which was equally
impressive for its imagery:

The metaphors used by one preacher in particular
were very striking. He compared the road to hell
to a railroad in which vice was a great black car
and the people were flocking in as quickly as colored people returning from Big Quarterly meeting. [31]

Sermons that attacked all forms of hatred and dissension and highlighted by the necessity for Christian unity and
harmony among all people, were also interlaced with imagery.
The Reverend Edward Chippey's sermon at Big Quarterly in
1879, in which he denounced all hatred and prejudice as "the
bulldogs of hell, " immediately comes to mind:

The preacher went on to show how when prejudice
and hatred had been entirely eradicated from the
heart, and love, peace, and faith had taken their
place, the Christian would go down to the brink of
the dark River of Jordan, without a doubt or fear,
happy in the confidence that his feet would soon
press the shores of the heavenly Canaan beyond.
The sermon was full of homely similes inculcating
the leading idea that all sectarian and other dissen-
sions should be eradicated and every Christian be
made to feel that he is a member of the same
great brotherhood. [32]

In many instances, the preachers borrowed their imagery from the Old Testament accounts of Moses and the
Hebrew tribal struggles and wanderings, to illustrate the
power of God as a deliverer of the afflicted. An example is

offered in a message given by the Reverend Abram George at the 1880 celebration:

> His style was very graphic and exceedingly dramatic. He referred to the "Kingdential Throne" in glowing terms, and eulogized Moses in his original way. After telling of the wonderful crossing of the Red Sea, he said "it was not Moses' Rod what did it, but the power of God. " The colored brethren would urge him on by crying out, "preach it!" "preach Jesus!" One old fellow in a white linen coat stood up in the aisle in front of him and by his exclamations and antics made himself almost as conspicuous as the preacher. [33]

The frequent shouts of "Amen, " "preach it, " and "preach Jesus" in response to George's message are illustrative of the fact that a key element in preaching at Big Quarterlies was the call-and-response pattern, which has been linked to the West African background. [34] The preaching always involved a constant dialogue between the preacher and the audience, suggesting that the folk sermon as a work of art was the product of a collective consciousness. The "Amens" and other passionate expressions often heard simply meant that the hearers were in agreement with the message of the preacher and that they perceived that message as an indication of the spirit acting upon him. Such responses in all cases depended upon the ability of the preacher to act out his sermon with the rhythm of his voice and the movement of his body. Some preachers were masters of this art. One such preacher was the Reverend Daniel J. Russell, Sr., who had been a close associate of Peter Spencer. At the 1883 Big Quarterly, he brought a large crowd of worshipers to a high pitch of emotional participation with his histrionic talent:

> He took a running text on "True Belief" and delivered his address without notes. His manner was earnest and enthusiastic, and the points of his sermon were emphasized by grotesque gestures. He divided his attention between the audience and brother ministers sitting in the pulpit, frequently turning to them for signs of approval. [35]

Black people who struggled daily to be free found special meaning in the sermons they heard at Big Quarterly. The struggles of Moses and the Hebrew Children became historical realities to which they could relate with familiarity. Such stories told by the preachers came alive in their existential situations and gave them the will and power to live.

The second most important ingredient in the Big Quarterly worship tradition was song. Some of the first slave spirituals assembled on these shores were improvised and sung at Big Quarterlies in the years prior to the Civil War, and others inspired by the slave experience were forged at these meetings in the late nineteenth century. A considerable number of these songs were remarkably similar to the sermon in that they strongly emphasized salvation, along with an invitation to sinners to join the company of the saved:

> Come with me, I'll do you good,
> Sinner, I'm on my way to God.

and:

> Sinner, you better run,
> You better run,
> Time is winding up. [36]

Others reflected the spiritual, physical, and psychological pain which came with serving in a strange land and revealed the degree to which black people were unflinching in their desire for freedom:

> In a strange land,
> Great ways from home.
> Heard a mighty rumblin',
> Didn't know where t'was from.

Another was:

> If once I get inside the door,
> You'll never find me here no more. [37]

In still others the black celebrants, in a manner remarkably similar to their West African ancestors, directed their hopes and dreams toward a heaven in which all of their friends and relatives would meet as a community:

> When the roll is called again,
> Will you meet me?
> When the roll is called again,
> Will you meet me over there?

and:

> My poor mother is dead and gone,
> There is a land of beauty lying over there.
> She told me also to come on,
> There is a land of beauty lying over there. 38

Song was a part of every ritual and ceremony associated with Big Quarterly in the nineteenth century. It always set the mood for love feast and prepared the worshipers for the sermon. Song increased the power of God's spirit among the celebrants as they, like their African forebears, expressed the whole range of their experience and emotion by dancing, shouting, footstomping, and hand-clapping. This was evident at Big Quarterly in 1882:

> Here the most powerful singers and shouters took possession of the center of the floor, drew their coats and got right down to business in a short time. They sang simple and oft-repeated octuplets, dwelling with all the strength of their voices in the chorus, slapping their hands together, stomping their feet and jumping up and down for half an hour at a stretch; while all around the church men and women, catching the infection, would join in the jumping and shouting and swing their arms around convulsively, while the shrieks of penitents and the hallelujahs of the saints joined to swell the sound until it became one complete and overpowering mass of voice. Then someone in the circle of exhausted shouters would swing his arms upward and breathlessly cry out: "Brethren, let's go down now," and the singing would give way to a short season of equally earnest prayer. 39

A similar occurrence marked the celebration in 1888, as the innate emotionalism of the black people found expression through call-and-response, rhythmic movement, and song:

> The revival songs, with their peculiar cadence and perfect melody, rose and fell. A large crowd surrounded each group, and many white people stood on the outskirts, looking on curiously. They started their hymn slowly, but as they got warmed up the perspiration streamed from their faces, coats came off, and the tune of the hymn accelerated. With uprisen hands one broke into the line

of an improvised or committed verse while all the others joined in the refrain with much throwing up and clapping of hands, nodding and bobbing of heads, movements of the body and jumping up and down, all in perfect time to their song. It was infectious, and many of the on-lookers unconsciously nodded their heads or moved their bodies in time. [40]

Next to song, the most important component of worship at Big Quarterly meetings was the frenzy, as W. E. B. Du Bois called it. The frenzy, which included both the shout and the holy dance, always evidenced the presence of God's spirit among the worshipers. The shout, unlike the dance, was normally a spontaneous act engaged in by both men and women any time they felt the spirit. [41] Two female shouters in the gallery of the Mother A. U. M. P. Church attracted the attention of a reporter of Wilmington's Every Evening at Big Quarterly in 1882:

One of the most vigorous jumpers was a young girl dressed in blue, who soon cleared out the pew in which she sat and then had plenty of room to exercise to her heart's content. One of her neighbors, who wore a pretty bonnet and white gloves, anxious for the safety of her apparel, got out of the way with amusing celerity. But at this point the elder of the two women, as if not to be outdone, sprang to her feet and commenced jumping up and down to the imminent risk of springing over the rail upon the heads of the throng below. The younger at once ceased her contortions and moved out of the way of her more active sister who had by this time mounted the bench and would have been over the rail had it not been for a man, who caught her by the arm and held her gently, as if she was something likely to break. The result was that she swung and twisted him around, among and over the benches at a lively rate, until an old auntie hurried to the spot and, taking hold of the shouting women with a grasp that meant business, put her down in a seat and held her there. [42]

The ring dance, to the same degree as other rituals and ceremonies at these early festivals, pointed to West Africa. The basic characteristics of African religious dance --with its music, singing, chanting, rhythmic movements, and spirit possession--were perpetuated during the nineteenth century in the religious dances of blacks who frequented Big Quarterly. Such of these dances as were observed were group affairs which consisted of men in most cases and which had a specified place in the order of worship. Occasionally there were instruments, and the dancers would move and sway to the music, singing, chanting, and hand-clapping. The Delaware State Journal printed an account of a ring dance ceremony performed by a large group of black men at the 1883 Big Quarterly, describing it as "a solemn, weird sort of chant resembling not a little an Indian war dance":

> In the basement of the church a hundred or more men formed a circle and swayed to and fro, sometimes fast and sometimes slow, according to the metre of the hymn sung. Those who formed the inner line of the human ring were the most violent in their movements and most of the time perspired so freely that they could not have been more wet if a hose had been turned upon them. Frantically, they urged one another to more violent feats of gymnastic devotion, clapping their hands, jumping and shouting, and occasionally groaning. When they grew weary they dropped upon their knees and prayers were offered. The women were modest and did not help form the rings. Instead they sang and watched the proceedings with interest. 43

In August 1886 Every Evening offered another description of this ceremonial dance in terms compelling enough to deserve extended quotation:

> After the regular services in the afternoon, two crowds of male Negroes, half frenzied by religious excitement, formed circles, where they began their most interesting exercises to spectators. One was selected as leader and forced into the circle, where he began some doggerel rhyme in a low chant. The others joined, the chorus swelled as they became excited, their hands began beating time, to which their feet soon followed, and they developed into one howling mass, in which each tried to out-shriek the other. This was continued for almost ten minutes, when hoarse and exhausted they would fall on their knees and one of them would pray. After prayer, and while still kneeling, the low chant would again start, and as the volume of

sound increased the men would rise again and the
same scenes would be repeated. This was continued uninterruptedly for hours at a time. As
soon as one would retire there were three or four
anxiously waiting to take his place. The majority
of them worked themselves into such a nervous
state that they were almost frenzied. One in particular was noticeable. He was a big heavy set
man and stood in the middle of the circle with his
eyes half closed. As the excitement increased, he
would jump and shout until the sweat rolled down
his dusky face in one continual stream. His sweet-
heart made an effort to rescue him from the crowd
by pulling him by one arm, but he continued his
frantic leaps and loud shouting until from mere
desperation the girl released him. [44]

Prayer was the fourth most essential element in the
Big Quarterly worship style. Like the song, prayer was
always intimately connected with all Big Quarterly rituals
and ceremonies. It, too, would pave the way for the coming
of the Holy Spirit and would prepare the celebrants for its
acceptance. It was not uncommon for one worshiper after
another to kneel in prayer to assist in creating the mood
for love feast, the Lord's Supper, or the sermon. Wilmington newspapers are replete with references to the passionate
and picturesque ways in which blacks expressed the deep
yearnings of their hearts at these festivals. As many as
five prayer meetings would be held simultaneously in the
church, the tent, and outdoors in the graveyard. This was
the scene at Big Quarterly in 1888, when "prayers were ut-
tered with surprising eloquence and were clothed in expressions pleasantly original":

After the afternoon services three prayer meetings
were begun, in which the brethren took part with
vigor and animation. Two of these were held under the trees in the rear of the church and the other in the lecture room. Gathered together in a
small circle, stirring prayers were made in the
sing-song manner peculiar to the race. [45]

Oftentimes, prayer would follow a plaintive song of inquiry
or invitation, as a reporter for The Morning News observed
in 1889:

The prayer which follows is a passionate appeal for

aid. It is fervent. It may be ungrammatical in its construction, but it is eloquent. The supplicant tries to lift the penitent to the skies. He implores aid, confesses sin and exhorts to the exercise of faith. His brethren around him aid with responses. Shouts of "no!" "yes!" "amen!" and "do Lord!" coach him and augment his effort until it often seems as if the man's heart would leap from his throat in excess of emotion. There are comical sides and shades to such a scene and such activities, but no one laughs, no one scoffs. Everyone looks with intense interest at the actors, fearing that some great thing will happen and they not see it. 46

The fifth most important ingredient in the Big Quarterly worship tradition was testimony. Many black people who attended these early festivals looked forward to sharing their conversion experiences with their fellow worshipers, and untold numbers would be moved by the spirit to do so. Testimony was a way of acknowledging the presence of God's spirit among them and of attesting to His goodness in their lives. It was not unusual for celebrants to sing, pray, shout, and even preach while giving their testimonies. This was all in accord with their manner as an emotional and spiritual people. 47

Faith-healing is the final ingredient to be considered in this discussion. It was not uncommon for African conjurers and medicine men to attend these early meetings. They joined preachers and other self-styled religious leaders and prophets in praying for the sick, and in laying hands on those who desired to be cured of special ailments or disorders. Singing and shouting were also intimately tied to this aspect of worship. The prominent place reserved for faith-healing in the Big Quarterly worship tradition was reflective of the indomitable faith of the thousands of African men and women who were the shapers of that tradition.

The Significance of the Festival

Big Quarterly was immensely important to black people on the Delmarva Peninsula in the nineteenth century for several reasons. First, the occasion provided a rare opportunity for slaves to worship God in communion with each other and with free blacks. The religious significance of the festival for the slaves who were permitted to attend in pre-Civil War times was vividly remembered by a reporter for Wilmington's The Morning News in 1889:

> That permission gave them one day of freedom; gave them the opportunity to talk over the long deferred promise of freedom which everyone of them felt was somehow ingrained in the religion of Jesus. It gave them an opportunity to sing and pray and shout together; to seek and find inspiration in communion with one another, telling to each a story of the hardships inflicted by the system of unpaid labor; told to each other how their necks chafed under the ox-yoke which bound to the soil with irrevocable bonds. To many of them this one day in the year was the one day in which they could meet their friends, talk and worship with them as free men and women. These are the circumstances which made this religious holiday important and sacred in their sight. [48]

When the slaves met in Wilmington, after weeks of being cursed and lashed, their burdens were eased for the moment as they celebrated their common joy in God's acceptance of them and their unshakable faith in His deliverance. The songs, sermons, and prayers they heard gave them new hope, lifted them into a transcendent moment, and provided them with what sociologists call "staying power."

Second, Big Quarterly had a social dimension which allowed some outlet for black people. Relatives from different geographical points held reunions, and acquaintances who had been separated for a whole year met and spent the day in pleasant chat upon the events of the past year. The social climate which prevailed at the festival in 1880 was typical:

> There were greetings, and smiles and laughter, occasional oaths, a fight now and then, gallons of perspiration, and even a few tears. Here and there two women would be seen locked in tight embrace, the hand of each pounding the back of the other, while the two expressed their delight at the meeting. As each train came in hundreds of heads were thrust out at the windows, while the air resounded with shouts of recognition. [49]

There were always those who showed up merely to show off their new costumes and to have a good time. Groups of black men would gather to tell tales, and African music, dance, and good humor would mingle with the spirited greetings and homestyle cooking. Homes were often turned into temporary restaurants, and booths and refreshment stands were set up. Chicken, ham, cabbage, spare-ribs, and other foods would be temptingly displayed, and hundreds of Jersey Cantaloupes, Peninsula peaches, and watermelons devoured by the pilgrims. The whole scene offered diversion and color in a time when there were all too few variations in the monotonous pattern of life. 50

Third, the festival was important in the pre-Civil War years not only because it provided in a limited way a public platform for free blacks to discuss colonization and other issues involving slavery, but also because it gave slaves a chance to slip away to freedom. The experience of a weekend of relative freedom, and the opportunity to associate with free blacks, proved tempting to many bondsmen whose only other alternative was to return to their masters. Abolitionists and Underground Railroad conductors of the stature of Thomas Garrett and Harriet Tubman were often in the Wilmington area to assist slaves who chose to escape. The Mother African Union Church, always the focal point of Big Quarterly, became a kind of gateway to freedom. In the late nineteenth century, The Morning News recalled those days:

> As the years passed the church enlarged. The day grew in importance and the number of visitors increased from a few hundreds to many thousands. The desire for freedom grew stronger and stronger, and pilgrims did not always return to their masters, but found homes in the free states and in Canada. Thus "Big Quarterly" came to be regarded with suspicion by slave owners. During the latter days of slavery, sheriffs, constables, and sometimes U. S. Marshalls were busy watching for runaways. The old people now refer to these meetings as big excursions on the Underground Railroad, and smile at the remembrance of the tricks to which they resorted to hide and aid the fugitives. 51

Fourth, the event marked a time to commemorate the founding of African Union Methodism. Those affiliated with the Spencer Churches were reminded of the bitter struggles

Top: Harriet Tubman, the Moses of her people; bottom: Thomas Garrett, the Quaker antislavery advocate.

of Peter Spencer, William Anderson, and the forty or so
other blacks who struck the great blow for religious freedom.
In August 1843 one month after Spencer's death, the tradition
was broadened to include wreath-laying ceremonies at his
gravesite.   Each year after 1843 slaves and free blacks
marched up the hill to the rear of the mother church and
stood at the grave "covered with old-fashioned marble slabs
lying on brick piers. "   The silence of the moment would be
broken as the pilgrims lifted their voices in song:

> Oh, where is Father Spencer?
> I wonder where he's gone?
> The Church is all in mourning,
> And he cannot be found.

And there were these lines:

> Father Spencer's body lies moldering
>   in the clay,
> Father Spencer's body lies moldering
>   in the clay,
> His Church is marching on. 52

Spencer's tomb became "the shrine of every lover of freedom, " and thousands went to great lengths "to make this
annual pilgrimage to the cradle of African Union Methodism,
and to help the memory of Father Spencer to live on and on
while his spirit marches on to new and greater triumphs. "53
Wilmington soon earned an enduring reputation as "the Mecca of African people":

> For nearly a century this city has been the Mecca
> of the African race in the United States.   A pil-
> grimage to the church here and to the grave of
> Peter Spencer was to them as sacred a duty as is
> the visit to the prophet's tomb, to the pious Mo-
> hammedan. 54

   Fifth, Big Quarterly was tremendously important because it functioned very early as a kind of general conference
for congregations in the Union Church of Africans.   Representatives from all of the congregations were usually present
at the festival, and this afforded an opportunity to transact
business matters which affected the entire connection.   After
the Civil War, the policy of holding general conferences
was adopted by the A. U. M. P. Church, and the uses of Big
Quarterly in this regard were minimized. 55

Finally, the celebration kept alive a spirit of ecumenism among black churchmen and women of various denominational backgrounds on the Delmarva Peninsula. Black churches in Wilmington and neighboring areas would always close down on Big Quarterly Sunday, and would assemble in Wilmington for a day of ecumenical worship and activities. In the late nineteenth century, Ezion Methodist Episcopal Church, the Mother A. U. M. P. Church, and the Mother U. A. M. E. Church--all having common roots in the Spencer movement--would engage in a joint effort to pay tribute to Spencer and to make the day successful. The doors of these and other churches in the vicinity of French Street were often opened to accommodate the thousands of worshipers who appeared. [56] Denominational unity and cooperation of this kind continued well into the twentieth century, as shall be revealed in a later chapter.

NOTES

1. The Morning News, Wilmington, Del. (August 26, 1889), p. 1.

2. The Morning News (August 27, 1883), p. 1; and "Wilmington's Oldest Folk Festival, " The Big Quarterly Program Booklet of the Mother A. U. M. P. Church, Wilmington, Delaware (August 27, 1978), pp. 1-4.

3. A fascinating reference to black people's festive and feeling-oriented approach to life is provided in Harvey Cox, The Feast of Fools: A Theological Essay on Festivity and Fantasy (Cambridge: Harvard University Press, 1969), pp. 16-17 and 25.

4. Alice Dunbar-Nelson, Big Quarterly in Wilmington (Wilmington: the author, 1932), p. 2; The Morning News (August 27, 1883), p. 1; The Morning News (September 1, 1884), p. 1; and The Morning News (August 26, 1889), pp. 1 and 8. Sources on Delaware history have not been in agreement as to the exact date of the origin of this festival. According to the Nelson account, the first great meeting of rejoicing occurred in August 1812. Pauline A. Young, another black Delaware historian and a relative of Alice Dunbar-Nelson, sets the beginning date at August 1813, in her "The Negro in Delaware, Past and Present, " in H. Clay Reed, ed. , Delaware: A History of the First State, 3 Vols. (New York: Lewis Historical Publishing, Inc. , 1947), II, pp. 604-605.

All of the Wilmington newspapers of the nineteenth and twentieth centuries--such as The Delaware Gazette, The Delaware State Journal, Blue Hen's Chicken, The Evening Journal, The Delmarva Star, and The Morning News--agree with Young's dating of Big Quarterly. It is believed that a festival of this kind was held by black Methodists in Wilmington as early as 1810, when Spencer and his followers were still at Ezion. The Union Church of Africans was not officialized until September 1813, which means that the first Annual Quarterly held in connection with this church took place in August 1814.

5. Nelson, Big Quarterly in Wilmington, pp. 2-3; and The Morning News (August 26, 1889), pp. 1 and 8.

6. The Morning News (August 30, 1880), p. 1; The Morning News (August 26, 1889), pp. 1 and 8; and The Sunday Morning Star, Wilmington, Del. (August 25, 1895), p. 1.

7. Nelson, Big Quarterly in Wilmington, pp. 2-3; Young, "The Negro in Delaware, Past and Present," p. 604; and The Morning News (August 26, 1889), pp. 1 and 8.

8. The Delaware Gazette and Peninsula Advertiser, Wilmington, Del. (September 26, 1816), pp. 1-2; The Delaware Gazette, Wilmington, Del. (September 1, 1857), p. 2; and The Morning News (August 26, 1889), pp. 1 and 8.

9. Minutes of a Regular Meeting of the Elders of the African Union Church in Wilmington, Delaware, August 18, 1863 (Wilmington: unpublished accounts housed in the Wilmington branch of The Historical Society of Delaware, 1863), pp. 1-2; The Delaware Tribune, Wilmington, Del. (May 28, 1868), p. 3; and Nelson, Big Quarterly in Wilmington, pp. 1-5.

10. The Morning News (August 26, 1889), pp. 1 and 8; and Nelson, Big Quarterly in Wilmington, pp. 2-3.

11. The Delaware State Journal, Wilmington, Del. (September 2, 1880), p. 1; The Delaware Gazette and State Journal, Wilmington, Del. (August 29, 1889), p. 3; and Nelson, Big Quarterly in Wilmington, pp. 1-3.

12. The Delaware State Journal (September 2, 1845), p. 3.

13. Blue Hen's Chicken, Wilmington, Del. (September 1, 1848), p. 2.

14. The Delaware Gazette (August 28, 1849), p. 2.

15. The Delaware Gazette (August 27, 1850), p. 2; Program Booklet of the 157th Anniversary of the Mother A. U. M. P. Church, 1813-1970, Wilmington, Delaware, August 30, 1970 (Wilmington: printed by the trustees of Mother A. U. M. P. Church, 1970), p. 17; and "Wilmington's Oldest Folk Festival," pp. 1-4.

16. The Morning News (August 29, 1881), p. 1; The Morning News (August 31, 1885), p. 1; Every Evening, Wilmington, Del. (August 31, 1891), p. 1; The Evening Journal, Wilmington, Del. (August 27, 1888), p. 4; and The Sunday Morning Star (August 26, 1900), p. 1.

17. The Delaware Gazette (August 29, 1865), p. 2.

18. The Delaware State Journal and Statesman, Wilmington, Del. (August 28, 1866), p. 2; and The Delaware Gazette (August 27, 1867), p. 2.

19. The Delaware Gazette (August 29, 1871), p. 2; and Every Evening (August 28, 1876), p. 4.

20. Every Evening (August 26, 1878), p. 1.

21. Every Evening (September 1, 1879), p. 1.

22. The Morning News (August 27, 1883), p. 1; The Morning News (August 31, 1885), p. 1; Every Evening (August 30, 1886), p. 1; The Morning News (August 29, 1887), p. 1; The Evening Journal (August 27, 1888), p. 4; The Morning News (August 26, 1889), pp. 1 and 8; and The Morning News (September 1, 1890), p. 1.

23. The Evening Journal (August 29, 1892), p. 1; and Every Evening (August 28, 1899), p. 2.

24. Nelson, Big Quarterly in Wilmington, p. 2.

25. The Morning News (August 27, 1888), p. 1.

26. The Evening Journal (August 26, 1895), p. 1.

27.   The Morning News (September 1, 1884), p. 1; and The Morning News (August 26, 1889), pp. 1 and 8.

28.   The Morning News (September 1, 1884), p. 1.

29.   The Morning News (August 26, 1889), pp. 1 and 8; and The Evening Journal (August 30, 1897), p. 1.

30.   Every Evening (August 27, 1883), p. 1.

31.   The Evening Journal (September 1, 1890), p. 1.

32.   Every Evening (September 1, 1879), pp. 1 and 4.

33.   Every Evening (August 30, 1880), p. 1.

34.   See Melville J. Herskovits, The Myth of the Negro Past (Boston: Beacon Press, 1958), pp. xxiii-xxv; and Alfloyd Butler, The Africanization of American Christianity (New York: Carlton Press, 1980), Chapter I.

35.   The Delaware State Journal (August 30, 1883), p. 1.

36.   The Evening Journal (August 27, 1888), p. 4.

37.   Every Evening (August 30, 1880), p. 1; The Evening Journal (August 27, 1888), pp. 4-5; and The Delaware State Journal (August 30, 1883), p. 1.

38.   The Morning News (August 26, 1889), pp. 1 and 8; and Every Evening (August 30, 1886), p. 1.   Black people in America were being typically West African in rejecting a kind of individualistic involvement in the afterlife.   African scholars such as E. Bolaji Idowu have demonstrated that in African traditional religion, "The place where the ancestors live permanently is the 'paradise' for which Africans yearn as their final home--a 'heaven' in which they have a happy, unending reunion with their folk who are waiting for them on the other side."   See Idowu, African Traditional Religion: A Definition (New York: Orbis Books, 1973), pp. 188-189.

39.   Every Evening (August 28, 1882), p. 1.

40.   The Evening Journal (August 27, 1888), p. 4.

41.   John Hope Franklin, ed., The Souls of Black

Folk in Three Negro Classics (New York: Avon Books, 1975; originally published in 1903), pp. 338-340. A distinction between the shout and the holy dance is given in Clifton H. Johnson, ed., God Struck Me Dead: Religious Conversion Experiences and Autobiographies of Ex-Slaves (Philadelphia and Boston: Pilgrim Press, 1969), p. 12.

42. Every Evening (August 28, 1882), p. 1.

43. The Delaware State Journal (August 30, 1883), p. 1; and The Delaware Gazette and State Journal (August 29, 1889), p. 3.

44. Every Evening (August 30, 1886), p. 1. This ring dance ceremony was obviously an essential part of the Big Quarterly worship style throughout the nineteenth century because numerous references to it are made in early Wilmington newspapers such as Every Evening, The Delaware Gazette, The Delaware State Journal, The Evening Journal, The Morning News, and The Sunday Morning Star.

45. The Evening Journal (August 27, 1888), p. 4; and The Delaware Gazette and State Journal (August 29, 1889), p. 3.

46. The Morning News (August 26, 1889), pp. 1 and 8.

47. The Delaware Gazette (September 1, 1846), p. 3; The Delaware Gazette (September 1, 1868), p. 2; and Every Evening (August 28, 1882), p. 1.

48. The Morning News (August 26, 1889), pp. 1 and 8.

49. The Morning News (August 30, 1880), p. 1.

50. The Evening Journal (August 27, 1888), p. 4; The Morning News (August 26, 1889), pp. 1 and 8; The Morning News (August 27, 1894), p. 1; The Evening Journal (August 29, 1898), p. 6; and Nelson, Big Quarterly in Wilmington, pp. 1-5.

51. The Morning News (August 26, 1889), pp. 1 and 8; Frances Cloud Taylor, The Trackless Trail: The Story of the Underground Railroad in Kennett Square, Chester County, Pennsylvania, and the Surrounding Community (Kennett Square,

Pa.: the author, 1976), pp. 4-6 and 32-34; and James A. McGowan, Station Master on the Underground Railroad: The Life and Letters of Thomas Garrett (Moylan, Pa.: The Whimsie Press, 1977), Chapters I-XI. This source examines the close relationship between Garrett and Tubman.

52. Daniel J. Russell, Jr., History of the African Union Methodist Protestant Church (Philadelphia: Union Star Book and Job, 1920), p. 12; and Program Booklet of the 157th Anniversary of the Mother A.U.M.P. Church, 1813-1970, pp. 3 and 17.

53. "Wilmington's Oldest Folk Festival," p. 4; and Edward R. Bell, et al., compilers, The Tomb of Peter Spencer: A Pamphlet (Wilmington, n.d.), p. 1.

54. The Morning News (August 26, 1889), pp. 1 and 8.

55. The Morning News (August 27, 1883), p. 1.

56. The Evening Journal (August 26, 1889), p. 3; The Morning News (August 30, 1897), pp. 1-3; and Nelson, Big Quarterly in Wilmington, pp. 1-5.

Chapter VI:

INSTITUTIONAL CHAOS AND DECLENSION:
THE SPENCER CHURCHES CONFRONT
THE TWENTIETH CENTURY

> Like St. Peter, let us not be satisfied with a
> stunted or stationary life, but rather let us
> grow in influence as we take what we have and
> make what we want ..., as we take our little
> country churches and make them into fit places
> for God's indwelling.... If we would have the
> state of the church exemplify the rock which
> PETER SPENCER must have been, then this
> conference must live, not within itself, but we
> must extend into the far corners with our
> churches.
>   --Walter C. Cleaver[1]

The twentieth century has not represented a success story as
far as the growth, expansion, and influence of the A. U. M. P.
and U. A. M. E. Churches are concerned. To be sure, institutional chaos and declension have been marked features of
both churches. Between 1900 and 1980 they suffered serious
losses in terms of memberships and church buildings. Very
significant for this trend were a host of problems relating
to leadership and organization. Thus, they have continued
to struggle in the backwaters of African Methodism.

Despite staggering losses, the A. U. M. P. and U. A. M. E.
denominations attempted to deal in a positive way with some
of the problems facing black people in America during the
first half of the century--problems stemming primarily from
the forces of migration, oppression, urbanization, and economic depression. They organized colleges and seminaries
for the first time in their histories and moved to support the
National Association for the Advancement of Colored People
(N. A. A. C. P.) and other groups aimed at solving the race
problem in this country. Such efforts, born of a keen sensi-

152

tivity to social issues and a deep awareness of social need, continued to some extent during the 1960s and 1970s as A. U. M. P. 's and U. A. M. E. 's confronted the new and different realities of civil rights, black power, and theological renewal.

The marks of the decline of the Spencer Churches are still evident today, and there are no strong indications that they will develop beyond a mere regional existence. However, A. U. M. P. and U. A. M. E. leaders are convinced that there are hopeful signs which suggest that their churches will grow and survive as black religious institutions. Furthermore, they are attempting to recover in a fresh way their religious heritages as well as the original sources of inspiration which lay beneath them.

The A. U. M. P. Church

The A. U. M. P. Church entered the twentieth century without the services of two of its most capable leaders. Daniel Russell, Sr., a former president of the Middle District, passed away on April 21, 1899. Edward H. Chippey, the most widely known figure in the church during the first four decades after the Civil War, died on August 10, 1900. Chippey's death was mourned by the entire city of Wilmington, Delaware, and Chippey Street was named for him. [2] The loss of these men did not set well with a denomination which was already suffering because of a serious shortage of strong, progressive-minded leaders. But despite the loss of these men, A. U. M. P. 's faced the new century with high hopes and great expectations. Some in the church regarded the new century as an evangelical opportunity to start anew in imparting the guiding light of the gospel to the unsaved. John H. Bell, A. B. Selvey, and Charles H. Walker, three of the most admired preachers in the church, spoke optimistically about the possibilities for growth and expansion, noting, "We have noticed that the beginning of the twentieth century has opened upon us with marvelous possibilities with regard to the country in general, and the A. U. F. C. M. P. Church in particular. "[3]

The high hopes for a productive future in terms of growth and expansion were soon dashed as internal bickering threatened once again to tear the church apart. The central figure in this dispute was James E. Sargent, who was the president of the First District, which embraced parts of Dela-

ware, Pennsylvania, and New Jersey, and chairman of the
General Board of presiding officers. In the fall of 1902,
Sargent, in compliance with the ruling of the general conference which met earlier that year, sought to increase the
quarterly taxation from 70 cents to a dollar, the proceeds
from which were to be placed in the general fund. In addition, he took steps to strengthen connectional authority by
declaring that the properties of local congregations were to
be deeded to the conference and that the general officers of
the church, not the members of local congregations, were to
serve as the trustees of those properties. [4] Most of the
preachers and lay persons were not in favor of these measures. Sargent, who recommended that the measures be
adopted in the first place, became the object of strong ridi-
cule and attack. On October 2, 1902, the congregations in
Philadelphia and South Jersey revolted against his administration and organized a new district called the Philadelphia and
New Jersey District of the A. U. M. P. Church. [5] A month
later, a special session of the annual conference of this district was called to discuss the problem. Sargent did not attend the conference. Daniel J. Russell, Jr. and Alexander
W. Woodards, two respected clergymen, led the attack on
the new measures. Russell argued along these lines:

> First, they have departed from the Constitution
> and Government of our fathers. Our Government
> has always been a republican form, but the new
> laws as enacted, will place our properties in the
> hands of strangers. The new laws say that the
> five General Officers shall be the trustees. By
> this code of law our local trustees will be handi-
> capped and our rights taken from us.
>   Second, they also adopted the dollar money
> which we protest against. There may be a time
> when it will be very acceptable, but not now. Our
> motto is to stand by the African Union Church as
> founded by the Rt. Rev. Peter Spencer. [6]

Woodards was far more harsh in his criticisms, blaming
Sargent with "causing this great trouble in our church...."
After indicating that vesting control in the conference at
large was contrary to the very principles so dear to Peter
Spencer, Woodards commented:

> I am opposed to buying property and having it
> deeded to any one man or set of men aside from
> the trustees of the local church who labor for the

money to buy the properties with. I am with the
people, and for the people, and when you turn
down the rights of the people, a conference is no
good. We would have had today a church [Ezion]
in Wilmington, Delaware, at the corner of Ninth
and Walnut Streets, had it not been that the Methodist Episcopal Conference controlled the property.
Therefore, we do not want that in our church any
more. 7

Despite being under heavy pressure, Sargent refused
to bow, believing that vesting control in the local trustees
was self-defeating in that it opened the door for the with-
drawal of churches which found the policies of the annual
and general conferences unacceptable. In a letter to the
conference, he insisted that he would not change his mind,
and that he was willing "to take my wife and children and
leave the connection" if necessary. 8 An acceptable compromise was not reached, and Sargent made good of his prom-
ise. The church had lost one of its strongest leaders.
Isaac B. Cooper, a promising young preacher from Summit
Bridge, Delaware, was elected president of the Philadelphia
and New Jersey District. 9 A major schism had been avoided,
but the effects of the dispute were felt for some time after-
ward. Later developments clearly proved that Sargent was
right on this issue.

The dispute of 1902 pointed to very serious institutional weaknesses, and it was a sure signal that the A. U. M. P.
Church was entering a period of decline. It is difficult to be
precise about the number of churches in the connection at the
time of the dispute, but it is known that several were in
danger of either dying out or being lost to other stronger
and more popular black denominations. According to Benjamin W. Arnett, who emerged as a bishop in the African
Methodist Episcopal Church in 1888, there were 68 churches
in the A. U. M. P. connection in 1904. 10 This figure is about
right when taken to include both congregations and small missions (made up of members who had not built churches, but
were worshiping in homes).

By 1910 a number of congregations and small missions
had been started in parts of Delaware, Maryland, Virginia,
Pennsylvania, New Jersey, and New York. However, this
proved not to be an indication that the church was entering
a period of significant growth and expansion. Strangely, the
A. U. M. P. Church experienced its most serious decline be-

tween 1910 and 1950, when large numbers of southern blacks
were migrating north to cities like Detroit, Philadelphia,
Washington, D. C. , Wilmington, and New York. Even though
the A. U. M. P. 's had congregations and small missions in
these cities, they did not profit to any great extent from the
scores of black people participating in the so-called "Great
Migrations. " There were simply no vigorous, organized effort to attract them into the fold. Many of them joined other
black denominations, while others affiliated with storefront
churches or emerging black cults and sects. Thus, instead
of growing and expanding, the A. U. M. P. Church declined
from about 69 congregations and small missions in 1910 to
only 36 congregations in 1950. 11 Several churches in Connecticut, Maryland, New Jersey, Pennsylvania, Rhode Island,
and Virginia were apparently lost to other black denominations. 12 The following either died out, became independent,
or affiliated with other denominations: St. Paul A. U. M. P.
Church, Passaic, New Jersey; The Green Mountain Valley
Mission, Green Mountain Valley, New Jersey; Bethany Mission, Paterson, New Jersey; St. John A. U. M. P. Church,
Chesilhurst, New Jersey; The Burlington Mission, Burlington,
New Jersey; St. Joseph A. U. M. P. Church, Mt. Pleasant,
Delaware; the Easton Mission, Easton, Pennsylvania; St.
Matthew A. U. M. P. Church, Detroit, Michigan; St. Stephen
A. U. M. P. Church, Hurley, New York; the Horsehead Mis-
sion, Horsehead, New York; the Guyencourt Mission, Guyen-
court, Delaware; and the St. John A. U. M. P. Church, Chat-
ham, Ontario, Canada. 13

Serious losses were incurred along the Eastern Shore
of Maryland, in the vicinity of the city of Salisbury. During
the early years of the century, there were about 30 A. U. M. P.
congregations and small missions functioning in this area.
Only fourteen congregations remained in the entire state of
Maryland in 1950. 14 Reese C. Scott, who served as president of the A. U. M. P. Conference from 1950 to 1967, and
bishop from 1967 to 1974, claims that many of the churches
along the Maryland Eastern Shore were lost to other black
Methodist denominations. He assessed the losses in these
terms:

> The decline was because they (A. U. M. P. leaders)
> had more religion than they had business qualifica-
> tions. If they had had the initiative to go to court
> when these churches were being snatched by the
> A. M. E. , the A. M. E. Zion, the C. M. E. , and the
> Methodist Churches--if they had had less religion

and more business qualifications, and went on to
court, we would have more churches than we have
now. But they always figured that the Lord would
take care of them. But God will do nothing for you
that you can do for yourself. I am the only one in
this conference to go to court to stop the taking of
our churches. But I became president fifty years
too late. 15

George A. Woodards, the General Secretary of the A. U. M. P.
Conference for some thirty years, agreed with Scott, noting
that "the presidents were always guided by the age-old conviction that 'I can't take my brother to court'." Woodards
added another reason why so many churches were lost in
Maryland. According to his version of the story, some of
the pastors and trustees, influenced in part by pecuniary motives, even sold some of the churches:

They sold the churches because they knew that the
conference wasn't going to do anything about it.
Today on the Eastern Shore of Maryland, in and
around the city of Salisbury, cornerstones still
stand with "A. U. M. P. CONFERENCE" engraved on
them, but no church is to be found. Some were
brought by churches of other denominations, and a
few were even sold to home-buyers. Yet the conference did nothing about it. 16

In the midst of such serious losses, a number of
preachers became deeply discouraged, and some even pre-
dicted that the day would soon come when there would be no
A. U. M. P. Church. President John H. Bell responded
angrily to such predictions at the annual conference of the
Middle District in 1920 and offered the following response:
"Let us stop saying the Church will die, die--no it cannot
die for Jesus said upon this rock I build my Church and the
gates of hell shall not prevail against it."17 But the
A. U. M. P. Church was dying, and something more than
rhetoric was needed to steer it away from this tragic course.

On close inspection, it becomes apparent that numerous factors conspired to make possible the serious decline
of the A. U. M. P. denomination. First, the dearth of vigorous leadership continued to be a critical factor. The church
maintained a miserable record in attracting and holding on to
strong, educated progressive-minded leaders. The loss of
James E. Sargent in 1902 illustrates this point. After all,

this small, struggling denomination had little to offer strong, intelligent, progressive-minded preachers who were sure to find a more congenial field in the A. M. E. Church, the A. M. E. Zion Church, the C. M. E. Church, or in the Central Jurisdiction of the Methodist Church. In 1920 John H. Bell, who had assumed the presidency of the Middle District a year earlier, reported on several such preachers who, apparently disheartened by the weak and demoralized state of the church and its leadership, gave up their charges and left in search of something better. Concerning appointments he had made in Goshen and Port Jervis, New York, he announced:

> The appointment at Goshen, New York was not successful. The Rev. W. A. Brown was the man appointed there, but did not stay. I then gave the work to the Rev. G. W. Brown in connection with Port Jervis. The Rev. G. W. Brown took the work in hand, but I did not hear from him until some time in November, when he came to my house and informed me that he was compelled to give the work up. I then placed Brother Adams in charge and he has done what he could. In the midst of life we are in death. [18]

Bell's report on the preacher placed over the charge in Canada was equally revealing:

> Sometime about October 5th through the Rev. Dr. Nichols (another president in the connection), I received a letter from Sister Isabella Jackson, Chatham, Ontario, to the effect that the Rev. Johnson was going to leave the work at St. John's A. U. Church. I left home on the 18th of October for Chatham, Ontario. I arrived there on Sunday at 2 p. m. and found the work in a bad condition; that is to say the people were without a pastor and as sheep without a shepherd they just were lost as to what to do. [19]

Stories are still told today of numerous good, solid preachers who left the A. U. M. P. Church as late as the 1960s and joined other denominations. Small wonder the church has suffered so drastically because of leadership problems.

[Opposite:] The preaching staff of the A. U. M. P. Conference around 1918 (from the photo collection of the late Bishop George F. Brown of the A. U. M. P. Conference).

John H. Bell, President of the Middle District of the A. U. M. P. Conference, 1919-1927 (from the photo collection of the late Bishop George F. Brown of the A. U. M. P. Conference).

Second, problems of organization constituted a serious factor. The districts of the church were frequently renamed, reorganized, and reshuffled, contributing inevitably to serious institutional weaknesses and instability. Between 1900 and 1980, numerous structural changes occurred as districts were reshaped along geographical lines, increased in number, decreased in number, and phased out altogether. The church never really functioned on the basis of a clear plan of organization. [20] Understandably, institutional chaos became the vogue. The blame for this chaos rested primarily with the leadership contingent of the church, which was obviously unprepared to adopt well-thought out, long-lasting structural changes which could be supported wholeheartedly by the general church membership. In 1927 a plan of organization that was sufficiently clearcut and attractive enough to endure was finally considered. It provided that all districts would remain separate in name and geography, but would be brought together within one presidential district, to be presided over by a General President with the assistance of a General Vice President. John W. Brown, who replaced John H. Bell as president of the Middle District in that year, became the first General President of the denomination. By 1938 this new plan of organization had been put into effect, and by 1942 it had been officially adopted and included in the Book of Discipline of the A. U. M. P. Church. In 1967, when the episcopal mode of government was officially adopted, the system remained intact as all districts were combined within one episcopal district. [21] Even so, it becomes evident that constant changes in organizational structure in this century have illustrated, perhaps more than anything else, the institutional chaos and weaknesses so characteristic of the A. U. M. P. denomination. Institutional growth, development, and stability have always been extremely difficult where chaos and weakness persist.

Third, the lack of strong connectional authority and supervision figured prominently in the decline of the church. The regulations which placed church properties under the control of local trustees weakened connectional authority and made effective presidential supervision almost impossible. Local congregations could easily break away from the connection at the slightest provocation. In some instances, congregations did follow this course of action. In 1916 the trustees of St. Matthew A. U. M. P. Church in Philadelphia moved into the A. M. E. Church, completely ignoring a provision, included in A. U. M. P. Disciplines since the immediate post-Civil War era, which allowed for the expulsion of members

John W. Brown, the first General President of the combined districts of the A. U. M. P. Conference (from the photo collection of the late Bishop George F. Brown of the A. U. M. P. Conference).

found guilty of conspiring against the connection with the intention of causing splits. Apparently, these trustees, supported by the general membership of St. Matthew, were discouraged beyond recovery by the kind of institutional chaos which had caused a bitter dispute in their district in 1902. 22 Around the same time, the trustees of the St. Luke A. U. M. P. Church of Norfolk, Virginia, also disheartened by a denomination which showed no strong possibilities for growth and progress, affiliated with the C. M. E. Church. 23 In 1937, after the demise of Daniel J. Russell, Jr., the last president of the Philadelphia and New Jersey District, the trustees of the St. Luke A. U. M. P. Church of Camden, New Jersey, and of the Russell Memorial A. U. M. P. Church of Penns Grove, New Jersey, led their congregations into the U. A. M. E. Conference. These churches, which had previously been a part of the Philadelphia and New Jersey District, were desirous of going their own way because they opposed some of the policies of the general conference of the A. U. M. P. Church, including the recently accepted measure which had combined all districts within one presidential district. 24

Once congregations were taken over by other African Methodist Churches, little, if anything, was done to regain them. The responsibility rested squarely on the shoulders of John H. Bell, Sylvester C. Blackledge, John W. Brown, J. Edward Nichols, Daniel J. Russell, Jr., Charles N. Walker, and others who served the A. U. M. P. Church as presidents during these years, and who demonstrated a stunning lack of diplomacy in refusing to take strong measures to maintain all of the congregations in their respective districts. After more than thirty churches had been lost, John W. Brown and his General Vice President, Anthony D. Hammond, did attempt to deal with this general falling away of congregations from the connection. They decided to make church maintenance a first priority. Hence, the decision to combine all districts into one presidential district. 25 After all was said and done, however, connectional authority and supervision were not strengthened, and the Brown administration, which lasted until 1950, was haunted by the further decline of the A. U. M. P. Church.

The rural nature of some congregations in the A. U. M. P. denomination may be considered a fourth factor contributing to its decline. A number of congregations in extremely rural, sparsely-populated areas of Delaware, Maryland, Pennsylvania, and New Jersey maintained only a sporadic fellowship and communion with congregations in their districts and with

Daniel J. Russell, Jr., educator, medical doctor, and the last president of the Philadelphia and New Jersey District of the A. U. M. P. Church (from History of the African Union Methodist Protestant, by Daniel J. Russell, Jr.).

those in other districts. In time, some of these rural churches became independent, while others became affiliates of other black Methodist bodies. A few simply died out as elderly members passed on and the younger ones moved to urban areas. 26

Finally, the crisis of economics was a contributing factor. Securing sufficient funds for the general upkeep and maintenance of local congregations was always a burdensome task. There were always too few funds for a viable church extension program at the domestic level, to say nothing of work in foreign fields.

In May 1950 the general conference nominated, elected, and installed Reese C. Scott as General President of the A. U. M. P. Church. Scott, a tough-minded churchman and politician, succeeded Brown, who retired after almost 24 years of service. Before him stood the challenge of rescuing his denomination from the darkest period in its history. 27 Walter C. Cleaver, who also possessed impressive leadership qualities, became the General Vice President. In his inaugural address, he vowed to work closely with Scott in rebuilding the A. U. M. P. Church. Cleaver's appeal for help to save the church was perhaps the most passionate one made by an A. U. M. P. leader in this century. He said in part:

> I plead today for our A. U. M. P. Conference. I plead that we revere the name of PETER SPENCER, not with our words alone, but by our very acts of extending his work into every hamlet and city. I plead that we, like St. Peter, be ambitious for the church, not that selfish ambition that puts one man against the other; but that ambition which envisions the whole church moving forward. Forward in the eyes of those who watch A. U. M. P. to see what it is doing now and has done in the years of its ministry; forward in the eyes of God's young men who might be attracted to A. U. M. P.; and forward in the eyes of those men who have stood with and by this conference through the storms and through the sunshine. 28

After taking office, Scott moved fast to strengthen connectional authority. The law of incorporation of the A. U. M. P. Church was carefully reviewed, and a ruling which placed the properties of local congregations under conference control was quietly passed. This step was taken not so much

Reese C. Scott, the second and last General President of the combined districts of the A. U. M. P. Conference (from the photo collection of the late Bishop George F. Brown of the A. U. M. P. Conference).

as a conscious effort to break with a tradition stretching back to Peter Spencer, but as a deliberate attempt to prevent local congregations from breaking away from the connection when they so desired. All congregations and districts were now subject to the general conference. The rules and regulations of annual conferences for the admission and government of members within their districts were to be considered valid and acceptable only after being approved by the general conference. 29 The traditional Methodist system of connectional authority had finally found official acceptance among A. U. M. P. 's.

These initial steps by the Scott administration proved to be very timely, because in 1954, only four years after he became General President, there was an attempt to break away with one of the congregations in the A. U. M. P. Church. Ironically, the instigator in this case was Walter Cleaver, who had spoken so eloquently of the need for unity within the A. U. M. P. Church and who had decried "that selfish ambition which puts one man against the other." At this time Cleaver, in addition to being General Vice President, was pastor of the St. Paul A. U. M. P. Church in Washington, D. C. When the time came to make new appointments in the conference, Scott decided to move Cleaver from Washington to another appointment. Cleaver, who preferred to remain at St. Paul, rejected the new appointment, and a bitter dispute resulted between the two men. St. Paul was split right down the middle as some supported Cleaver, while others rallied on behalf of Scott. Cleaver decided that he was going to lead the church out of the conference and become independent. This enraged Scott, who warned that Cleaver could leave the A. U. M. P. Church with his supporters, but that he could not take the building and property. The dispute was carried before the U. S. Civil Court in Washington, where the two men battled each other for three years. In 1957 a decision was rendered against Cleaver, and he was forced to pay the entire cost of the court. St. Paul remained in the A. U. M. P. connection, and Cleaver and his followers went out and built the St. Paul Christian Community Church, an independent body. Scott later recalled some of the problems he encountered during this long legal ordeal:

> When I took Cleaver to court, the older men of
> this conference told me I was wrong. "You ought
> not take your brother to court, " they told me. I
> vowed never to turn around or back up. I told
> them that I was going to take him to court before

> he took me to hell, because I was not going to lose
> that church. My whole cabinet was against me. I
> let them know that I, not them, was installed as
> president to guard the doors of the A. U. M. P.
> Church. In the end, I won the battle. 30

In the heat of the quarrel, Sherman B. Hawkins was
installed as the new General Vice President. The dispute,
occurring as it did between the two top officials of the
A. U. M. P. Church, brought to light once again the kind of
problems which haunted this small denomination. In the end,
Scott proved himself to be a strong and courageous leader--
perhaps the strongest and most courageous to assume the
presidency of the A. U. M. P. Church in this century. For
the first time in A. U. M. P. Church history, a president had
gone so far as to exhaust legal means in order to save a
church. During Scott's 24 years as General President and
bishop not a single congregation was lost. As he, himself,
put it: "As far as I was concerned, those days were
over. "31

The Move to the Episcopacy

At the 1966 general conference of the A. U. M. P. Church,
there were serious discussions at the leadership level concerning the need to adopt the episcopal form of polity. In
the past, the possibility of adopting such a system had been
discussed, but the general church body had not supported the
idea wholeheartedly. Peter Spencer and William Anderson
had rejected the episcopacy for reasons already discussed.
The issue had received nodding attention after the death of
Spencer and during the late nineteenth century. The general
conference of 1914, which convened in Chester, Pennsylvania,
voted to recognize bishops, but Daniel Russell, Jr., then the
president of the Philadelphia and New Jersey District, was
the only church official actually interested in assuming the
title of bishop. In 1922 he was consecrated bishop at his
request. The presiding officers of the other two districts
chose to continue under the title of president. 32 In 1966
the issue was brought to the floor of the general conference
by Edward R. Bell, the General Treasurer of the conference,
and George A. Woodards, the General Secretary of the conference. For further consideration of this proposal, a resolution was passed extending the general conference into the
next annual conference. At the annual session of 1967, which
was held May 16-21 at the Ebenezar A. U. M. P. Church in

Norristown, Pennsylvania, the conference voted to elect and consecrate two bishops. The following resolution was passed:

> Be it resolved, that the titles of the two general elected officers; namely, the General President and the General Vice President, be changed to read Senior Bishop and Junior Bishop, or Presiding Bishop and Conference Bishop. Those who now serve the church as General President and General Vice President shall, upon being consecrated, be henceforth known as Bishops of the A. U. F. C. M. P. Conference.
>
> Be it further resolved that seniority be the determining factor in the selection of candidates for these offices. 33

Those persons involved in the consecration of bishops had to be conference members who had traveled successfully as pastors for at least ten years. Reese C. Scott was consecrated Senior Bishop, and Robert F. Walters, who had replaced Sherman B. Hawkins as General Vice President in 1962, was consecrated Junior Bishop. 34

Several concerns prompted the change to the episcopacy. First, many in the conference were convinced that the episcopal system was more in accord with scripture. Second, some agreed that the office of president, due in part to the serious decline of the A. U. M. P. Church during the preceding half century, was losing its prestige. Third, it was strongly suggested that the episcopacy was more in line with the structure of traditional Methodism. Fourth, the presidential title, according to Edward R. Bell, gave the church the appearance of a club and made it difficult for him, as treasurer, to transact business matters with banks and other firms. Finally, all seemed to agree that the episcopal structure would make it more possible for their denomination to attain proper recognition as a member of the Methodist family of churches. 35

The consecration of Scott and Walters meant that both the A. U. M. P. and U. A. M. E. denominations were now similar in polity to the A. M. E., the A. M. E. Zion, and the C. M. E. Churches. The U. A. M. E. Church had adopted the episcopacy more than a half century earlier. Although the move to the episcopacy on the part of these Union Churches represented an example of a drift back to patterns of polity and

Sherman B. Hawkins, the first Presiding Elder of the combined districts of the A. U. M. P. Conference (from the photo collection of the late Bishop George F. Brown of the A. U. M. P. Conference).

ministry that Spencer and Anderson opposed, it did not neces-
sarily signal a drastic move away from founding principles.
These churches have retained a distinctive African Methodist
posture.   Both continue to find a special or unique expression
by emphasizing strong lay involvement, the active participation of women in ministry, and the need for black Americans
to assume primary responsibility for their own liberation. 36

During the 158th Annual Session of the A. U. M. P.
Church, held in 1971, the office of presiding elder was created to strengthen the conference administratively.   A resolution was adopted calling for the appointment of a presiding
elder annually.   The appointee, who was eligible for reap-
pointment, had to be active as a pastor. 37   Sherman B.
Hawkins, pastor of the Chippey Chapel A. U. M. P. Church,
Hockessin, Delaware, and a former General Vice President
of the conference, was named the first presiding elder of
the combined districts of his denomination by presiding Bishop Reese C. Scott. 38   Years earlier, Peter Brookins had
served as presiding elder under Daniel J. Russell, Jr.
Hawkins died in 1973, and the presiding eldership remained
vacant until 1979.   At the 166th Annual Session, held in
Salisbury, Maryland, in May 1979, Maynard Smith, the pastor of St. James A. U. M. P. Church, Head of the Creek,
Maryland, and Freedmen's A. U. M. P. Church, Tyaskins,
Maryland, was chosen by Presiding Bishop Robert F. Walters
to fill the position.   After serving only three months, Smith
complained that the work was too demanding for one person
and requested that another presiding elder be appointed.
During the 1979 Big Quarterly celebration, Thomas E. Moon,
pastor of the St. Paul A. U. M. P. Church, Washington, D. C.,
was designated by Walters as a second presiding elder.   To
accommodate his appointment, all of the districts were re-
arranged and divided into two presiding elder districts within
one episcopal district.   Smith was given charge of the First
District, which covers congregations in Delaware, Maryland,
and Pennsylvania.   Moon was delegated authority over the
Second District, which consists of churches in New Jersey,
New York, and Washington, D. C. 39

In 1974, Bishop Reese C. Scott retired, forcing other
changes at the administrative level.   Robert F. Walters became the presiding bishop of the conference, and George F.
Brown, who had pastored the Mother A. U. M. P. Church in
Wilmington since 1955, was consecrated Junior Bishop at the
general conference in September 1974.   His untimely death
a year later left the conference with only one active bishop. 40

Robert F. Walters, the present Presiding Bishop of the combined districts of the A. U. M. P. Conference (from the photo collection of Bishop Robert F. Walters).

A proposal to elect another bishop at the 1978 general conference was not well-received.   Today, the A. U. M. P.
Church, consisting of 36 congregations, functions under one
presiding bishop, Robert F. Walters of Norristown, Pennsylvania. 41

Mission Priorities and Self-Help

Throughout this century the A. U. M. P. Church has directed
its modest resources and domestic mission efforts toward
addressing the dual concerns of salvation and liberation.   In
this respect, its raison d'être has not differed from that of
other black churches.   It has proclaimed the good news that
God loves, affirms, forgives, saves, and acts in the histories of people to whom He has given life, irrespective of
color, race, creed, or nationality.   It has also made contributions on behalf of improving the quality of black life in
areas such as education, human development, and civil rights.
The need for such services will not diminish in the near future and could possibly increase as there are still signs that
black Americans must continue to fight the same battles
fought by their forebears.

Education has remained important to the majority of
A. U. M. P. 's.   They have moved, with a little more authority than in the nineteenth century, to support secondary and
higher education.   At the beginning of the century, Spencer's
African Union Methodist Protestant College and Seminary
was established in Viola, Delaware.   In 1904, Russell's
Bible Training School was started in Philadelphia by Daniel
J. Russell, Jr. , who was highly respected among A. U. M. P. 's
as a physician and theologian. 42   These schools were never
as strong as those financed by the A. M. E. 's, A. M. E. Z. 's,
and C. M. E. 's, and therefore were not even in a position to
serve sufficiently the educational needs of A. U. M. P. 's.
They practically collapsed in the aftermath of the Great Depression.   In 1938, Reese C. Scott, then the president of
the A. U. M. P. Sunday School Association, organized the African Union School of Religion in St. James A. U. M. P. Church
in Wilmington.   In 1950, when Scott took over as General
President of the conference, he introduced policies designed
to improve its educational work.   First, he placed the school
under the supervision of an executive committee of the general conference.   Second, Annual Conference Ministerial Programs were planned for men and women interested in forms
of Christian ministry.   The present-day African Union School

of Religion functions largely on the basis of this plan, having
a Board of Directors. [43]

The publishing activities of the A. U. M. P. Church has
served as an indicator of its abiding interest in education and
the printed word. During the early years of the century,
publishing activity was carried on by the A. U. M. P. Book
Room and Publishing House in Philadelphia, with Daniel J.
Russell, Jr. as Business Manager. [44] One of the very first
pieces issued by this publishing house was a brief history of
the Spencer movement completed in 1914 by Jacob F. Ramsey, a U. A. M. E. Bishop, who entitled it, Father Spencer:
His Work for the Church and Race. In time this publishing
house printed and circulated a number of denominational
periodicals which, aside from discussing the day-to-day
activities of congregations, featured commentaries on the
Bible, Christian educational concerns, and social issues.
The Union Star, started as the first A. U. M. P. periodical in
1882, and The Flash Light, first published at the beginning
of the century, became monthly journals. By the beginning
of World War II, The Morning Star and The Union Youth
Messenger were being issued by the denomination. These
periodicals have been produced by A. U. M. P. 's throughout
this century. [45]

In recent years A. U. M. P. 's have stressed the need to
support black youth who pursue higher education. Through
their Sunday School Association, they have awarded annual
scholarships to promising high school graduates. At the
155th Annual Session of the A. U. M. P. Church, held in May
1968, a resolution was passed which stated, "Unless the
church specifically provides for college-age youth, it is in
danger of losing them altogether. " Such sentiments have
emerged out of a mounting awareness of the need for more
educated young blacks to serve the church and the race as
leaders. [46]

The issue of what roles women should play in the life
of the church has also remained important. Since 1900,
women have entered more freely into the programs and activities of the A. U. M. P. Church, serving as missionaries,
church officials, conference evangelists, and pastors. Lydia
Archie, who was a pastor and conference delegate early in
the century, remained very active in those capacities up until the 1920s. Clara Wright pastored the Friendship A. U. M. P.
Church in Kennett Square, Pennsylvania, for some thirty
years before passing on in 1950. [47] Women who were active

Clara Wright, pastor of the Friendship A. U. M. P. Church, Kennett Square, Pennsylvania, for some 30 years (from the photo collection of Albert Haley, a former son-in-law).

Ann B. Henderson, presently the Director of Church Extension for the entire A. U. M. P. Conference (from the photo collection of Ann B. Henderson).

as conference evangelists around this time included Mary R.
Bishop, Elizabeth Clayton, Pearl King, Lucinda Morgan, and
Minnie Wadsworth. Lay women who served the local congregations and the conference in numerous capacities between
1920 and 1960 were Margaret E. Bell, Mae Blackledge,
Martha Brister, Ada M. Brown, Annis G. Chippey, Eleanor
Chippey, Sara Gardner, Margaret A. Hill, Sarah Johns, El-
len Russell, and Mamie Stubblefield. Because of women like
these, conference auxiliaries such as the Grand Body of the
Daughters of Conference and the Home Mite Missionary Soci-
ety have continued to be active forces in the church. During
the 1960s and 1970s, women like Alice Whye, Jimmie L.
McClinton, and Irene Taylor, all preachers, served on the
Board of Directors of the African Union School of Religion.[48]
At this writing, five women were holding key positions in the
A. U. M. P. Conference: Mildred Demby, the Conference
Statistician; Ann B. Henderson, Director of Church Extension;
Corina Montgomery, president of the Sunday School Associa-
tion; Ellen Holtz, Assistant Secretary of the Conference; and
Eleanor Dailey, Acting Assistant Secretary of the Conference.
Ann Henderson has also been active as a pastor. Presently,
there are about eighteen female ministers in the A. U. M. P.
Conference, constituting almost half of the total number of
preachers.[49]

The problem of racism and the struggle for equal
rights have been equally significant for A. U. M. P.'s. The
severe oppression of black Americans during the early years
of the century, particularly in the south, drew sharp criti-
cism from A. U. M. P. preachers like Samuel Watson Chippey,
the son of the popular late nineteenth-century A. U. M. P.
president, Edward H. Chippey. In 1907, during the annual
session of the Middle District in Chester, Pennsylvania, the
sentiments of Chippey and others found expression in a sharply worded resolution which called for an immediate halt to
"the barbarous practice of lynching" and other racist acts
designed to intimidate blacks:

> We deeply deplore the spirit of mob violence,
> lynching and other disgraceful, yes, barbarous
> treatment practiced against the Negro on account
> of his color and past condition. We pray the God
> of Nations to make bare his arms and in His ap-
> pointed time, raise up a deliverer as He did in
> the darkest days of slavery.[50]

In 1925 Sylvester C. Blackledge, the last president of

Samuel Watson Chippey, a dynamic preacher and leader of his race (from the photo collection of Bishop Robert F. Walters of the A. U. M. P. Church).

Sylvester C. Blackledge, educator, race leader, and the last
president of the Maryland District of the A. U. M. P. Conference
(from the photo collection of his wife, Mae Blackledge).

the old Maryland District, wrote <u>An Open Book on Hidden Mysteries</u>, in which he provided a stinging critique of the congenital corruption of white Christianity and the American society. He not only attacked the lynchers of black people, but also the American legal system which he felt gave sanction to such outrageous practices:

> The Negro is today an outcast dwelling among strangers when it comes to dealing with the law. And every Negro should know that his chances for justice are slim in the common courts of the land. For instance, we will take the extreme South, where men and boys from fourteen years old and upward are taken from their homes and mobbed and lynched; one half of whom are innocent of the crimes they are accused of; and still no permanent action is taken either by the state or nation to prosecute these brutish violators and transgressors of both the law and the Constitution. [51]

Observing that "All other races may unite and worship wherever they choose, but the Negro cannot," Blackledge went on to charge that such racial bigotry was unimaginable in a country that boasted of its role as a Christian leader among nations:

> I imagine that it is quite embarrassing to our ministers, missionaries, and Christian workers in China, Japan, and Africa, who are striving to convert the "heathen," when they are told that they had better go back and convert their own people who are doing far worse than they are. [52]

In a nationalistic vein, Blackledge insinuated that black people should reject the examples and values of the majority culture and build their own foundations and values for freedom. "The Negro," he wrote, "should realize the fact that all plans and examples set by the white man are set for the white race only, and would not work out to any advantage to the Negro, even if applied." Therefore, "every Negro should endeavour to get at least a common school education, so that he might read and learn for himself, and not have to depend upon others to set his course in life. "[53]

The A. U. M. P. Church was an early supporter of the N. A. A. C. P., which was organized in 1909 to fight for the rights and freedom of black people. A. U. M. P. periodicals

George F. Brown, social and political activist, journalist, and A. U. M. P. Bishop (from the photo collection of the late Bishop George F. Brown).

and conference minutes made a regular feature of news on
N. A. A. C. P. activities, and the church contributed what it
could in the way of funds to the work of this agency.   During
the civil rights movement of the 1960s, A. U. M. P. 's were
allied not only with some of the social action strategies of
the N. A. A. C. P. , but also with the work of the Student Non-
violent Co-ordinating Committee (S. N. C. C.) and of the Martin Luther King movement as a whole.   George F. Brown,
who pastored the Mother A. U. M. P. Church in Wilmington between 1955 and 1974 and who became only the fourth bishop
in the history of his denomination in the fall of 1974, stood
as a bright symbol of his church's involvement in such cam-
paigns.   In May 1963, while annual conference was in session
at the mother church, he began a sit-in movement in Wilmington in conjunction with John H. Woodlin, pastor of Emmanuel
A. U. M. P. Church, Ambler, Pennsylvania; Sherman B. Hawkins, pastor of Bethlehem A. U. M. P. Church, Newport, Delaware; L. S. Stewart, pastor of Wickham A. U. M. P. Church,
Port Jervis, New York; and Edward C. Morton, pastor of
St. John A. U. M. P. Church, Goshen, New York.   They were
encouraged by General President Reese C. Scott, who in his
annual address had urged the delegates to give full support to
the N. A. A. C. P. in its struggle to end racial discrimination.
The five clergymen entered Victoria's Luncheonette at
Twelfth and King Streets on May 16 and asked to be served.
Victoria Smentkowski, the owner, who had refused to sign
the affidavit of non-discrimination required to obtain a city
business license, charged Brown and the others with tres-
passing and obtained warrants for their arrest.   Upon refusing to leave the premises, they were arrested, booked, and
soon released pending an appearance in court.   Morton, one
of the most outspoken in the group, later defended their action:

> It is not enough to stand and preach God's word.
> The leaders must act upon this.   It is no more a
> question of being my brother's keeper.   The out-
> standing fact is that I am my brother's keeper.
> When he is hungry, I, too, suffer hunger.   I, my-
> self, will continue to sit in, ride in, walk in.   I
> will go until there is nothing left of me to go....
> If this nation is going to remain, it is time for us
> to clean it up and make it fitting.   If this takes
> sacrifice on the part of a few, the sacrifice will
> be made.   If it takes sacrifice on the part of many,
> the sacrifice will be made.   Our leaders have given
> the call.   We will respond. 54

George F. Brown, Edward C. Morton (in police wagon), Sherman B. Hawkins (being searched), Lewis S. Stewart (standing directly behind policeman), and John Woodlin (standing on sidewalk beside policeman) are arrested for refusing to leave Victoria's Luncheonette (from the photo collection of George F. Brown).

The case against the clergymen was dismissed in early June 1963 by Judge Sidney J. Clark, who concluded that the clergymen had been denied service at Victoria's solely because they were black. [55] In the meantime, the sit-in movement caught momentum as Brown joined Maurice Moyer, a clergyman and president of the local N. A. A. C. P. , in staging sit-ins in several Delaware cities. Despite numerous arrests and court appearances, some success was achieved. Victoria's Luncheonette was forced to close under pressure, and the Brandywine Diner and other Wilmington restaurants were desegregated. The sit-in activities of Brown, Moyer, and others also forced the desegregation of restaurants and hotels in parts of lower Delaware, such as Middletown, Newark, Dover, Delaware City, Milford, and Smyrna. [56] In mid-June 1963 Brown was arrested for refusing to leave the Deer Park Hotel in Newark after he was denied service under The Delaware Inn-Keepers Law, by which a proprietor could deny service to anyone he felt would injure his business. The case reached the State Supreme Court, which decided that although the Inn-Keepers Law was valid, it could not be constitutionally enforced. Louis L. Redding, the widely respected black civil rights attorney of Wilmington, later said of Brown, his client: "He took a commendable and almost heroic stand. He took a great risk in being arrested and facing the possible consequences. "[57]

The A. U. M. P. Conference encouraged Brown and representatives from all congregations in the connection to become involved in the civil rights movement at the national level. The conference sent a bus load of demonstrators to participate in the great march on Washington in August 1963. The group was led by Brown and several other ministers. [58] In the spring of 1965, Brown represented the conference in the Selma to Montgomery march. When Martin Luther King, Jr. was assassinated in April 1968, Presiding Bishop Reese C. Scott sent Brown and Edward C. Morton to attend the funeral in Atlanta, Georgia. [59]

Although A. U. M. P. 's were not actively involved in all of the developments associated with the black power movement in the late Sixties, their sympathy with some of its goals, such as institution-building and the promotion of self-help projects, was made known in a resolution adopted at the annual conference in May 1968, one month after the King assassination. It read: "We must enter massive programs of training and retraining to lift ourselves up, literally. "[60] Those words obviously stemmed from the conviction that black people must take the lead in effecting their own liberation.

The U. A. M. E. Church

The U. A. M. E. Church was under considerable pressure when the twentieth century began. The resources of the church were barely sufficient to meet the multiple needs of its own constituents, let alone to sponsor programs of Christian nurture that would address the realities and urgencies of an increasingly urban situation. Furthermore, the church had not grown to an appreciable extent, and there was cautious optimism about its chances for significant growth and expansion in the future. The following is suggestive as to how the U. A. M. E. Church compared to other African Methodist bodies in terms of numerical strength in 1900:

Church	Membership
African Methodist Episcopal	500, 000
African Methodist Episcopal Zion	300, 000
Colored Methodist Episcopal	150, 000
*Union American Methodist Episcopal	5, 000
African Union Methodist Protestant	4, 000
Reformed Methodist Union Episcopal	4, 000
Reformed Zion Union Apostolic (Methodist)	2, 500
Colored Methodist Protestant	2, 000
Independent African Methodist Episcopal	1, 000[61]

Amidst all the uncertainty, Bishops Jacob F. Ramsey, Benjamin T. Ruley, and James C. Wilmore, the episcopal heads of the U. A. M. E. Church during the first decade of the century, believed that the new century would afford a great evangelical opportunity for the U. A. M. E. 's to spread out to the far corners of America and the entire world with the gospel of salvation. The Women's Home Missionary Society and the Southern Volunteer Workers were developed in connection with the general conference to conduct missionary activity, which took on the aspects of church extension. Orlando S. Watts of Camden, New Jersey, oversaw foreign mission work, and W. L. Castelle of Media, Pennsylvania, took charge of domestic missions. The relative poverty of the U. A. M. E. Church made it difficult to achieve major, lasting successes in domestic missions, to say nothing of foreign missions. It is interesting to note, however, that the report for 1926 showed 24 missionaries employed, and the sum of

$9, 660 contributed for missions.   Foreign mission work was being carried on only in Canada. 62   Thus, the U. A. M. E. Church was slightly more progressive in this area than the A. U. M. P. Church, which had no foreign mission program at this time.

Between 1900 and 1930, a few congregations and small missions were formed in Alabama, Arkansas, Delaware, Florida, Georgia, Louisiana, Michigan, Mississippi, New Jersey, New York, Pennsylvania, and Texas.   Three congregations were organized in Canada, increasing the number in that dominion to six. 63   It is important to understand that these successes did not contribute substantially to the number of congregations in the connection because they were accompanied on the other hand by serious losses.   The U. A. M. E. Church experienced a period of decline in terms of membership and the number of congregations between 1906 and 1916.   Between 1916 and 1930, steady increases were reported by U. A. M. E. bishops, as the number of congregations increased by six, and the membership increased by some 6, 645.   The general summary of statistics given below shows the alternating rates of increase and decline for the Spencer Churches and the three largest African Methodist Churches between 1906 and 1926: 64

African Methodist Episcopal	1906	1916	1926
Churches	6, 608	6, 633	6, 708
Members	494, 777	548, 355	545, 814
African Methodist Episcopal Zion			
Churches	2, 196	2, 716	2, 466
Members	184, 542	257, 169	456, 813
Colored Methodist Episcopal			
Churches	2, 365	2, 621	2, 518
Members	172, 996	245, 749	202, 713
*Union American Methodist Episcopal			
Churches	77	67	73
Members	4, 347	3, 524	10, 169
African Union Methodist Protestant			
Churches	69	58	43
Members	5, 592	3, 751	4, 086

The period between 1930 and 1970 brought severe losses for the U. A. M. E. Church. The denomination declined from 79 congregations to 54 congregations. The six congregations in Canada died out. The few congregations and small missions scattered throughout parts of Alabama, Arkansas, Florida, Georgia, Louisiana, Michigan, Mississippi, and Texas either died out, became independent, or were sold because there were not enough members to keep them going. 65

The decline of the U. A. M. E. Church was brought on by some of the same factors which caused the decline of the A. U. M. P. Church. First, the dearth of vigorous leadership remained a serious problem. Between 1900 and 1970, the church produced very few able leaders, among them Jacob F. Ramsey, Benjamin T. Ruley, James C. Wilmore, Philip A. Boulden, Herbert T. Ryder, Benjamin M. Fernanders, Orville W. Forward, John P. Predow, and David M. Harmon. All of these men rose to the episcopal office and never ceased to take their responsibilities seriously, but almost everything--accidents of history, the lack of money, an increasingly urban and mobile black population, the lack of fully developed administrative structures, and the church's own sense of uncertainty--militated against the success of their attempts to develop and maintain their congregations as a strong, disciplined, and fully committed body. Additionally, the U. A. M. E. Church had a terrible time attracting and holding on to good, solid, well-trained, progressive-minded clergymen to serve as administrators and local pastors. Beginning in the late nineteenth century with the loss of Lorenzo Dow Blackson, the extremely bright clergyman who ended up in the A. M. E. Zion Church, the U. A. M. E. Church almost became notorious for losing vigorous preachers. As late as 1978, Charles Davis, a remarkably bright young minister who worked as an administrator in the general office of the U. A. M. E. Church in Camden, New Jersey, left the church and joined the A. M. E. Zion Church after running unsuccessfully for the episcopacy against Earl L. Huff. 66

Second, problems of organization contributed to the decline of the church. Frequent changes in the geographical shape and composition of the districts were made, beginning early in the century. Consequently, institutional weaknesses were exposed and the task of developing stable administrative structures was made more difficult. Strangely, frequent organizational changes were not only a contributor to, but a result of, peculiar patterns of church growth and decline. 67

Organizational problems were further illustrated by the constant personality clashes and bickering among undisciplined corps of clergymen, some of whom wanted to be bishops instead of presiding elders and local preachers. Sadie Bulah, the wife of Bishop Benjamin Fernanders during his active service from 1939 to 1954, claims that "there were always those who wanted to be superiors--who wanted to cause disruption by breaking up the connection."[68] Conflict became commonplace and schisms were not unusual. The great dispute that surfaced at the general conference in 1934 could be cited as an example. At this conference, which convened at Mother U. A. M. E. Church in Wilmington in October, the issue of whether or not new bishops should be elected was hotly debated. Bishops Benjamin T. Ruley, Jacob F. Ramsey, and Herbert T. Ryder had passed on, and Philip Boulden remained as the only active bishop. Trouble broke out when Daniel B. Ennis, Edward S. Rice, and Orlando S. Watts ran unsuccessfully for the episcopacy. Ennis, who was stubborn in his claim that God had chosen him to be the next U. A. M. E. bishop, accused Bishop Boulden and the majority present of "rejecting, annulling, refusing, and fighting against God's choice." A serious rift ensued between Boulden and the three candidates. Ennis, Rice, and Watts led their supporters out of the conference. Watts and some of his supporters soon rejoined the U. A. M. E. Church. In 1935 Ennis, Rice, and their supporters organized the Reformed U. A. M. E. Church, a rival body which was incorporated in 1937. Wilmington, Delaware, became the headquarters of this new church, and Ennis and Rice assumed the title of bishop. The Reformed U. A. M. E. Church existed for only a few years before falling apart. The group presided over by Ennis was led into the A. M. E. Zion Church. Rice continued to exercise pastoral charge over his supporters in West Chester, Pennsylvania, until he lost his sight in 1955. His membership was then accepted into the A. U. M. P. Conference at his request. [69]

The geographical makeup of the denomination could be cited as a third factor in its decline. During the period of the greatest decline of the church, most of its congregations were concentrated in Delaware, Maryland, Pennsylvania, and New Jersey. The majority of these congregations survived, and so did the congregations in Connecticut, New York, and Rhode Island. However, the very thin net of congregations located in Alabama, Arkansas, Florida, Georgia, Louisiana, Michigan, Mississippi, Texas, and Canada were either too rural or too separated geographically from the mainstream of hurch activity to remain securely a part of the connection. Many of these churches were simply abandoned and sold. [70]

Finally, the relative poverty of the U. A. M. E. Church proved to be a contributing factor. The necessary resources of manpower, money, and ingenuity were simply unavailable to render successful the missionary and church extension enterprises of the church. The foreign missions program had virtually collapsed by mid-century. On the domestic scene, mission and church extension efforts were not effective to the point of reaching the great harvest of black souls who migrated into the major industrial centers of the nation during the periods immediately before and after World Wars I and II.

By 1975 strong interest in foreign missions had been revived. John D. Douglas was named Presiding Elder of Foreign Affairs for the U. A. M. E. Church. Under his direction, mission work was started in West Omerri Central Station, Nigeria. Mission activity was also started in Kingston and Browntown, Iron Hills, Jamaica. In 1977 Bishops David E. Hackett and David M. Harmon led a small delegation to the West Indies to investigate the progress of church work in that part of the world. Ministers were ordained and given the responsibility of overseeing the building of new churches. A U. A. M. E. Church in Browntown, Iron Hills, Jamaica is nearing completion. [71]

Interest in reviving domestic missions and church extension work is also growing. Bishop David E. Hackett and Presiding Elder George W. Poindexter, both of the First and Fourth Districts of the U. A. M. E. Church, recently suggested that more initiative needs to be dispensed in this area. They support, as an immediate goal, the establishment of new churches in Baltimore, Washington, D. C. , and in parts of the South and Southwest. Hackett expressed the feelings of most clergy and lay persons in the church in saying that "we have not gotten very far as a church, so we must concentrate on growing and expanding as a first priority. If we can hold what we have and build on it, we're going places."[72]

Presently, there are 55 congregations in the U. A. M. E. denomination. The 28 congregations comprising the First and Fourth Districts are located in Delaware, Maryland, and Pennsylvania. These districts are under the care of Bishop Hackett and Presiding Elder Poindexter. The 26 congregations making up the Second and Third Districts are situated

in Connecticut, New Jersey, New York, and Rhode Island.
These congregations are presided over by Bishop Earl L.
Huff and Presiding Elder James H. Purnell. The church in
Browntown, Iron Hills, Jamaica, in addition to the other
small missions in Kingston and Nigeria, fall under the Fifth
District. This district, which is said to be making wonder-
ful progress under John Douglas, is under the joint super-
vision of Bishops Hackett and Huff. [73]

The following statistics are important for understanding where the U. A. M. E. and A. U. M. P. Churches stand in
comparison to the A. M. E., A. M. E. Zion, and C. M. E.
Churches in 1980: [74]

Church	Districts	Congregations	Members	Active Bishops
A. M. E.	18	8, 000	1, 600, 000	19
A. M. E. Z.	12	6, 000	1, 350, 000	12
C. M. E.	9	3, 500	800, 000	9
U. A. M. E.	5	55	7, 000	2
A. U. M. P.	2	36	3, 500	1

An Agenda for Change and Self-Help

Throughout this century the U. A. M. E. Church has been one
of the agencies of self-help in black America and, in a manner similar to other black churches, it has played a vital
role in maintaining group cohesion. It, too, has provided a
forum for black leadership, recognition, and self-expression,
and has fostered self-respect by proclaiming the good news
that the God of the Bible is the God of blacks as well as
whites. Aside from the proclamation of the gospel, its mission agenda has included 1) education, 2) benevolences,
3) the increasing involvement of laity in mission, 4) the
growing participation of women in the life of the church,
5) more youth involvement in church activities, and 6) civil rights.

The U. A. M. E. Church has been as much interested
in promoting education as the larger and more popular
branches of black and white Methodism. However, being
seriously limited in terms of resources, it has not been in
a position to compete in this area on a level with the
A. M. E. 's, the A. M. E. Z. 's, the C. M. E. 's, and the United
Methodists. Nevertheless, U. A. M. E. 's have recognized fully

the importance of education in the advancement of black people and have moved to establish schools and seminaries. At the beginning of the century, they built the Union Industrial School in Wilmington. They also built the Local Preachers Training School in Camden, New Jersey, with an extension center in Philadelphia. This school was renamed the Spencer Training School and Seminary around 1920, and Philip A. Boulden, one of the U. A. M. E. bishops, became its dean. These schools all but collapsed during the Great Depression, and the educational efforts of the church were later combined through the Boulden Academy and Seminary which became a tribute to the vision, faith, and sacrifice of Bishop Boulden. 75 Since 1939, the year of Boulden's death, the school has operated out of extension centers in Newark, New Jersey; New Haven, Connecticut; Camden, New Jersey; and Wilmington, Delaware. In 1967 a $250,000 addition to it was completed in Wilmington. Soon afterward, fire was set to the school several times, vandalism occurred, and the new building eventually had to be torn down. Today, courses for ministers, missionaries, and Christian educators are taught at the episcopal residences in Camden and Wilmington. In 1970, for the first time, the general conference resolved that all U. A. M. E. ministers should have college and seminary training prior to ordination. 76

The publishing activities of the church is another indication of its interest in education and the printed word. During the early years of the century, men like W. H. King, Herbert T. Ryder, and Orlando S. Watts served as editors of The Union Recorder and Messenger, The Southern Pioneer, and The Union Herald. These were U. A. M. E. periodicals which featured articles on concerns of a Christian and educational nature. In recent years, The Union Messenger, published quarterly, has been the major periodical of the church. However, the editors have been less than consistent in printing and circulating this periodical on schedule. 77

Benevolences have also been a dominant item among the church's mission priorities. Interest in this area has found expression on two levels: programs that provided food and clothing for the needy; and low-income housing. In the periods immediately before and after the Great Depression, U. A. M. E. congregations made modest but important contributions to programs designed to assist southern black migrants who settled in the urban centers of the North. The Christian Endeavor Society and the Spencer League functioned under the auspices of the church to help in providing food, clothing,

Philip A. Boulden, educator, race leader, and U. A. M. E.
Bishop (from the photo collection of the late Bishop George
F. Brown of the A. U. M. P. Conference).

shelter, and financial assistance for the destitute. During
the worst years of the Depression, some U. A. M. E. congregations served hot meals for fifty cents or less. [78] In 1953
the Peter Spencer Memorial Home, a 15-unit structure on a
seven-acre tract of land, was purchased in Kennett Square,
Pennsylvania, to accommodate elderly blacks and others who
were financially unable to secure decent housing of a rental
or purchase nature. In 1955 the Georgiana Ramsey Memorial
Home, an 18-unit structure, was purchased in Camden, New
Jersey, for the same purpose. [79] In 1962 Bishops David M.
Harmon and John P. Predow established a Department of
Urban Affairs to enlarge the general commitment of the

Top: John P. Predow, educator, social activist, and U. A. -
M. E. bishop; bottom: David M. Harmon, social activist and
U. A. M. E. Bishop (from the photo collection of Bishop John
P. Predow).

church to provide living quarters under the Federal Housing Act for low-income families. Two non-profit corporations were formed. First, the U. A. M. E. Church Non-Profit Housing Corporation, headquartered in Wilmington, was set up to develop housing in the First and Fourth Episcopal Districts. Second, the U. A. M. E. Church Apartments, Inc., situated in Camden, New Jersey, was organized to develop housing in the Second and Third Episcopal Districts. By 1971 the Predow Apartments, named for Bishop Predow, were completed at a cost of $811,000. At that time, Predow and Harmon stated their purpose for providing low-income housing:

> This housing project is an expression of our faith in helping others to live "the more abundant life." As the Cross has vertical and horizontal bars, so will our Christian outreach. We reach up to God through worship, thanksgiving, and praise. We reach out to our fellowman through practical deeds of human endeavor. May all who live here thank God for shelter and daily bread. [80]

U. A. M. E. 's have been equally concerned about the involvement of laity in mission. Strong lay participation has always been one of the most significant aspects of the life of the Spencer Churches, but in recent years U. A. M. E. 's have stressed to a greater extent the need for more better trained lay persons to exercise independent responsibilities on behalf of the mission of the church. This need was forcefully expressed in a recent edition of The Union Messenger: "There are a number of lay members in our church who have good potential, and with the proper training, can become good leaders. "[81]

The participation of women in the life of the church has commanded more attention from U. A. M. E. 's in this century. Women have always been a force in the history of the church, but after 1900 interest in utilizing the full service of women increased. First, a significant number of women became ordained preachers and pastors for the first time. Second, female members were given the right to participate in the election of all officers in their respective congregations. Third, female lay representatives at conferences were granted many of the same privileges as men. [82] Presently, there are at least twenty female ministers in the denomination, constituting almost a third of the total number of clergy persons. Some are pastoring churches. The Reverend Irene C. Dutton, who pastors the historic Mother

Irene C. Dutton, U. A. M. E. historian and pastor of Mother
U. A. M. E. Church, Wilmington, Delaware (from the photo
collection of the Rev. Mrs. Dutton).

U. A. M. E. Church in Wilmington, and who serves the conference in numerous capacities, is an example of the great extent to which women have entered the ranks of church life and activity. 83

A concern for youth and their place in the church has attracted the attention of many U. A. M. E. 's. Bishop David Hackett recently alluded to the church's titanic, ideological struggle to recapture the allegiance and full participation of young people who have been turned off by the "routineness" of church life. Earlier in this century, Sunday Schools were the major vehicles used by the Spencer Churches to keep young people interested and involved in the church and to prepare them for greater service to the church. 84 The youth of today are demanding new and more radical programs of Christian nurture that address the realities and urgencies of an increasingly urban, technological society. As Hackett observed, a part of this effort to reach the young will involve translating the gospel into the idioms and symbols of their language:

> We've got to tell the same old story in a different language. Jesus told Nicodemus--"You must be born again." My father told me to get converted and join the church. We've got to find the kind of language to tell the same story of salvation. We are going to have to make the church more relevant, not only by words, but by actions. The church is going to have to reach further out into the community and embrace these young people. Presently, the church is afraid to go on the corner, in the pool halls, and in other places where youth hang out. 85

Finally, U. A. M. E. 's have devoted some attention to advancing the interests of black people by participating in the general struggle for equal opportunity. Men such as Bishops Philip Boulden, Jacob F. Ramsey, and Benjamin M. Fernanders spoke up for the rights of their people when floggings and lynchings were commonplace. Their church was an early supporter of the N. A. A. C. P. 86 This long-standing witness against racism and discrimination continued down through the 1960s as U. A. M. E. 's joined the sit-ins and demonstrations staged by black people across the country. In August 1963 bus loads representing U. A. M. E. congregations from Camden (New Jersey), Wilmington (Delaware), and other places participated in the great march on Washington. The church contributed financially to the families of the four black girls who were killed when the Sixteenth Street Baptist Church in Birmingham, Alabama, was bombed a month later, and it paid special tribute to Jimmy Lee Jackson, James Reeb, Viola Liuzzo, and others who gave their lives for the cause in 1965. [87] Issues of The Union Messenger often featured commentaries on the racial conflict. David E. Hackett, who was the pastor of the St. Paul U. A. M. E. Church in New Haven, Connecticut, during the sixties, was one of the few very active U. A. M. E. clergymen in the movement. In 1965, while serving as the president of a ministerial alliance in New Haven, he united with students from Yale University on a trip to Selma, Alabama, to participate in civil rights demonstrations. When Martin Luther King was assassinated in April 1968, Hackett and several other black ministers were summoned to console angry, panic-strickened blacks in New Haven. A day after the assassination, he, like scores of black leaders around the country, honored King's memory by celebrating the accomplishments he made on behalf of human liberation. Standing before an angry crowd of blacks, he declared:

> King sought to inspire others to share enthusiasm and worked to the very last moment of his busy life for the interest of others. Our world is richer because Dr. Martin Luther King, Jr. lived here, worked here, and died in the faith of the Lord Jesus Christ. Today, his life is richer, fuller, and more blessed. His earthly light has been blown out, but his spirit light shall burn FOREVER. [88]

The civil rights and black power crusade affected U. A. M. E. 's to the same degree as other black churches. Many within the church were led to a new collective understanding of themselves and their mission in light of the events that had taken place. The dawning of this new self-understanding was manifested in a number of ways. Some became more mindful of the social dimensions of the gospel and how it related to the racial realities of the time. Others gained a deeper sense of the importance of agencies like the Urban League and the N. A. A. C. P. and developed closer ties with them. Still others were compelled to recover in a fresh way their heritage as a black religious institution. The published history of the U. A. M. E. Church, issued in 1973, was a product of this new collective consciousness. [89]

Bottom: David E. Hackett, civil rights activist and present Bishop of the First and Fourth Districts of the U. A. M. E. Church; top: Earl L. Huff, Bishop of the Second and Third Districts of the U. A. M. E. Church (from the photo collection of Bishop Earl L. Huff).

Ecumenical Directions for the Spencer Churches

The Spencer Churches showed signs of becoming more sensitive to the need for interdenominational unity and cooperation after 1960. Union discussions between the U. A. M. E. 's and A. U. M. P. 's seemed to take on a more serious tone. In August 1964 union discussions between the two bodies took place at the Mother A. U. M. P. Church in Wilmington. General President Reese C. Scott, General Vice President Robert F. Walters, and General Secretary George A. Woodards represented the A. U. M. P. Conference, and Bishop Orville W. Forward, Bishop David M. Harmon, Bishop John P. Predow, and Presiding Elder John E. Harris represented the U. A. M. E. Church. The representatives discussed methods of achieving unity, property rights, and the possible reactions of clergy and lay persons to the idea of a merger between the two churches. Several agreements were made. First, agreement was reached on the episcopacy and on a uniform order of worship. Second, the representatives agreed to hold joint founder's day programs until union was consummated. Finally, they agreed on the possible transfer of ministers in 1966 as an experimental step. 90 This meeting was very important not merely because it was the most serious and substantive one held between the two bodies since the great schism more than a hundred years earlier, but because it pointed to the possibility of a closer relationship between the Union Churches. Bishop Hackett noted that prior to that time "many of the old heads in both churches vowed that they would never go back together. "91 Unfortunately, the agreements made in 1964 have not yet materialized.

In October 1977 the U. A. M. E. Church, the A. U. M. P. Church, and the C. M. E. Church met in a union coalition service at Holsey Temple C. M. E. Church in Philadelphia. The occasion was designated "Reformation Day. " The leading representatives present were Bishops David E. Hackett and David M. Harmon of the U. A. M. E. Church, Bishop Robert F. Walters of the A. U. M. P. Church, and Bishop Henry C. Bunton of the C. M. E. Church. Instead of focusing seriously on the possibility of a merger, the representatives decided on a working agreement that would allow the three bodies to continue their independent structures, but at the same time to work toward some common goals in a unified fashion. The further advancement of black people was cited as one of the chief goals toward which the churches should work. The City Council of Philadelphia passed a resolution extending congratulations to the churches on the celebration of this occasion. It read in part:

>Resolved by the City Council of Philadelphia, that
>we hereby extend felicitations to the New York-
>Washington Conference of the Christian Methodist
>Episcopal Church, the Union American Methodist
>Episcopal Church, the African Union Methodist
>Protestant Church, and its convener, Bishop Henry
>Clay Bunton, on the occasion of Reformation Day.[92]

The participants in this meeting agreed to meet for a second
annual Reformation Day in October 1978, but the meeting was
canceled after Bishop Harmon died in the summer of that
year. The Churches have not met since the 1977 meeting.[93]

The Spencer Churches' growing sensitivity to ecumenical concerns has found very little expression on the level of
functional cooperation with the other branches of Methodism.
The bishops of the U. A. M. E. and A. U. M. P. Churches did
not join the bishops of the A. M. E., A. M. E. Zion, C. M. E.,
and the Methodist Churches in signing the Black Power Statement of the National Committee of Negro Churchmen issued in
July 1966.[94] They were absent in 1979 when several bishops
of the A. M. E., the A. M. E. Zion, the C. M. E., and United
Methodist Churches met in an attractive display of ecumenism
in Atlanta, Georgia. A statement came out of that meeting
in March 1979, which suggested that "some formal arrangements be developed for the regular consulting together by
these four churches which have so much in common."[95] The
Spencer Churches have also remained aloof from current
union talks between the A. M. E. Z.'s and C. M. E.'s.[96] On
the level of national and worldwide ecumenism, they have remained almost completely out of touch with developments.
Unlike the other branches of African Methodism, the U. A. M. E.
and A. U. M. P. denominations have not moved to establish
firm ties with ecumenical agencies like the National Council
of Churches and the World Council of Churches. As long as
they remain outside of the mainstream of such activities,
they cannot expect to emerge out of the backwaters of black
Methodism.

NOTES

1. The Official Journal of the 137th Annual Session
of the A. U. F. C. M. P. Church, Mother A. U. M. P. Church,
Wilmington, Delaware, May 17-21, 1950 (Wilmington: T. E.
Bolden, printer, 1950), pp. 19 and 35.

2. Daniel J. Russell, Jr., History of the African Union Methodist Protestant Church (Philadelphia: Union Star Book and Job, 1920), p. 27; Every Evening, Wilmington, Del. (August 11, 1900), p. 3; and The Sunday Morning Star, Wilmington, Del. (August 12, 1900), p. 6.

3. Minutes of the 93rd Session of the Annual Conference of the African Union First Colored M. P. Church, of the Middle District, St. John's A. U. F. C. M. P. Church, Chester, Pennsylvania, May 15-20, 1907 (Wilmington: Hubert A. Roop, printer, 1907), p. 22.

4. Minutes of a Special Session of the Annual Conference of the Philadelphia and New Jersey District of the African Union M. P. Church, New Jerusalem A. U. M. P. Church, Claysville, New Jersey, November 12-13, 1902 (Wilmington: unpublished records housed in the headquarters of the A. U. M. P. Church, 1902), pp. 1-4.

5. Ibid.; and Daniel J. Russell, Jr., A Short History of the Life and Death of Rev. I. B. Cooper (Philadelphia, 1919), p. 9.

6. Minutes of a Special Session of the Annual Conference of the Philadelphia and New Jersey District of the African Union M. P. Church, 1902, pp. 2-3.

7. Ibid., pp. 3-4.

8. Ibid., p. 4.

9. Russell, A Short History of the Life and Death of Rev. I. B. Cooper, p. 9. The record is not clear as to what church Sargent affiliated with after the dispute.

10. Benjamin W. Arnett, ed., The Budget: Containing the Annual Reports of the General Officers of the African M. E. Church (Philadelphia, 1904), p. 235.

11. Ibid.; Minutes of the 108th Session of the Annual Conference of the African Union First Colored M. P. Church, Mother A. U. M. P. Church, Wilmington, Delaware, May 19-21, 1920 (Wilmington: Charles L. Story, 1921), pp. 58-60; Daily Journal of the 138th Annual Session of the A. U. F. C. M. P. Church, St. John A. U. M. P. Church, Chester, Pennsylvania, May 16-20, 1951 (Chester, Pa., 1951), p. 31; and The Official Journal of the 137th Annual Session of the

A. U. F. C. M. P. Church, 1950, p. 39. In light of such losses, it is difficult to understand how Daniel J. Russell, Jr., president of the Philadelphia and New Jersey District, would list 575 churches and 20,000 members for the A. U. M. P. Church for the year 1918. Apparently, these erroneous figures resulted from typographical errors made during the printing of Russell's study. He most likely listed 57 churches and 2,000 members. See Russell, History of the African Union Methodist Protestant Church, p. 23.

12. Minutes of the 108th Annual Session of the Annual Conference of the African Union First Colored M. P. Church, 1920, p. 19; Russell, History of the African Union Methodist Protestant Church, p. 34; "A Brief History of St. Matthew A. M. E. Church," Souvenir Journal; The 163rd Session of the Philadelphia Annual Conference of the A. M. E. Church, St. Matthew A. M. E. Church, Philadelphia, Pennsylvania, May 23-27, 1979 (Philadelphia, 1979), p. 5; Private Interview with the Rt. Reverend Reese C. Scott, Wilmington, Del., January 22, 1979; and Private Interview with the Reverend George A. Woodards, Newark, Del., August 27, 1979. The Rev. Scott has served as both General President (1950-67) and bishop (1967-74) of the A. U. M. P. Conference. The Rev. Woodards has been the General Secretary of the Conference for some thirty years.

13. Minutes of a Special Session of the Annual Conference of the Philadelphia and New Jersey District of the African Union M. P. Church, 1902, pp. 4-5; and Minutes of the 108th Session of the Annual Conference of the African Union First Colored M. P. Church, 1920, pp. 58-60.

14. The Official Journal of the 137th Annual Session of the A. U. F. C. M. P. Church, 1950, p. 39.

15. Private Interview with the Rt. Rev. Reese C. Scott, Wilmington, Del., August 26, 1979.

16. Private Interview with the Rev. George A. Woodards, Newark, Del., August 27, 1979.

17. Minutes of the 108th Session of the Annual Conference of the African Union First Colored M. P. Church, 1920, p. 17.

18. Ibid., p. 15.

19. Ibid. , pp. 16-17.

20. Journal of the Proceedings of the Eleventh General Conference of the African Union First Colored Methodist Protestant Church, St. Luke A. U. M. P. Church, Norfolk, Virginia, September 12-20, 1906 (Wilmington: Hubert A. Roop, printer, 1906), pp. 23-30; Minutes of the Twenty-Second Annual Conference of the Philadelphia and New Jersey District of the African Union First Colored M. P. Church, Russell Memorial A. U. M. P. Church, Penns Grove, New Jersey, May 28-June 3, 1924 (Wilmington, 1924), pp. 1-6; The Doctrine and Discipline of the African Union M. P. Church of the United States of America, or Elsewhere, 16th Revised Edition (Wilmington: Charles Gray, printer, 1927), pp. 45-46; A Supplement of the 1942 Discipline of the African Union M. P. Church (Wilmington, 1942), pp. 6-7; Minutes of the 129th Annual Conference of the African Union M. P. Church, St. Paul A. U. M. P. Church, Washington, D. C. , May 20-25, 1942 (Wilmington: T. E. Bolden, printer, 1942), pp. 20ff.; and The Doctrine and Discipline of the African Union First Colored M. P. Church and Connection of the United States of America, or Elsewhere, 17th Revised Edition (Wilmington, 1958), pp. 16 and 42-43.

21. A Supplement of the 1942 Discipline of the African Union M. P. Church, 1942, pp. 6ff.; and Telephone Interview with the Rt. Reverend Robert F. Walters, March 18, 1980. The Rt. Rev. Walters is presently the presiding bishop of the A. U. M. P. Conference.

22. "A Brief History of St. Matthew A. M. E. Church, " p. 5; Private Interview with the Rt. Rev. Reese C. Scott, Wilmington, Del. , August 26, 1979; and Private Interview with the Rev. George A. Woodards, Newark, Del. , August 27, 1979.

23. Private Interview with the Rt. Rev. Reese C. Scott, Wilmington, Del. , January 22, 1979; and Private Interview with the Rev. George A. Woodards, Newark, Del. , February 20, 1980.

24. Our Heritage: The History of the Union American Methodist Episcopal Church (Hackensack, N. J. : Custombook, 1973), pp. 34 and 37; and Private Interview with the Rev. George A. Woodards, Newark, Del. , February 20, 1980.

25. Private Interview with the Rt. Rev. Reese C.

Scott, Wilmington, Del., August 26, 1979; Private Interview with Rev. George A. Woodards, Newark, Del., August 27, 1979; and Telephone Interview with the Rt. Rev. Robert F. Walters, March 18, 1980.

26. Private Interview with the Rev. George A. Woodards, Newark, Del., August 27, 1979.

27. Private Interview with the Rt. Rev. Reese C. Scott, Wilmington, Del., August 26, 1979.

28. The Official Journal of the 137th Annual Session of the A. U. F. C. M. P. Church, 1950, pp. 19 and 35.

29. Private Interview with the Rt. Rev. Reese C. Scott, Wilmington, Del., January 22, 1979; and The Doctrine and Discipline of the African Union First Colored Methodist Protestant Church and Connection, 1958, pp. 55ff.

30. Private Interview with the Rt. Rev. Reese C. Scott, Wilmington, Del., January 22, 1979 and August 26, 1979; and A Letter from Louis L. Redding, Attorney at Law, Wilmington, Del., to Reese C. Scott Regarding W. C. Cleaver et al. vs. Reese C. Scott and the A. U. F. C. M. P. Conference, Wilmington, Del., February 7, 1957.

31. Private Interview with the Rt. Rev. Reese C. Scott, Wilmington, Del., August 26, 1979.

32. Private Interview with Mr. Edward R. Bell, Wilmington, Del., May 22, 1978; Private Interview with the Rt. Rev. Reese C. Scott, Wilmington, Del., January 22, 1979; Private Interview with the Rev. George A. Woodards, Newark, Del., August 27, 1980; Russell, History of the African Union Methodist Protestant Church, pp. 20-21; and Minutes of the Twenty-Second Annual Conference of the Philadelphia and New Jersey District of the African Union First Colored M. P. Church, 1924, pp. 1-10. Mr. Bell, a long-time Wilmington mortician, served the A. U. M. P. Conference as General Treasurer for some thirty years.

33. Private Interview with Mr. Edward R. Bell, Wilmington, Del., May 22, 1978; Private Interview with the Rt. Rev. Reese C. Scott, Wilmington, Del., January 22, 1979; Private Interview with the Rev. George A. Woodards, Newark, Del., August 27, 1980; and George A. Woodards, compiler, Resolution No. 4: Records of the A. U. F. C. M. P.

Conference (Wilmington: printed by the general conference of the A. U. F. C. M. P. Church, 1978), I, p. 96, and II, p. 146.

34. Private Interview with the Rt. Rev. Reese C. Scott, Wilmington, Del., August 26, 1979; Private Interview with the Rev. George A. Woodards, Newark, Del., August 27, 1979; and Telephone Interview with the Rt. Rev. Robert F. Walters, March 18, 1980.

35. Private Interview with Mr. Edward R. Bell, Wilmington, Del., May 22, 1978; Private Interview with the Rt. Rev. Reese C. Scott, Wilmington, Del., January 22, 1979; Private Interview with the Rev. George A. Woodards, Newark, Del., August 27, 1979; Telephone Interview with the Rt. Rev. Robert F. Walters, March 15, 1980; and Private Interview with the Rev. Albert N. Jarman, Wilmington, Del., January 21, 1979. The Rev. Jarman is the pastor of Mother A. U. M. P. Church, Wilmington, Del.

36. Ledger of the 159th Annual Session of the A. U. F. C. M. P. Conference, Inc., Ebenezer A. U. F. C. M. P. Church, Norristown, Pennsylvania, May 16-21, 1972 (Wilmington, 1972), pp. 3ff.; Minutes of the 166th Annual Session of the A. U. F. C. M. P. Church, Inc., St. James A. M. E. Zion Church, Salisbury, Maryland, May 15-20, 1979 (Wilmington, 1979), pp. 4-26; and Minutes of the 167th Session of the A. U. F. C. M. P. Church, Inc., Mother A. U. M. P. Church, Wilmington, Delaware, May 16-20, 1980 (Wilmington, 1980), pp. 2ff.

37. Minutes of the 158th Annual Session of the A. U. F. C. M. P. Church, Mother A. U. M. P. Church, Wilmington, Delaware, May 18-23, 1971 (Wilmington, 1971), pp. 1ff.; and Woodards, compiler, Resolution No. 1: Records of the A. U. F. C. M. P. Conference, 1978, I, pp. 1-2.

38. The Morning News, Wilmington, Del., (May 29, 1971), p. 10; and Private Interview with the Rt. Rev. Reese C. Scott, Wilmington, Del., January 22, 1979.

39. Delaware County (Pa.) Daily Times, Delaware County, Pa. (March 27, 1973), p. 4; Private Interview with the Rev. George A. Woodards, Newark, Del., February 20, 1980; Telephone Interview with the Rt. Rev. Robert F. Walters, March 15, 1980; Private Interview with the Rev. Thomas E. Moon, Wilmington, Del., February 16, 1980; and Private Interview with the Rev. Maynard Smith, Wilmington,

Del., February 16, 1980. Moon and Smith presently serve the A. U. M. P. Conference as presiding elders.

40. Private Interview with the Rt. Rev. Reese C. Scott, Wilmington, Del., January 22, 1979; Telephone Interview with the Rt. Rev. Robert F. Walters, March 15, 1980; Private Interview with Mrs. Elizabeth Brown, Wilmington, Del., January 20, 1979; and Evening Journal, Wilmington, Del., (August 11, 1975), p. 29. Mrs. Brown is the widow of the late Bishop George F. Brown.

41. Telephone Interview with the Rt. Rev. Robert F. Walters, March 15, 1980.

42. Russell, History of the African Union Methodist Protestant Church, p. 24.

43. "History of the A. U. M. P. School of Religion, " in Program Booklet: Service of Recognition, St. James A. U. M. P. Church, Wilmington, Delaware, April 26, 1979 (Wilmington, 1979), p. 4; The Annual Ministerial Studies Program of the A. U. F. C. M. P. Conference (Wilmington: printed by the Conference Standing Committee on Ministerial Studies, 1955), pp. 1ff.; and the Minutes of the 167th Annual Session of the A. U. F. C. M. P. Church, 1980, p. 10.

44. Russell, History of the African Union Methodist Protestant Church, p. 24; and O. Watson, ed., Yearbook of the Churches (Washington, D. C.: The Federal Council of the Churches of Christ in America, 1923), p. 160.

45. Russell, History of the African Union Methodist Protestant Church, p. 24; The Union Youth Messenger of the A. U. F. C. M. P. Church, Vol. I, No. 5 (May 30, 1945), pp. 1-4; and The Flashlight of the A. U. F. C. M. P. Church, Vol. I (January 1956), pp. 1ff.

46. The Delaware Valley Defender, Wilmington, Del. (June 18, 1977), pp. 1-2; The A. U. F. C. M. P. Sunday School Association News, Vol. I, No. 7 (October 1977 to April 1978), pp. 1-4; and The Morning News (May 23, 1968), p. 18.

47. Russell, History of the African Union Methodist Protestant Church, p. 51; and The Official Journal of the 137th Annual Session of the A. U. F. C. M. P. Church, 1950, p. 13.

48. Russell, History of the African Union Methodist Protestant Church, pp. 37ff.; The Morning News (August 27, 1945), p. 4; Ledger of the 159th Annual Session of the A. U. F. C. M. P. Conference, 1972, pp. 9ff.; Private Interview with Mrs. Ada M. Brown, Wilmington, Del., January 22, 1979; and Private Interview with Mrs. Martha Brister, Wilmington, Del., January 22, 1979. Mrs. Brown is the widow of former General President John W. Brown of the A. U. M. P. Conference, and a long-time member of the A. U. M. P. Church. Mrs. Brister has been a member of the Mother A. U. M. P. Church in Wilmington for about 88 years.

49. Minutes of the 166th Annual Session of the A. U. F. C. M. P. Church, 1979, pp. 24-25.

50. Minutes of the 93rd Session of the Annual Conference of the African Union First Colored M. P. Church, 1907, p. 22.

51. Sylvester C. Blackledge, An Open Book on Hidden Mysteries (Elkton, Md.: the author, 1925), pp. 95-96.

52. Ibid., p. 98.

53. Ibid., pp. 103-104.

54. The Morning News (May 17, 1963), pp. 1ff.; Private Interview with Mrs. Elizabeth Brown, Wilmington, Del., January 20, 1979; and Private Interview with Ms. Grace Thomas, Wilmington, Del., February 20, 1980. Ms. Thomas was one of George F. Brown's closest associates in the Delaware sit-in movement.

55. The Morning News (June 5, 1963), pp. 1-3.

56. The Evening Journal (June 5, 1963), pp. 1-3; The Morning News (June 11, 1963), p. 33; and The Morning News (June 15, 1963), pp. 1ff.

57. The Evening Journal (August 11, 1975), p. 29; and The State of Delaware vs. George F. Brown, Argued Before the Supreme Court of Delaware, New Castle County, November, 1963 (Wilmington, 1963), Cr. A. No. 887, No. 64, pp. 1-16.

58. The Delaware Defender, Wilmington, Del. (August 30, 1963), pp. 1 and 5; Private Interview with Elizabeth

Brown, Wilmington, Del., January 20, 1979; and Private Interview with the Rt. Rev. Reese C. Scott, Wilmington, Del., January 22, 1979.

59.　Private Interview with the Rt. Rev. Reese C. Scott, Wilmington, Del., January 22, 1979; and Private Interview with Mrs. Elizabeth Brown, Wilmington, Del., January 20, 1979.

60.　The Morning News (May 23, 1968), p. 18.

61.　Figures have been rounded out to the nearest thousand. For assistance in arriving at these estimates, the author checked The United States Department of Commerce, Bureau of Census: Religious Bodies, 1926: Statistics, History, Doctrine, Organization, and Work (Washington, D.C.: The U.S. Government Printing Office, 1929), pp. 995–1046. The estimates provided in this study are more accurate than those given in Frederick A. Norwood, The Story of American Methodism: A History of the United Methodists and Their Relations (Nashville and New York: Abingdon Press, 1974), p. 359. Norwood's estimate of 16,000 U.A.M.E.'s in 1900 is excessive, to say the least. His figures do not include the African Union Methodist Protestant Church, the Colored Methodist Protestant Church, the Reformed Methodist Union Episcopal Church, the Reformed Zion United Apostolic (Methodist) Church, and the Independent African Methodist Episcopal Church. The histories of the last three churches mentioned are relatively unknown. The Reformed Methodist Union Episcopal Church developed as a result of a split within the A.M.E. Church in 1884. The Reformed Zion Union Apostolic (Methodist) Church was started in 1869 by black Methodists in southeastern Virginia, who at the close of the Civil War found themselves in a peculiar situation in that they were no longer permitted to gather for worship in white churches, had no educated clergy, and were not in sympathy with the ecclesiasticism of the black Methodist denominations. The Independent African Methodist Episcopal Church was organized in Jacksonville, Florida, between 1897 and 1910. It, too, resulted from a schism within the A.M.E. Church.

62.　The United States Department of Commerce, Bureau of Census, Religious Bodies, 1926, pp. 1017-1021; The Evening Journal (April 26, 1916), p. 2; and The Evening Journal (May 1, 1919), p. 17.

63.   Our Heritage, pp. 7-37; Arnett, ed. , The Budget: Containing the Annual Reports of the General Officers of the African M. E. Church, 1904, p. 231; The United States Department of Commerce, Bureau of Census, Religious Bodies, 1926, pp. 1018-1021; Frank R. Zebley, The Churches of Delaware (Wilmington: the author, 1947), pp. 106, 200, and 269; and The Evening Journal (May 2, 1925), p. 6.

64.   The United States Department of Commerce, Bureau of Census, Religious Bodies, 1926, pp. 995-1034. These figures were approved in 1926 by Professor J. R. Hawkins, General Financial Secretary of the A. M. E. Church; S. M. Dudley, Secretary-Treasurer of the Church Extension and Home Missions Board of the A. M. E. Zion Church; Bishop R. S. Williams, Official Statistician, Colored Methodist Episcopal Church; Bishop Philip A. Boulden, Chancellor of Union College of the U. A. M. E. Church; and C. N. Walker, President of the A. U. M. P. Church.

65.   Our Heritage, pp. 2-4; and Private Interview with the Rt. Reverend David E. Hackett, Wilmington, Del. , May 10, 1979.   The Rt. Rev. Hackett is a U. A. M. E. bishop.

66.   The Discipline of the Union American Methodist Episcopal Church, Thirty-First Edition (Chester, Pa. : printed by the General Conference of the U. A. M. E. Church, 1976), p. 4; and Private Interview with the Rev. George W. Poindexter, Marshallton, Del. , May 9, 1979. The Rev. Poindexter is a presiding elder in the U. A. M. E. Church.

67.   The Discipline of the Union American Methodist Episcopal Church (Wilmington: T. E. Bolden, printer, 1942), pp. 1ff. ; and The Discipline of the Union American Methodist Episcopal Church, 1976, pp. 25ff.

68.   Private Interview with Mrs. Sadie Harris Fernanders Bulah, Hockessin, Del. , May 9, 1979.   Mrs. Fernanders is the widow of the late Bishop Benjamin Fernanders.

69.   John P. Predow, A Brief History of the Spencer Movement (Wilmington: unpublished paper, the Predow Collection, the Boulden Academy and Seminary, 1979), pp. 6-7; Private Interview with the Rt. Rev. David E. Hackett, Wilmington, Del. , May 10, 1979; and Telephone Interview with the Rt. Rev. John P. Predow, April 14, 1980.   The Rt. Rev. Predow is the only living retired bishop of the U. A. M. E. Church.

70.   Private Interview with the Rt. Rev. David E. Hackett, Wilmington, Del., May 10, 1979; and Telephone Interview with the Rt. Rev. John P. Predow, April 14, 1980.

71.   The Union Messenger of the U. A. M. E. Church, Vol. I, No. 1 (January 1975), p. 1; Private Interview with the Rt. Rev. David E. Hackett, Wilmington, Del., May 10, 1979; Private Interview with the Rev. George W. Poindexter, Marshallton, Del., May 9, 1979; and Telephone Interview with the Rt. Rev. Earl L. Huff, March 15, 1980. The Rt. Rev. Huff is a U. A. M. E. bishop.

72.   Private Interview with the Rt. Rev. David E. Hackett, Wilmington, Del., May 10, 1979; and Private Interview with the Rev. George W. Poindexter, Marshallton, Del., May 9, 1979.

73.   Our Heritage, pp. 3ff.; Telephone Interview with the Rt. Rev. Earl L. Huff, March 15, 1980; and Private Interview with the Rt. Rev. David E. Hackett, Wilmington, Del., May 10, 1979.

74.   These figures have been rounded out to the nearest thousand. They were determined after receiving estimates from the Rt. Rev. Richard A. Hildebrand, Presiding Bishop of the First Episcopal District of the A. M. E. Church; Bishop Herman L. Anderson and the Rev. Earl Johnson, Department of Statistics and Records of the A. M. E. Zion Church; the Headquarters of the Christian Methodist Episcopal Church, Memphis, Tennessee; the Rt. Rev. Earl L. Huff, Presiding Bishop of the Second and Third Districts of the U. A. M. E. Church; and Mildred Demby, General Statistician of the A. U. M. P. Conference.

75.   The United States Department of Commerce, Bureau of Census, Religious Bodies, 1926, p. 1021; The Evening Journal (May 2, 1925), p. 6; and The First Anniversary Booklet of the Great Charter Day of the New Boulden Academy and Seminary, Inc., of the U. A. M. E. Church, Wilmington, Delaware, February 14, 1960 (Wilmington, 1960), pp. 1-8.

76.   Predow, A Brief History of the Spencer Movement, pp. 3-6.

77.   The United States Department of Commerce, Bureau of Census, Religious Bodies, 1926, p. 1021; The

Union Messenger, Vol. II, No. 1 (January 1964), pp. 1-4; The Union Messenger (May 1969), pp. 1-4; and The Union Messenger of the U. A. M. E. Church, Vol. V, No. 1 (January 1975), pp. 1-4.

78. The Evening Journal (May 2, 1925), p. 6; and Private Interview with Sadie Harris Fernanders Bulah, Hockessin, Del., May 9, 1979.

79. John P. Predow and David M. Harmon, compilers, The Handbook of the Predow Apartments: The U. A. M. E. Church Non-Profit Housing Corporation (Wilmington: printed by the U. A. M. E. Church Non-Profit Housing Corporation, 1971), p. 13.

80. Ibid., pp. 2 and 14; and The Union Messenger (May 1969), p. 1.

81. The Union Messenger of the U. A. M. E. Church, Vol. V, No. 1 (January 1975), pp. 2-3.

82. The Discipline of the Union American Methodist Episcopal Church, 1942, pp. 124-125.

83. Our Heritage, pp. 22ff.; and Private Interview with the Rev. Irene C. Dutton, Wilmington, Del., May 11, 1979. The Rev. Mrs. Dutton is an active pastor and historian in the U. A. M. E. Church.

84. The United States Department of Commerce, Bureau of Census, Religious Bodies, 1926, pp. 1018ff.

85. Private Interview with the Rt. Rev. David E. Hackett, Wilmington, Del., May 10, 1979; and The Union Messenger of the U. A. M. E. Church, Vol. V, No. 1 (January 1975), p. 3.

86. The Evening Journal (May 2, 1925), p. 6.

87. The Morning News (March 16, 1965), p. 3; The Morning News (September 23, 1963), p. 1; and Private Interview with the Rt. Rev. David E. Hackett, Wilmington, Del., May 10, 1979.

88. David E. Hackett, compiler, A Book of Inspirational Poems and Wayside Messages, 1943-1977 (Wilmington: the author, 1977), p. 28; and Private Interview with the Rt. Rev. David E. Hackett, Wilmington, Del., May 10, 1979.

89. _Our Heritage_, pp. 1-40.

90. _The Evening Journal_ (August 1, 1964), pp. 1ff.

91. Private Interview with the Rt. Rev. David E. Hackett, Wilmington, DeL, May 10, 1979.

92. "A Resolution Extending Felicitations to the New York-Washington Conference of the Christian Methodist Episcopal Church, the Union American Methodist Episcopal Church, and the African Union Methodist Protestant Church, on the Celebration of 'Reformation Day'," passed by the City Council, Philadelphia, Pa., October 6, 1977.

93. Private Interview with the Rt. Rev. David E. Hackett, Wilmington, Del., May 10, 1979; and Private Interview with the Rt. Rev. Robert F. Walters, Wilmington, DeL, February 16, 1980.

94. See C. Eric Lincoln, _The Black Church Since Frazier_ (New York: Schocken Books, 1974), pp. 176-178.

95. See _NOW: Black Methodists for Church Renewal_, VoL II, No. 4 (April 1979), pp. 1 and 3.

96. _The A. M. E. Zion Quarterly Review_, Vol. XCII, No. 2 (July 1980), pp. 7-19; and _The Christian Index_ of the C. M. E. Church, Vol. 113, No. 13 (July 1, 1980), pp. 3-7.

Chapter VII:

BIG QUARTERLY IN THE TWENTIETH CENTURY: A TRADITION IN TRANSITION

> It is an anachronism, a flareback atavism,
> what you will, this Big Quarterly, but it holds
> within it incredible possibilities of suggestion
> for those who might wish to investigate a rich
> mine of folklore, custom, and tradition among
> this growing Negro people.
> --Alice Dunbar-Nelson[1]

In the twentieth century Wilmington, Delaware, has remained the home of Big Quarterly, the nation's oldest continuously celebrated black religious street festival. The festival continues to reflect a curious blend of religion, culture, and history and is closely connected to the political struggle of Delaware blacks for freedom. It remains an occasion of great pride, of festivity, and of celebration to those who know of its origin and significance in the struggle for black religious freedom.[2]

The Pilgrims

Despite claims to the contrary, the attendance and enthusiasm at Big Quarterly celebrations continued to reach high levels in the early twentieth century.[3] An average of three thousand visitors attended the festival between 1900 and 1905. The ten thousand or so who appeared in 1907 and 1908 were the largest crowds for the first decade of the century. The average attendance increased sharply during the second decade. Twenty thousand are said to have jammed French Street for Big Quarterly in 1912, and almost twenty-five thousand showed up in 1917.[4] The fifteen thousand who gathered in 1925 were a record high for the 1920s. In that year visitors from as far north as New York and as far south as North Carolina came via boat, train, and motor car

213

A Big Quarterly crowd on French Street in the 1950s (from the photo collection of the late Bishop George F. Brown of the A. U. M. P. Conference).

to participate in the event.   Between 1929 and 1935 there was a noticeable drop in the average attendance due primarily to the lingering effects of the Great Depression.   After the more drastic effects of the depression subsided, attendance reached normal proportions once more. [5]   Nine thousand visitors were attracted to Wilmington from many geographical points in 1935:

> Hundreds of automobiles bearing the license plates of New Jersey, New York, Pennsylvania, Maryland, District of Columbia, Virginia, West Virginia, North Carolina, South Carolina, Tennessee, Ohio, Indiana, and Illinois were observed parked on east side streets.   Hundreds of Delaware automobiles lined the curbs. [6]

Fourteen thousand were at Big Quarterly in 1940, setting a record for the fourth decade of the century. A total of eight thousand were present in 1950 and 1955, and ten thousand appeared in 1956 and 1957. The 1959 Big Quarterly witnessed the appearance of eight thousand. 7

After 1960, the festival began to show clear signs of decline for reasons to be addressed later. The five thousand who gathered in Wilmington in 1963 were the largest crowd recorded for the 1960s. The 1964 and 1965 celebrations drew almost three thousand each. Fewer than two hundred attended in 1967. Rainy weather undoubtedly contributed to this unusually poor showing. 8 Only about one hundred persons showed up for the 1969 Big Quarterly, which was reported to be the last one held on French Street. The dismal showing resulted largely from widespread uncertainty as to whether Big Quarterly was to be held, especially since the Mother A. U. M. P. Church was being relocated in accordance with urban renewal plans. 9

Prayers are offered by the faithful at the grave of Peter Spencer at a Big Quarterly celebration in the 1960s (from the photo collection of the late Bishop George F. Brown of the A. U. M. P. Conference).

What was it about Big Quarterly that drew an average of ten thousand people each year between 1900 and 1969? There is no simple answer to this question because "the festival," as Sara Gardner observed, "was different things to different people."[10] Those directly affiliated with the Spencer Churches were continuously drawn in large numbers because Big Quarterly honored Peter Spencer and commemorated the founding of African Union Methodism. The pilgrimage to the grave of Peter Spencer was always considered the sacred duty of the faithful. As established by custom, presiding officers and pastors of the Spencer Churches would pay high tribute to Spencer as a champion of black rights and religious freedom. At the 1929 celebration he was compared to the early apostles.[11] During the 1958 Big Quarterly, Grand Master Bishop A. H. Ransom of the York Free and Accepted Masons made a very special and memorable salute to Spencer, honoring him as one of the earliest supporters of the black masonic movement in this country. A wreath was placed on Spencer's grave by Ransom and his staff.[12] The tribute given Spencer at the festival in 1966 was equally special and memorable, as Reese C. Scott, president of the A. U. M. P. Conference, reminded all present that he fought for civil rights long before Martin Luther King, Jr. did:

> Human rights marches didn't start with Martin Luther King. Humanity regardless of creed has always sought equal human rights. Spencer just wanted equal rights, the opportunity to be free and to worship God according to the dictates of his own conscience. And that's what we want today--equal rights--the right to go where we want to go, live where we want to live, and worship God.[13]

The religious aspect of Big Quarterly continued to be an attractive feature for many. Black churches of all denominations within a hundred mile radius of Wilmington often canceled services on the last Sunday in August in order to take part in the Big Quarterly worship experience. Worship services with all the old-time vigor would be held concurrently in the Mother A. U. M. P. Church, in tents alongside the church, in the Mother U. A. M. E. Church, and in Ezion Methodist Church. The worship experience never ceased to give a place to emotion and feeling in religion as gospel, jazz, and spiritual songs blended curiously with the preaching, chanting, and shouting.[14]

It has been suggested that most blacks and whites who

frequented Big Quarterly in the first six or so decades of this century were attracted by a motive of a social nature. People came to socialize--to see old friends, to meet new people, and to hold family reunions. Elderly residents of Wilmington tell of days of grandeur when there were large crowds, fashion parades, and "plenty of story-telling, laughter, spirited greetings, and home-style cooking. "[15] To black children Big Quarterly was a circus, while many young men and women regarded it as an occasion to make merry, to meet mates, and to show off the latest styles in costumes. "It was," according to Pauline A. Young, "just a happy occasion for everybody. "[16]

The Worship Experience

Noticeable changes in the Big Quarterly worship style have occurred in the twentieth century. The traditional love feast, regarded in earlier times as one of the highlights of the festival, was rarely held after 1955 and was almost completely abandoned during the 1960s. Today the love feast is not a part of Big Quarterly at all. Alfred Collins, an elderly member of the Mother A. U. M. P. Church, recently complained bitterly about the discontinuance of the love feast at Big Quarterly celebrations:

> It is a shame that we no longer have love feast.
> Years ago, it was unthinkable to celebrate Big
> Quarterly without that love feast, which was always
> held very early on that Sunday morning. People
> looked forward to it, and hundreds would arrive in
> Wilmington on the Saturday night before August
> Quarterly Sunday just to be present for that love
> feast. Now we only have the welcome address. [17]

Most of the ceremonies and practices linked to the African background either died out completely or were celebrated with less frequency in this century. The ceremonial ring dance, which was so much a part of the Big Quarterly worship style in the nineteenth century, had been completely abandoned by 1920. Conjurers and medicine men slowly passed off the scene, and faith-healing was being practiced on a smaller scale by 1940.

Toward the middle of the century, gospel songs displaced the spirituals as the most popular type of black sacred music heard at the festivals, signaling still another change in

the Big Quarterly worship tradition. Impromptu gospel services along both sides of French Street became the mode, and popular singing groups such as the Coronette Gospel Singers, Clara Ward and the Ward Singers, the Celestial Gospel Singers, and the Spiritual Travelers showed up in increasing numbers each year. Gospel music was popularized at the Mother A. U. M. P. Church by Willard B. Chippey, the organist, and one of the descendants of a long line of Chippeys in the history of African Union Methodism. [18]

Preaching, vocal and instrumental music, the frenzy, prayer, and testimony continued to be the principal elements of worship at Big Quarterlies. In this respect, there was no major departure from what had been the vogue in the nineteenth century.

The sermon remained the center of worship. Worshipers at Big Quarterly services often spent half the day listening to doctrinal preaching and fiery exhortation in the churches and on street corners. The number of so-called "French Street evangelists" increased each year, drawing groups of curious whites with cameras. At the 1929 celebration "exhorters held their places on the streets and preached sermons that rose to the dizzy heights of emotion." During the 1940 festival "oddly dressed evangelists of both sexes, many bearing signs, 'BLIND,' took their stands on street corners, automobile hoods, and wooden boxes. They preached fervently of the judgement to come, urging repentance from sin and recommending that the people seek God's mercy."[19] The sermons of such evangelists were frequently accompanied by music and singing. In 1936, Big Quarterly attracted "a number of evangelists with retinues of white-robed women with tambourines and choruses of 'Hallelujas.'" The 1959 gala was no exception, as "street preachers in their bizarre garb proclaimed the gospel to the tune of drum beats and brass accompaniment."[20] At the 1967 festival, a Prophet Parker and his revival band attracted wide attention with their street preaching and foot-tapping religious selections. [21]

[Opposite:] A sidewalk preacher chants his sermon to a group of Big Quarterly listeners in 1966 as a guitarist in the background strums accompaniment (from the photo collection of the late Bishop George F. Brown of the A. U. M. P. Conference).

Willard B. Chippey, the popular musician who was renown
for his "good spiritual and gospel music" at Big Quarterlies
in the 1950s and 60s (from the photo collection of the late
Bishop George F. Brown of the A. U. M. P. Conference).

"Prophet" Alexander Parker beats out time to lively revival music with his cymbals at the 1967 Big Quarterly (from the photo collection of the late Bishop George F. Brown of the A. U. M. P. Conference).

Some of the evangelists who appeared at Big Quarterly meetings openly engaged in faith-healing. In 1929 "faith doctors or healing evangelists held their clinics and, for a small sum, healed the afflicted of such disorders as stomach trouble, and liver and kidney ailments."22 Elder James Seawright of Somerset, New Jersey, appearing at Big Quarterly in 1964, stood on a small kitchen chair and offered healing to a few believers. "I'll be on my knees praying at 11 o'clock tonight," he said to those listening, "and no matter where you are, you point to where you ail, and, if you believe, you'll be healed."23

The continuing importance of music, song, and the chant at Big Quarterlies was clearly recognized by all who attended the festivals. A reporter of The Evening Journal wrote the following in reference to the celebration held in 1909:

> The spirit of the day caught the older worshippers and the singing and chanting rang through the open windows and were heard far down the street. It was the characteristic chant that makes all colored folks happy, and the happiness swelled and overflowed into joyous shouts that revived memories of the greatest camp meetings.24

The festival of 1918 was equally fervent, "as the lusty chanting and singing of the worshippers could be heard blocks away."25 "'The Old-Time Religion' that was Good for Daniel, Paul, Silas, and the Other Biblical Characters was the theme song" at the celebration of 1929. Men and women dressed in bizarre costumes sang and chanted "as if the Day of Judgment was at hand, and their transient congregation joined with a joy and enthusiasm that would have sent the average preacher into ecstasy."26

Musical instruments of almost every variety were commonly used by those who sang spirituals and gospel songs at these meetings. At the 1940 celebration, strolling minstrel evangelists played black spirituals and favorite hymns on guitar, drum, cymbals, tambourine, and cornet. "Lord, make me strong some day," "When the gates swing open, let me in," and "Lord receive a sinner" were among the hymns most often heard.27 Of the variety of instruments used at the 1950 Big Quarterly, The Morning News stated:

> Music, struggling above the hub-bub of hundreds of

Members of a band relax with instruments at a Big Quarterly meeting in the 1960s (from the photo collection of the Rev. George Woodards of the A. U. M. P. Conference).

voices, reflected both the cadence of a primitive past and the lyrical quality of the Negro spiritual. The rattle of the tambourines, the beat of drums, and the music of violins, guitars, and banjos, created a medley of sounds to punctuate the exhortation of preachers in pulpit and on street corner. 28

At the 1956 festival "Gospel chants and the lifting rhythm of brass and drum furnished those in the street with a form of sacred music which has become an American folk classic. "29 The curious mixture of vocal and instrumental music heard at the 1964 gala was described in a very picturesque manner by one observer:

An elderly man strummed a Hawaiian guitar, and sang softly to himself. A hard-lettered cardboard

sign on a window ledge above proclaimed he was
"Bro. Elijah Beckham, " a near-blind disc jockey.
Few passersby were watching him, however.   Their
attention was on three women who offered a rousing
curbstone rendition of "When the saints go marching
in. "   While one sat on a chair rhythmically beating
a worn brass drum--as a housewife beats a cake
mix--her fellow musicians pumped out the tune on
a trombone and a baritone horn.   About fifty persons watched silently and an elderly, grim-faced
man stood with arms folded across his chest de-
terminedly tapping out the beat with one foot while
Miss Corine Millens and her Philadelphia group
played.   Farther up French Street toward Ninth,
Mrs. Flora Molton, 55, of Washington, D. C. , was
reminding listeners that "Jesus is on the mainline,
tell Him what you want. " She stole the show from
two other elderly women who sat on camp chairs
across the street feebly beating tambourines. 30

The powerful sermons and rich musical sounds at
Big Quarterlies often set the stage for dancing and shouting,
thus illustrating the ability of Black people to celebrate with
real abandon.   A classic example of such frenzied behavior
occurred at the celebration in 1917:

This service was largely of the old fashioned type.
At times 100 or more of the men and women would
be seen shouting, singing, and leaping into the air,
so imbued were they with religious fervor.   Many
of them continued in this manner of worship until
compelled to desist from pure exhaustion, and give
way to others, and seemingly there were plenty of
others at all times to fill up the enforced gaps in
the ranks of the religious enthusiasts. 31

The swaying of black bodies up and down and back and forth,
like the levers of a mighty engine, was a common sight at
these gatherings.   The dancing and shouting frequently began
in the churches and tents and reached the streets before the
excitement eased.

Intimately tied to this kind of emotionalism and ex-
pressionism was the element of prayer.   Prayer meetings
were generally held throughout the day on Big Quarterly Sun-
days--in the churches, tents, and at the gravesites of Peter
Spencer and the other early saints of African Union Methodism.

One after another, the celebrants would kneel in response to
the invitation to "continue in prayer."[32] Prayer was always
a central ingredient of the healing ministries of the evangelists who lined up along French Street each year. Like
the sermon, song, and the frenzy, it remained a communal
happening. It continued to reflect the hopes, the dreams,
and the inner yearnings of an oppressed people who expressed
their joy freely and collectively with shouts of "Amen," "hal-
lelujah," "praise the Lord," and "thank you, Jesus." Big
Quarterly played a significant role in developing, nourishing,
and sustaining what Harold A. Carter has called "the prayer
tradition of black people."[33]

Prayer and testimony were always closely related.
Each year worshipers testified to the goodness of God in
sparing them to attend another Big Quarterly and bore witness to their determination to "keep their eyes on the prize
and hold on." Testimonies commonly preceded and followed
the prayers offered. Both the content of what was said and
the manner in which it was communicated illustrated beyond
doubt the struggle of a people for liberation and wholeness.[34]

The Decline of the Festival

On August 28, 1967, an issue of Wilmington's The Evening
Journal displayed the headline: "Big Quarterly a Big Question
for Next Year." The article that followed read in part:

> Whether there will be a Big Quarterly next year
> or, for that matter, a Mother A. U. M. P. Church
> at 819 French Street to hold it in, is uncertain.[35]

By this time it had become clear to many Big Quarterly supporters that the annual celebrations would soon be past history. Demolition for the Civic Center Urban Renewal Pro-
ject had already begun in the 800 block of French Street.
A. U. M. P. Church leaders such as George F. Brown and
Reese C. Scott speculated that future Big Quarterlies would
probably be devoted to simple founder's day programs rather
than the usual festivities.[36] The 1969 Big Quarterly, the
last one held on French Street before the relocation of the
Mother A. U. M. P. Church, attracted an amazingly small
crowd of about one hundred persons. Only one block of
French Street, between Eighth and Ninth, was closed to traf-
fic for the fete. This was a far cry from what had occurred
in the past, when the street was blocked off from Fourth

Street to Tenth Street, and the entire six-block length was
literally jammed with people. The young people who attended
this last celebration seemed unanimously unimpressed with
what was happening. A few curious adults showed up to see
if anything at all would take place. "People in Philadelphia
told me there wasn't anything down here, anymore," said
Bennett Ashford, who had supported the festival in the past.
"I wouldn't take their word, though, I had to come down and
see for myself."[37]

Many of the elderly blacks present used the occasion
to reflect upon Big Quarterlies of past years. "By this time
of day (3:30 p.m.) there used to be about 25,000 people
here," recalled Bennett Ashford. "You couldn't even see the
street, and you had to push your way through the crowds to
get anywhere," he continued. "It used to be like a regular
camp meeting," reminisced Mrs. Charles Benson, who sat
in a folding chair alongside the Mother A. U. M. P. Church.
Eighty-eight-year-old Harry Ruffin of Baltimore, Maryland,
who had been in charge of a food stand at the festival for the
previous thirty years, nodded his head in agreement. Andrew Lambert, a 70-year-old Delawarean, added: "There
used to be nothing but people as far as you could see. It
would take two hours to make your way through the crowd."
Stephen Nichols, Lambert's 76-year-old companion, bore witness to his claim. "And there was always lots of music and
hundreds of outdoor preachers," he said. The following Mon-
day, Wilmington's The Morning News added a sad footnote to
the testimonies of these old-timers as its headline read:
"Big Quarterly, One-Time Black Gala, Expires."[38]

According to the accounts of Wilmington newspapers,
and the testimonies of Big Quarterly supporters, several factors combined to force the eventual decline of the French
Street festival. First, the increasing lack of interest and
support on the part of the younger generations of blacks who
had been introduced to Big Quarterly by their parents, grandparents, and great-grandparents proved to be a crucial factor. As early as 1908 The Evening Journal reported, "The
younger generation of colored people is not, of course, quite
so interested in Big Quarterly as were their grandparents."[39]
In 1933, The Delmarva Star concluded that "The waning was
inevitable after the young colored folk lost their strong devotion to church practice and turned to worldly emotional out-
lets."[40] Five years later, The Sunday Morning Star related,
"The real significance and purpose of Big Quarterly are
missed by many of this third generation."[41] In 1964 The

Morning News re-echoed this sentiment, noting that "the
thinner crowds in recent years are due to the lack of interest among the young. "[42] As recent as 1979, Anna Ferrel
complained, "The young people have not been concerned about
carrying on the tradition. Many left the Wilmington area,
accepted jobs, and simply refused to return for Big Quarterly. "[43] Other young blacks undoubtedly shared the opinion of
29-year-old William Potts of Wilmington, who characterized
the festival as the stereotypical, out-dated remains of slave
culture: "The event's an anachronism, and they should have
quit it when the slaves were freed. It's nothing but memories
of the past. We should let it go. "[44]

Second, a growing number of Wilmington's black intellectuals not only ceased to support Big Quarterly, but called
for its abolishment with an increasingly loud voice each year.
As far back as the 1880s the more sophisticated blacks of
the city began to abandon the festival, to denounce the folk
qualities associated with it, and to join impatient and uneasy
whites in questioning its importance. During the early
years of the twentieth century, black leaders continued to express "the hope that someday soon Big Quarterly will disap-
pear completely. "[45] Bill Frank, a Jewish columnist for
The Morning News, remembers the 1930s when Alice Dunbar-
Nelson, teacher, civil rights activist, and wife of the great
Paul Laurence Dunbar, who lived in Wilmington, urged black
leaders to work toward abolishing the annual folk fiesta. [46]
Before her death, however, she was compelled to confront
the fact that her wish would not materialize in the near future. She wrote:

> Big Quarterly is too deeply rooted in the minds
> and hearts of the Negroes of the Eastern Shore of
> Maryland and Virginia, of Delaware and south-
> eastern Pennsylvania, to be broken up or rooted
> out by the mere disgust of a few intelligentsia. [47]

As late as 1965 Bill Frank was approached by a number of intellectually-inclined blacks who "told me that they,
too, would like to see it go into oblivion and that the goings
on embarrass them. " Frank reacted in this manner:

> As one who is attached to the remaining folklore of
> our town, I fail to see why Big Quarterly should
> be abolished. It is rooted in Delaware Negro his-
> tory, although I grant you very few Negroes of
> Delaware know the history of their people. [48]

Alice Dunbar-Nelson, teacher, civil rights activist, and wife of the great Paul Laurence Dunbar, wrote about Big Quarterly in the 1930s (from the photo collection of her niece, Pauline A. Young, a Wilmington historian).

He went on to write:

> I hate to see such a well-established folk festival
> as Big Quarterly shuffled into nothing. If it is true
> that it is doomed, then it is another one of our lo-
> cal folk patterns that is being discarded. Little by
> little, city life is becoming dull, and ordinary, and
> standardized. The picturesque ways of life are
> passing, but I don't suppose there is any way of
> preventing this. On the other hand, is it possible
> that new folk ways are being developed?[49]

Third, the decline of Big Quarterly has been attributed
in part to commercialism. In the early years of the century
there were those who felt that the festival was developing into a commercial enterprise. This concern was expressed in
1927 by 86-year-old James A. Anderson, a watchman at the
public building in Wilmington:

> When it was originated, there was a certain sacred
> significance attached to the observance and at that
> time visitors were required to have a pass to en-
> ter the state. Reunions of families from other
> parts of the country at that time were free from
> commercialism, and when these reunions were held,
> the visitors were always provided with food by the
> relatives and friends. [50]

In 1964, almost forty years later, black people in Wilmington
blamed commercialism for the drop in attendance and enthusiasm at the festivals:

> By commercialism they meant the baskets, pans,
> and up-turned hats that lay waiting for coins in
> front of the singing groups and others who peddled
> food, drink, and religious tracts. [51]

In recent conversations with this author, Edward R. Bell and
Matthew Gardner, long-time supporters of the Big Quarterly
festival, explained how elements outside the church, with less
than honorable motives, often appeared to dampen the enthusiasm of well-intentioned worshipers. Bootleggers and gamblers
turned out, and so did religious charlatans and fakers. Their
very presence cast suspicion upon Big Quarterly and undoubtedly caused more and more people to stay away. [52]

Fourth, scores of Big Quarterly pilgrims who had attended the festival in the late nineteenth and early twentieth centuries, among whom were a few ex-slaves, became discouraged by what they saw as a developing interest in socializing at the expense of the religious aspect of the festival. They felt that the sacredness of the occasion was being increasingly undermined by those who spent the day having fun. In 1929, 83-year-old John T. Sency of Quenne Anne County, Maryland, who had attended the last 47 Big Quarterlies, declared that "where the visitors once came for the purpose of religious experience only, hundreds now come only because of curiosity and for the sociability and dressed up part of the day."[53] John H. Bell, president of the A. U. M. P. Conference, voiced similar sentiments at the 1935 celebration, charging, "Too many are losing sight of the deep religious significance of Big Quarterly. Lots of folk come here every year for a good time but they don't know why."[54] More than a decade later, Delaware historian Pauline A. Young indicated that "The carnival aspect is often more pronounced today than the religious."[55] By the 1960s, most black people on the Delmarva Peninsula had come to regard Big Quarterly as a social extravaganza, and many who were devoutly religious refused to participate in the celebration.

Fifth, Big Quarterly became more closely identified with activities of a political nature, and greater numbers of black and white people stayed away because they feared that riots or racial violence might occur. The festival had provided a public platform for national issues involving black people since the pre-Civil War years, when the issues of slavery and colonization were at the top of the black agenda. In the late nineteenth and early twentieth centuries concerns like education and voting rights were addressed at these annual gatherings. At the 1907 meeting, J. E. McGirt of Philadelphia, editor of McGirt's Magazine, spoke to an immense crowd at the Mother A. U. M. P. Church, noting that the ballot was the solution to the race problem. McGirt was the secretary of The Constitutional Brotherhood, an organization which claimed 24,000 ministers and professors whose purpose was the organization of the black voters in the doubtful states with the intention of casting their votes for only such candidates as would champion equal rights for black people. He spoke to the racial situation in this manner:

> There are two gigantic spirits upon the battle plain
> of America's arena; the two spirits constitute what
> is falsely known as the Negro problem. I say
> "falsely" because the problem is not the Negro's

> but America's problem. It is made up of the spir-
> it of the white man versus the spirit of the black
> man. Thus I say to you that the ballot is the
> antidote and the only one for all the atrocities put
> upon us. For with the ballot goes everything--
> freedom of manhood, the honor of our wives, and
> the chastity of our daughters. [56]

During the second and third decades of the twentieth
century, representatives of the Garvey movement appeared
at Big Quarterly from time to time in search of contributions
for the back-to-Africa crusade. During the 1935 celebration
"several fiery speakers who urged the Negroes to support
the cause of Ethiopia mingled with the street exhorters and
singing bands. "[57] In the 1960s civil rights activities were
associated with Big Quarterly. At the 1961 meeting, a near-
riot involving 3,000 persons took place when overly-zealous
white policemen attempted to use force in clearing French
Street at the close of the festivities. An 80-year-old woman
was knocked to the ground, two policemen were hurt, and a
number of black youths were arrested. [58] Racial tension in
Wilmington was heightened throughout the 1960s due to the
demonstrations and sit-ins led by the Reverend George F.
Brown and the Reverend Maurice Moyer, president of the
city branch of the N.A.A.C.P. The civil rights battle song,
"We Shall Overcome," was frequently heard at Big Quarterly
celebrations. The atmosphere was charged at the 1963 gathering by the fiery speeches of several black ministers who
had just returned from the great march on Washington, where
Martin Luther King, Jr. delivered his famous "I Have a
Dream" speech. [59] The 1964 Big Quarterly ended with a
civil rights rally at the Mother A.U.M.P. Church. Such
activities apparently convinced many that it was no longer
safe to appear at the festival.

City officials and church leaders confronted the problem forthrightly by attempting to soothe the fears of those
who thought it best to remain at home. Each year police
set up barricades closing off French Street from about Sev-
enth to Ninth Streets. Participants in the festivities were
often compelled to honor a 6:30 p.m. curfew, thus creating
a situation which resembled martial law. President Reese
C. Scott of the A.U.M.P. Conference did his best to allay
doubts and fears surrounding Big Quarterly. He reassured
those present in 1964 that the observance was nothing more
than what it had been in the past:

> You don't have to be afraid of what's going to hap-
> pen. We will only worship God this day, and hon-
> or the founder of our church. This day was never
> designed for any type of demonstration. There will
> be no civil rights demonstrations--there will be no
> racial demonstrations where this day is concerned. 60

To those who associated Big Quarterly with a growing tendency toward racial tension and violence, Scott said:

> We are against violence of any kind. We do not
> condone violence by any organization. We are all
> devoted to the acceptance of law and order. You
> don't need to argue; you don't need to fight. When
> you have learned to respect yourself, other people
> will be forced to respect you. 61

Such assurances did little to revive widespread support for
an already waning Big Quarterly. The cloud of doubt and
suspicion remained and attendance continued to decrease.

Sixth, there was a serious decline in the support given
the festival by black churches, particularly those with roots
in the Spencer tradition. Prior to the 1960s it had been a
custom for black churches in parts of Delaware, Maryland,
Pennsylvania, and New Jersey to cancel services on the last
Sunday in August in order to be in Wilmington for Big Quarterly. The Mother A. U. M. P. Church, the Mother U. A. M. E.
Church, and Ezion Methodist Church were usually filled to
capacity with the ministers and lay persons from various
churches. This all changed with the coming of the civil
rights era. Black churches in Delaware and neighboring
states abandoned the festival, and the U. A. M. E. Church and
Ezion Methodist Church no longer engaged in a strong joint
effort with the A. U. M. P. Church to make Big Quarterly a
lasting tribute to the life and work of Peter Spencer. 62 The
festival has become primarily an event held by the Mother
A. U. M. P. Church, with only scanty support from other
A. U. M. P. congregations, U. A. M. E. 's, and black churches
of other denominations.

Finally, the relocation of the Mother A. U. M. P.
Church from French Street to North Franklin Street in Wilmington in November 1969 was a prominent factor in the decline of Big Quarterly. This move, which happened in accordance with urban renewal plans, largely destroyed the communal solidarity which had been the life of the festival for so

many years. The relocation of the church broke the link with the past and dealt a serious blow to the spirit and enthusiasm of most of the elderly members who had struggled to keep alive the religious character of Big Quarterly. According to Sara Gardner, who has been a member of the Mother A. U. M. P. Church for more than a half century, "The older members died like flies when we left French Street. The old Church, which had been our Mecca since slavery times, had been their home. "63

The relocation of the church was apparently the result of trends long in the making. Even though the church had been renovated in 1956, the Wilmington Board of Health charged in June 1960 that the building, due supposedly to defective wiring, was in violation of the Housing and Zoning Codes of the city. 64 Early in 1965, the Wilmington Housing Authority, caring little for the cultural and historical significance of the church, insisted that the building be torn down to make way for a public mall. George F. Brown, who was pastoring the mother church at that time, used every available means to save the building. Louis L. Redding, Delaware's most reputable black lawyer, was contacted to explore legal channels by which the church could be saved. A proposal was submitted by Brown through Redding to the Housing Authority requesting a reconsideration of Urban Renewal Plans. On March 13, 1967, the Housing Authority sent a letter to Redding stating, "It has been determined that it is not possible to change the Urban Renewal Plan to allow the church to remain in its present location. " The letter continued:

> The Authority's action on the church's proposal, after very careful deliberation, is based on its nonconformity with the Urban Renewal Plan. The plan designates the church as property to be acquired and its site as a public mall. The open spaces in the "government complex" have been designed to provide a common focal point for the large structures to be built around it. An attractive vista is developed from King Street across French Street to the new city building. The retention of the church would seriously curtail the pedestrian traffic flow down the steps from King to French Streets and would block the attempt to internally orient the new buildings around strongly defined open spaces through the use of common building soffit lines, pedestrian walkways, and the malls. 65

The old Mother A. U. M. P. Church, 819 French Street, Wilmington, Delaware, was the focal point of Big Quarterly for more than a century and a half before it was torn down in 1969 (from the photo collection of the late Bishop George F. Brown of the A. U. M. P. Conference).

The old Mother U. A. M. E. Church, 1206 French Street, Wilmington, Delaware, was second only to the Mother A. U. M. P. Church in terms of its importance as a focal point of Big Quarterly (from the photo collection of Rev. Irene C. Dutton, pastor).

Dudley T. Finch, the Executive Director of the Authority, went on to say in this letter:

> Recognizing the important place held in Delaware history by Peter Spencer, and the heritage represented by the Mother A. U. M. P. Church, we will explore the possibilities of creating some type of memorial at public expense on the mall. When the design of the mall area is prepared it may be possible to preserve the remains of the founder on the site or, if that is not feasible, at least erect a suitable monument. We will pursue this proposal further if requested to do so by the church. [66]

The Board of Trustees of the Mother A. U. M. P. Church responded to this proposal in a letter addressed to Peter Larson, the City Planner of the Authority, dated April 10, 1967. It stated:

> In light of the fact that we have agreed to relocate, being officially notified by the Housing Authority and informed by the City Planner that a public plaza has been planned for this present site.
>
> In the conceptual plan, we have within our grasp an opportunity to create a beautiful image and demonstrate in a tangible way the major contributions made by both Negro and white Delawareans.
>
> Peter Spencer, the founder of our church, was one of the colored Methodists who left Asbury Church in 1805, and assisted in forming Ezion Church. In 1813 he founded the Union Church of Africans, being the first church in the United States organized and entirely controlled by colored people.
>
> We would suggest at this time that the Civil Center Plaza be named for Peter Spencer, the founder of our church.
>
> We further recommend that our architect, Mr. Calvin Hamilton, be permitted to work with the planner in designing the plaza.
>
> As a part of the same memorial and in commemoration of the founder, as a special project, we would strike a commemorative medal, the size of a silver dollar, to be priced for sale at a nominal cost. [67]

In the fall of 1969, George F. Brown, Edward R. Bell, and the trustees of the Mother A. U. M. P. Church finalized a deal to purchase the building of the all-white Second Baptist Church, which was located on North Franklin Street in Wilmington. Because the members of Second Baptist were making plans to move to a new location, they agreed to sell the building for $225,000. [68] The trustees of the Mother A. U. M. P. Church then made a deal with Mayor Harry G. Haskell, Jr. and the Housing Authority to sell the building on French Street for $380,000. [69] As a part of the sales agreement, the remains of Peter Spencer, Annes Spencer, Ferreby Draper, William Anderson, Daniel Bailey, Moses Chippey, and six others were to be exhumed and interred in a single vault in the new city plaza. Plans also called for the erection of a statue on the plaza as a lasting tribute to Spencer and African Union Methodism. [70]

During the first week of June 1970, the Mother A. U. M. P. Church building was destroyed as a few looked on with tearful eyes. George F. Brown later fought back tears as he reflected:

> To be sure, the walls of old Mother A. U. M. P. Church came tumbling down, but the deeper significance and the idealism of its founder will forever remain the hearts of thousands of blacks who have lived in Delaware, and throughout the nation. [71]

An effort to erect a suitable monument to the memory of Peter Spencer on French Street was continued by George F. Brown after the relocation to North Franklin Street. Edward R. Bell, the General Treasurer of the A. U. M. P. Conference, who is also a mortician in Wilmington, exhumed the remains of Spencer and the other early saints and kept them in storage until work began on the plaza. These remains were later interred at the site chosen for the Spencer monument. [72] In August 1973 "Father and Son," a 14-foot statue by Charles Parks, was unveiled at the dedication ceremonies for the Wilmington Civic Center Plaza. [73] One year later, the Wilmington City Council voted to officially name the plaza "Peter Spencer Plaza" and drew up an ordinance to that effect. [74]

In 1976 plans were implemented by high level officials in the city government to erect another monument to the memory of Harriet Tubman and Thomas Garrett--figures who along with Spencer epitomized Delaware's role in the black freedom struggle. A plaque was placed in Peter Spencer Plaza in the spring of that year. [75] In the fall of 1976, State

Senator Herman Holloway and Representative Henrietta Johnson, both from the Wilmington area, presented a resolution before the Delaware Legislature requesting that French Street be renamed Spencer Street. This was the second time Holloway had been involved in a legislative effort to give due recognition to African Union Methodism for its long and proud history. [76] The resolution calling for the renaming of French Street has not yet met with official approval.

Big Quarterly After 1969

The Big Quarterly festival became merely a founder's day program after 1969. In August 1970 a small group gathered to watch Bishop Reese C. Scott place a wreath on Spencer's gravesite. [77] Governor Russell W. Peterson of Delaware paid special tribute to the event in a statement which read as follows:

> The "Big Quarterly" originated at the Mother A. U. M. P. Church in 1813 as a religious celebration instituted and designed by the Rev. Peter Spencer and his followers.
>
> Each year, this event has brought many people together in a common bond of brotherhood and fellowship.
>
> This year, even though the Mother A. U. M. P. Church has moved to a new location, this tradition will be continued with the holding of the 157th annual "Big Quarterly" in Wilmington, Delaware.
>
> Accordingly, it is a pleasure for me, as Governor of the State of Delaware, to designate Sunday, August 30, 1970, as a day of tribute to "Big Quarterly" in Wilmington, and to salute all involved in this observance and its perpetuation over the years. [78]

The celebrations held between 1971 and 1974 were attended by very small crowds, most of whom were devoted members of the Mother A. U. M. P. Church. There were no major activities on French Street in 1975 and 1976. A

[Opposite:] A. U. M. P. 's gather at the Spencer Monument in Peter Spencer Plaza for the August 1974 celebration (from the photo collection of the late Bishop George F. Brown of the A. U. M. P. Conference).

measure of excitement was generated at the meeting in 1977 as a small crowd watched the unveiling of a large portrait of Spencer done by Simmy Knox. [79] In 1978 a fairly strong effort was made to revive Big Quarterly, beginning the Saturday before the last Sunday in August. The program began with a Saturday night candlelight procession from old Asbury Center at Third and Walnut Streets in Wilmington to the Peter Spencer Plaza. After the opening remarks by Robert F. Walters, presiding bishop of the A. U. M. P. Conference, choirs from a few churches in the city performed at the plaza in a "Joy Night" celebration. The festivities of the following Sunday were marred by unpleasant weather. [80] The 1979 Big Quarterly was perhaps the most impressive of the decade. Pauline A. Young, the highly regarded black Delaware historian, and officials representing the city government and the local N. A. A. C. P. , were among those who gathered at Peter Spencer Plaza for the activities. Speeches were offered in tribute to Spencer, and the importance of the Mother A. U. M. P. Church in Delaware history was cited. The highlight of the observance occurred when Albert N. Jarman, Sr. , who succeeded George F. Brown as pastor of the mother church in 1975, placed a wreath on Spencer's gravesite. In a brief but powerful statement, he paid tribute to the father of African Union Methodism and the inaugurator of Big Quarterly:

> Spencer lives in the hearts and minds of all who feel the bond of heritage stretching down through the years. For one who did so much, we would be derelict in our duty if we did not let the world know that we love him, that we appreciate him, that we remember him. [81]

The 1980 Big Quarterly involved a return to French Street and provided a basis for hope that the festival can be fully revived. About 500 showed up for the affair. Memories of the past were evoked as booths and tables were set up along the 800 block of French Street. Many types of "soul food" were displayed and consumed in large quantities. Singing groups performed in Peter Spencer Plaza. Stirring sermons were delivered at the Radisson Hotel in Wilmington by Bishop Robert F. Walters and Dr. Harold A. Carter, a nationally known author and revivalist from Baltimore. The festivals held in 1981 and 1982 showed even more signs of life as celebrants gathered on French Street.

More recently, Cultural Encounters, Inc., a minority media production company based in Kennett Square, Pennsylvania, has launched an effort to produce a film concerning Peter Spencer and the Big Quarterly festival. The film, which was in progress at this writing, will be called, "Peter Spencer: The Lasting Connection." If completed, it should add another dimension to Delaware history in particular, and American history in general, by depicting the human capacity for festivity and celebration and by highlighting the power of the human desire for religious freedom as a force for positive social change. 82

Meanwhile, the question of what will happen to Big Quarterly in the future still looms before us. The writing of this history and the effort to produce a film about the festival have aroused greater support and activity on behalf of making Big Quarterly "big" again. But the extent to which the festival is revived will depend in large measure upon the support given it by the churches that share roots in the Spencerian tradition; namely, the A. U. M. P. Church, the U. A. M. E. Church, and Ezion-Mount Carmel United Methodist Church. No one can predict what will happen. However, one can say with certitude that Big Quarterly will never be what it was when the Mother A. U. M. P. Church stood at 819 French Street in Wilmington.

NOTES

1. Alice Dunbar-Nelson, Big Quarterly in Wilmington (Wilmington: the author, 1932), p. 5.

2. Ibid., pp. 1-5.

3. Accounts in the various local newspapers during this time erroneously suggest that Big Quarterly was seriously declining. See The Morning News, Wilmington, Del. (August 27, 1900), p. 1; The Evening Journal, Wilmington, Del. (August 31, 1903), p. 4; The Evening Journal (August 30, 1909), p. 8; The Morning News (August 26, 1918), p. 3; and The Evening Journal (August 30, 1920), p. 2.

4. The Evening Journal (August 27, 1900), p. 1; The Evening Journal (August 26, 1901), p. 1; The Morning News (August 31, 1903), pp. 1 and 4; The Evening Journal (August 28, 1905), p. 8; The Morning News (August 26, 1907), pp. 1 and 7; The Evening Journal (August 31, 1908), p. 8;

The Evening Journal (August 26, 1912), p. 1; and Every Evening, Wilmington, Del. (August 27, 1917), p. 6.

5. The Evening Journal (August 31, 1925), p. 9; Every Evening (September 1, 1930), p. 5; and The Evening Journal (August 29, 1932), p. 3.

6. Every Evening (August 26, 1935), p. 13.

7. The Morning News (August 26, 1940), p. 1; The Morning News (August 28, 1950), pp. 1 and 4; The Morning News (August 29, 1955), pp. 1 and 3; The Morning News (August 27, 1956), p. 1; Every Evening (August 26, 1957), p. 10; and The Morning News (August 31, 1959), pp. 1 and 3.

8. The Delaware Defender: Delaware's Only Negro Weekly, Wilmington, Del. (August 30, 1963), pp. 1 and 5; The Evening Journal (August 31, 1964), p. 1; The Morning News (September 1, 1965), p. 20; and The Morning News (August 28, 1967), p. 21.

9. The Morning News (August 28, 1967), p. 21; and The Morning News (September 1, 1969), p. 11.

10. Private Interview with Sara Gardner, Wilmington, Del., January 27, 1979. Mrs. Gardner is a long-time member and historian of the A. U. M. P. Church.

11. The Evening Journal (August 26, 1929), p. 8.

12. The Morning News (September 1, 1958), pp. 1 and 9.

13. The Morning News (August 29, 1966), p. 9; and Private Interview with the Rt. Reverend Reese C. Scott, Wilmington, Del., August 26, 1979. Reverend Scott was the presiding Bishop of the A. U. M. P. Conference until his retirement in 1974.

14. Nelson, Big Quarterly in Wilmington, pp. 1-5; Private Interview with the Reverend George A. Woodards, Newark, Del., August 27, 1979; and Private Interview with Mrs. Blanche Wells, Kennett Square, Pa., August 28, 1979. Reverend Woodards has been the General Secretary of the A. U. M. P. Conference for some thirty years. Mrs. Wells is a long-time member of the Bethel A. M. E. Church, Kennett Square, Pa.

15. Nelson, Big Quarterly in Wilmington, pp. 1-5; and Private Interview with Edward R. Bell, May 22, 1978. Mr. Bell, a Wilmington funeral director, was the General Treasurer of the A. U. M. P. Conference for some thirty years.

16. Private Interview with Mrs. Pauline A. Young, Wilmington, Del., August 27, 1979. Mrs. Young, the niece of Paul Laurence Dunbar and Alice Dunbar-Nelson, is a black Wilmington historian.

17. Private Interview with Mr. Alfred Collins, Wilmington, Del., January 21, 1979. Mr. Collins served as a trustee of the Mother A. U. M. P. Church for some 60 years.

18. The Morning News (August 27, 1956), p. 1; The Morning News (September 1, 1958), pp. 1 and 9; The Morning News (August 31, 1959), pp. 1 and 3; Every Evening (August 27, 1960), p. 13; The Delaware Defender (August 30, 1963), pp. 1 and 5; and Private Interview with Sara Gardner, Wilmington, Del., January 27, 1979.

19. The Evening Journal (August 26, 1929), p. 8; Every Evening (August 26, 1940), p. 13; and The Morning News (August 26, 1940), p. 1.

20. The Morning News (August 31, 1936), p. 18; and The Morning News (August 31, 1959), pp. 1 and 3.

21. The Morning News (August 28, 1967), p. 21.

22. The Evening Journal (August 26, 1929), p. 8.

23. The Evening Journal (August 31, 1964), p. 1.

24. The Evening Journal (August 30, 1909), p. 8.

25. The Morning News (August 26, 1918), p. 3.

26. The Evening Journal (August 26, 1929), p. 8.

27. The Morning News (August 26, 1940), p. 1.

28. The Morning News (August 28, 1950), pp. 1 and 4.

29. The Morning News (August 27, 1956), p. 1.

30. The Morning News (August 31, 1964), p. 3.

31.　Every Evening (August 27, 1917), p. 6.

32.　The Morning News (August 27, 1956), p. 1; The Morning News (August 31, 1964), p. 1; and Private Interview with Mr. Alfred Collins, Wilmington, Del., January 21, 1979.

33.　See Harold A. Carter, The Prayer Tradition of Black People (Valley Forge, Pa.: Judson Press, 1976), pp. 1ff.

34.　Private Interview with Mr. Alfred Collins, Wilmington, Del., January 26, 1979; and Private Interview with Mr. Edward R. Bell, Wilmington, Del., May 22, 1978.

35.　The Evening Journal (August 28, 1967), p. 3.

36.　The Evening Journal (August 28, 1967), p. 3; Private Interview with the Rt. Reverend Reese C. Scott, Wilmington, Del., August 26, 1979; and Private Interview with Mrs. Elizabeth Brown, Wilmington, Del., January 27, 1979. Mrs. Brown is the widow of the late Rt. Reverend George F. Brown, bishop of the A. U. M. P. Conference.

37.　The Morning News (September 1, 1969), p. 11.

38.　The Morning News (September 1, 1969), pp. 11ff.

39.　The Evening Journal (August 31, 1908), p. 8.

40.　The Delmarva Star, Wilmington, Del. (August 27, 1933), p. 10.

41.　The Sunday Morning Star, Wilmington, Del. (August 28, 1938), p. 28.

42.　The Morning News (August 31, 1964), p. 3.

43.　Private Interview with Mrs. Anna Ferrel, Wilmington, Del., August 27, 1979. Mrs. Ferrel is a long-time member of the Mother A. U. M. P. Church.

44.　The Evening Journal (August 31, 1964), p. 1.

45.　The Morning News (September 1, 1965), p. 20.

46.　The Morning News (September 1, 1965), p. 20ff.

47.   Nelson, Big Quarterly in Wilmington, pp. 1-2.

48.   The Morning News (September 1, 1965), p. 20.

49.   The Morning News (September 1, 1965), pp. 20ff.

50.   Every Evening (August 29, 1927), p. 4.

51.   The Morning News (August 31, 1964), p. 3.

52.   Private Interview with Mr. Edward R. Bell, Wilmington, Del., May 22, 1978; and Private Interview with Mr. Matthew Gardner, Wilmington, Del., January 20, 1979.   Mr. Gardner is a long-time resident of Wilmington, Del.

53.   The Evening Journal (August 26, 1929), p. 8.

54.   Every Evening (August 26, 1935), p. 13.

55.   Pauline A. Young, "The Negro in Delaware, Past and Present," in H. Clay Reed, ed., Delaware: A History of the First State, 3 Vols. (New York: Lewis Historical Publishing, 1947), II, pp. 604-605.

56.   The Morning News (August 26, 1907), pp. 1 and 7.

57.   Every Evening (August 26, 1935), p. 13.

58.   The Morning News (August 29, 1961), p. 1; The Morning News (September 6, 1961), p. 1; The Morning News (September 14, 1961), p. 30; and The Evening Journal (September 28, 1961), p. 3.

59.   The Delaware Defender (August 30, 1963), pp. 1 and 5; and Private Interview with Mrs. Elizabeth Brown, Wilmington, Del., January 27, 1979.

60.   The Morning News (August 31, 1964), p. 3; and Private Interview with the Rt. Reverend Reese C. Scott, Wilmington, Del., August 26, 1979.

61.   The Morning News (September 1, 1964), p. 16; and Private Interview with Reese C. Scott, Wilmington, Del., August 26, 1979.

62.   Private Interview with the Reverend George A.

Woodards, Newark, Del., August 27, 1979; and Private Interview with Mrs. Sara Gardner, Wilmington, Del., January 27, 1979.

63. Private Interview with Mrs. Sara Gardner, Wilmington, Del., January 26, 1979; and Private Interview with Mrs. Pauline A. Young, Wilmington, Del., August 27, 1979.

64. The Flashlight of the A. U. F. C. M. P. Church (January 1956), p. 5; and A Letter from James C. Strong, M. D., Health Commissioner, Wilmington, Del., to Mother A. U. M. P. Church, June 14, 1960.

65. A Letter from Dudley T. Finch, Executive Director of the Wilmington Housing Authority, Wilmington, Del., to Louis L. Redding, Attorney-at-Law, March 13, 1967.

66. Ibid.

67. A Letter from the Trustees of Mother A. U. M. P. Church, Wilmington, Del., to Peter Larson, City Planner, April 10, 1967.

68. The Evening Journal (January 13, 1968), pp. 1ff.; The Morning News (October 23, 1969), p. 1; The Morning News (November 21, 1969), p. 18; and Private Interview with Mr. Edward R. Bell, Wilmington, Del., April 21, 1980.

69. The Morning News (October 23, 1969), p. 1; The Morning News (November 21, 1969), p. 18; and Private Interview with Mr. Edward R. Bell, Wilmington, Del., May 22, 1978.

70. The Morning News (October 23, 1969), pp. 1-2.

71. The Morning News (June 5, 1970), pp. 3 and 23.

72. Private Interview with Mr. Edward R. Bell, Wilmington, Del., May 22, 1978; and The Delaware Spectator, Wilmington, Del. (September 5, 1974), p. 6.

73. The Morning News (August 18, 1973), pp. 1ff.

74. The Delaware Spectator (September 5, 1974), p. 6; The Evening Journal (August 23, 1974), p. 34; and "An Ordinance to Name the Government City Plaza 'Peter Spencer Plaza,'" passed by the City Council, Wilmington, Del., August 22, 1974.

75. The Evening Journal (April 1, 1976), p. 58.

76. The Delaware Valley Defender, Wilmington, Del. (September 18, 1976), pp. 1 and 7.

77. The Morning News (August 31, 1970), p. 2.

78. "A Statement from the Honorable Russell W. Peterson in Tribute to 'Big Quarterly,'" presented at Wilmington, Del., August 30, 1970.

79. The Morning News (August 29, 1977), p. 4.

80. The Evening Journal (August 28, 1978), p. 4; and The Evening Journal (August 31, 1978), pp. 1ff.

81. From a Speech delivered by the Reverend Albert N. Jarman, Sr. at the Peter Spencer Plaza, Wilmington, Del., August 26, 1979.

82. Private Conversations with Marc Pevar and Oliver Franklin, Wilmington, Del., August 29, 1981. Pevar and Franklin are filmmakers and directors of Cultural Encounters, Inc.

Chapter VIII:

SUMMARY AND PROSPECT

Summary

This work of original research brings to consciousness the histories of the African Union Methodist Protestant and Union American Methodist Episcopal Churches, previously neglected because professional church historians, theologians, and sociologists of religion have known virtually nothing about these churches. In fact, this is the very first study that deals in an analytical fashion with the Spencer Churches. The treatment provided in "Invisible" Strands in African Methodism is especially new because 1) it sets forth the thesis that the Union Church of Africans, the parent body of the A. U. M. P. and U. A. M. E. denominations, was the first African Methodist Church organized and completely controlled by black people in the United States; 2) it seeks at many points to establish a comparative context with the Spencer Churches and other branches of African Methodism; and 3) it attempts to interweave the stories of the A. U. M. P. and U. A. M. E. Churches into the tapestry of Afro-American religious history.

The general focus has been in three areas: 1) the origin and development of the Spencer Churches as "dissenting movements" within the larger context of American Methodism; 2) the manner in which these churches found a special or unique expression; and 3) the question of why they have languished for so long in the backwaters of African Methodism. From this cursory review we will be reminded that the histories of the A. U. M. P. and U. A. M. E. Churches have been characterized by a strange amalgam of failures and successes, pain and pleasure, conflict and reconciliation, unity and divisiveness, and sin and saintliness.

The study begins with John Wesley, Methodism's founder, and his relationship to black people. From that point the Methodist appeal to early Africans is discussed, with some attention given to the manner in which Africans responded to that appeal and to the extent to which they, in their overt expressiveness, contributed to the Methodist style and ethos. It was determined that Africans responded enthusiastically and in large numbers to the Methodist appeal because 1) the Methodist preachers and/or circuit riders displayed an abiding concern for their spiritual lives; 2) the evangelical style and ethos so typical of Methodism appealed to them; 3) the Methodist practice of accepting blacks as preachers was attractive to them; and 4) they found the early antislavery stance of the Methodists to be consistent with gospel principles and with their own yearnings to be free human beings.

We saw how Africans were involved in the Methodist story in America almost from the beginning. An African woman named Betty was present at one of the earliest Methodist society meetings in America, held in the Philip Embury home in New York in 1766. The journalistic accounts of early Methodist preachers--among them Francis Asbury, Nathan Bangs, Richard Boardman, Thomas Coke, William Colbert, Joseph Pilmore, and Thomas Rankin--document the presence and participation of Africans in early Methodist societies and class meetings in such places as Baltimore, Philadelphia, and New York. Even at the historic Christmas Conference of 1784, which witnessed the official organization of the Methodist Episcopal Church, Africans were represented in the presence of Richard Allen and Harry "Black Harry" Hoosier. The full story of the development of Methodism in America will not be known until Africans like Betty, Richard Allen, and Harry Hoosier are included in all of the historical accounts related to the Methodist Episcopal tradition.

In the late eighteenth century, the relationship between Africans and the M. E. Church, which had previously been mutually enriching and seemingly unbreakable, was threatened as the church softened its stand against slavery and succumbed to the growing custom of segregating blacks in worship. A movement of African dissent in American Methodism resulted. That movement was born in the mind of Richard Allen, a Delaware ex-slave who, as early as 1786, entertained the idea of a separate organization for African Methodists. A year later Allen and his associates formed the Free African Society, which was an early example of black power or nationalism. In 1793 Allen led a group of blacks out of the predominantly white St. George's M. E. Church in Philadelphia in protest over racially proscriptive policies.

This signaled the beginning of a movement as African Methodists walked out of white racist M. E. Churches in New York, Baltimore, Charleston, Wilmington (Delaware), Attleborough (Pennsylvania), and Salem (New Jersey).

The African Methodist movement took the form of several independent ecclesiastical structures, one of which was the Union Church of Africans. In 1813 this body, which developed out of a movement started by Peter Spencer and William Anderson in Wilmington, Delaware, in 1805, became the first African Methodist Church completely owned and controlled by people of African descent in this country. In 1816 the African Methodist Episcopal Church assumed a similar status under Richard Allen in Philadelphia. In 1821 the African Methodist Episcopal Zion Church became the third body of African Methodists to break all ties with the white Methodist structure. Though influenced by the Wesleyan and Methodist tradition, the Union Church of Africans, the A. M. E. Church, and the A. M E. Zion Church emerged with institutional forms that distinguished them most decisively from white Methodism. These churches found a special or unique expression by embracing the idea of a God who is no "respecter of persons" and by providing a framework for self-help, expression, recognition, and leadership in a society where black people have been traditionally excluded from most areas of economic, social, and political life. In this sense, the African Methodist Churches became 1) visible manifestations of black theology and 2) classic examples of black power or nationalism.

By all odds the Union Church of Africans was the most unique of the early African Methodist Churches. This claim is made because Spencer and Anderson were remarkably creative and original in planning the structure of this church. They adopted the articles of religion, general rules, and discipline of the Methodist Episcopal tradition, but rejected its system of bishops and presiding elders because of its inherent undemocratic tendencies. Yet they considered themselves to be Methodists, both constitutionally and emphatically. Their adoption of the titles of elder minister and teaching or ruling elder in reference to church officials seemed to suggest a Presbyterian influence. From New England Congregationalism they borrowed the tradition of congregational freedom and authority. Their emphasis on strong lay involvement, which later became a unique feature of the A. M. E. Zion Church, developed naturally as a result of their views on congregational control. Spencer and Ander-

son's acceptance of women as preachers and their inaugura-
tion of that spectacular expression of both culture and worship called Big Quarterly may be attributed largely to early
Quaker influences.   Most of these traditions have survived
to become significant aspects of the lives of the A. U. M. P.
and U. A. M. E. denominations.

Despite being the first African Methodist Church completely under the care and control of blacks, the Union
Church of Africans did not grow and develop on a level with
the A. M. E. and A. M. E. Zion Churches.   Dearth of vigorous
leadership, severely limited resources, the lack of an itinerant ministry, and problems of organization stemming largely from weak connectional authority were among the reasons
for the exceedingly slow growth and development of the church.
These problems remained to haunt the Spencer Churches
throughout their histories, thus explaining why they have
struggled in the backwaters of African Methodism.

One of the most tragic events in the life of the Union
Church of Africans occurred between 1851 and 1856, less
than two decades after the deaths of Spencer and Anderson.
A major dispute erupted when Ellis Saunders, an elder minister from Christiana, Delaware, was denied the right to
preach and to administer the ordinances at the Mother Union
Church of Africans in Wilmington as he saw fit.   This dispute, which was carried before the courts of Wilmington,
eventually resulted in a schism as Saunders and Isaac Barney
broke away with most of the congregations of the Union
Church of Africans and organized a rival body which became
known as the Union American Methodist Episcopal Church.
In 1866 the congregations that remained with the parent body
were united with several congregations of the First Colored
Methodist Protestant Church, and the resulting body became
the African Union First Colored Methodist Protestant Church
of the United States of America and Elsewhere, ordinarily
called the African Union Methodist Protestant Church.

The A. U. M. P. and U. A. M. E. Churches grew slowly
in the years after the Civil War.   The slow growth of these
churches is especially apparent when measured in comparison
with the mushrooming of the A. M. E. , A. M. E. Zion, and
C. M. E. Churches.   In 1900 the A. U. M. P. and U. A. M. E.
bodies combined consisted of fewer than 10, 000 members located primarily in the states of Delaware, Maryland, Pennsylvania, and New Jersey.   By that time, the A. M. E. , A. M. E.
Zion, and C. M. E. Churches had become national bodies.

The A. M. E. Church embraced at least 500, 000 members;
the A. M. E. Zion Church consisted of around 300, 000 members; and the C. M. E. Church had in the neighborhood of
150, 000 members. Thus, the regional significance of the
Spencer Churches became quite evident against the national
character of the A. M. E. Church, the A. M. E. Zion Church,
and the C. M. E. Church.

In the twentieth century, this pattern of slow growth
so characteristic of the Spencer Churches was radically reversed as institutional decline became a marked feature of
both bodies. The A. U. M. P. Church declined from some 69
congregations and small missions in 1910 to only 36 congregations in 1980, and from some 4, 000 members in 1900 to
about 3, 500 members in 1980. The U. A. M. E. Church increased from a membership of about 5, 000 in 1900 to a little more than 10, 000 in 1926, but had dropped to a membership of about 7, 000 by 1980. Furthermore, this church declined from some 79 congregations in 1930 to only 55 congregations in 1980. Such serious records of decline attest to
the weak and demoralized state of the Spencer Churches in
this century, and they help explain why these churches have
not entered the mainstream of African Methodism.

Perhaps the most interesting feature of the A. U. M. P.
and U. A. M. E. Churches in this century has been the ways
in which they, despite institutional weaknesses and seriously
limited resources, have contributed to the moral, spiritual,
and social uplift of black people. In this sense, they have
continued to function essentially on the agenda left by Peter
Spencer. They have emphasized the proclamation of the
Word and have placed great stress on temperance, the sanc-
tity of the marriage vow, and other fundamental moral principles. Additionally, they have expressed in both word and
deed the need for black people to elevate themselves in the
economic, educational, and political areas of life.

Prospect

As we come to what can only be a conclusion in this history,
we turn to a glance at the future to try to suggest what
course the Spencer Churches must take in order to grow and
to find a truly respectable place within the mainstream of
African Methodism particularly and American Methodism generally. Obviously, the greatest challenge facing the A. U. M. P.
and U. A. M. E. Churches in the years ahead has to do with

their growth, development, and relevance as religious institutions. Can these churches recover fully from the many seasons of agony brought on by the serious decline of their institutional structures in this century? Will they develop beyond a mere regional existence to become national bodies like the A. M. E., the A. M. E. Zion, and the C. M. E. Churches? Do they have the necessary potential for meeting the demands of social relevance? These questions become all the more pressing considering that the A. U. M. P. and U. A. M. E. Churches are still suffering from a serious malady of spirit and resolve which could threaten what little remaining stamina they have. These churches are not growing with much authority, they remain virtually closed out of ecumenical activities at the national and international levels, and they are still seriously hampered by weak mission priorities, underdeveloped structures, and severely limited financial resources. Perhaps they have wallowed in "smallness" for too long.

The foregoing is not to suggest that the survival of the A. U. M. P. and U. A. M. E. Churches is in great jeopardy. These churches are and will remain the only accessible institutions for those whose identities and sense of belonging in both a human and divine sphere are tied up with the Spencerian tradition. What is in jeopardy is the capacity of these churches to attract large numbers of urban blacks, particularly young blacks who are raising more and more questions about the influence and relevancy of religious institutions generally. If they are to meet with any success at all in this regard, they must work harder to establish and support ministries and missions oriented toward combating crime, poverty, drug abuse, illiteracy, and other problems associated with an increasingly urban black situation. This will necessitate developing resources, financial and otherwise. It will also require seeking out young, gifted, and well-trained black men and women who can serve the churches as effective clergy and lay persons and who are willing to fill dominant positions in their hierarchies.

The A. U. M. P. and U. A. M. E. Churches would do well to consider organic union as an important step in furthering their development and effectiveness. I can think of no period in the histories of these churches when it would have been more beneficial for them to unite. There are important reasons why this course of action should be followed. First, these churches share a common orientation in that they trace their heritages back to Peter Spencer. Second, they are uniform in terms of doctrine and polity, having similar articles of religion, general rules, disciplines, and administrative structures. Finally, a merger would strengthen them tremendously in terms of influence and resources. Through their combined structures, they would stand a much better chance of mustering the necessary resources, both in terms of manpower and finances, to assist in addressing the multitude of needs confronting their own constituents and the black community as a whole. They would also be in a better position to conduct foreign mission programs.

In the past, bitter feelings over who were responsible for the great schism in the 1850s and strong disagreements concerning who are the rightful heirs of Peter Spencer seem to have been the main barriers to union and full cooperation between the A. U. M. P. and U. A. M. E. denominations. At best, such concerns are outrageously trivial and totally irrelevant. The people responsible for the great split in the Spencer movement have been dead for years, and both churches have a rightful claim to the Spencer tradition because they share common roots in it. Hatchets must be buried, and the disputes of the past must be left to the past. Those who comprise these churches--most importantly, their leadership contingents--must remember that an African Union Methodism that fails to be faithful to the Spencer legacy of ecclesiastical unity is not African Union Methodism at all, but a poor carbon copy of the real thing which in time will perish.

On a broader scale, the A. U. M. P. and U. A. M. E. Churches should consider cooperation, if not organic union, with the larger and more popular branches of African Methodism; namely, the A. M. E. , the A. M. E. Zion, and the C. M. E. Churches. To reiterate a point made by Harry V. Richardson in Dark Salvation: The Story of Methodism as It Developed Among Blacks in America, cooperation between the various branches of African Methodism would make it possible for the churches to accomplish in a large, unified fashion what they have been doing in small ways. First, with their combined resources they would be able not only to finance massive publishing enterprises which could make available a wide range of sources of a Christian educational nature, but also to create employment within those enterprises for thousands of talented and well-trained black men and women. Second, these churches would be in a better position to finance nurseries, educational programs and institutions, drug programs, low-income housing projects, and other essentials designed to move black people from a condition of oppression and dependency to one of liberation and self-sufficiency. Finally, the combined resources of these churches would enable them to be more effective in foreign missions. Presently, there is little indication that the five African Methodist Churches will work toward common goals in a unified manner.

At last, those affiliated with the A. U. M. P. and U. A. M. E. Churches must take a long, hard look at the past and what it has meant in terms of the decline and demoralization of their institutional structures. After scrutinizing the past, they would be wise to resolve never to repeat it, because the endurance of the Spencer heritage depends to a great extent upon the perseverance of their churches. In the meantime, a luta continua ("the struggle continues").

AN ESSAY ON SOURCES

The histories of the African Union Methodist Protestant and Union American Methodist Episcopal Churches are enormously important in the understanding of African Methodism in particular and black religion in general.   Based on the contents of this study, no professional theologian, church historian, or sociologist of religion can honestly challenge this contention.   One wonders, then, why the A. U. M. P. and U. A. M. E. Churches have been ignored as critical dimensions of the Afro-American religious experience by black and white scholars alike.

Apart from suggesting answers to this question, the purpose of this essay is threefold.   First, it examines the level of attention given Peter Spencer and the A. U. M. P. and U. A. M. E. Churches in studies of American Christianity, in works on general American history, and in surveys of Afro-American history, the black church and black religion, and Delaware history.   Second, it offers recommendations for further research in this area.   Finally, it gives direction as to where important sources on Spencer and African Union Methodism can be found.

Protestant church historians who have surveyed the history of American Christianity have totally ignored Peter Spencer and the churches which grew out of his movement. Robert Baird, Religion in the United States (London, 1842), made a fleeting reference to the early A. M. E. and A. M. E. Zion movements, but offered nothing on the early Union Church of Africans.   In his America: A Sketch of the Political, Social, and Religious Character of the United States of North America (New York, 1855), Philip Schaff made brief mention of the influence of Methodism among blacks, but gave virtually no evidence of knowledge concerning the branches of African Methodism in existence during the time he was writing.   The same can be said of H. K. Carroll, The Religious Forces of the United States (New York, 1893). This serious pattern of omission regarding African Union Methodism, and Afro-American religion generally, continued to a great extent in the twentieth century with Leonard Bacon, Peter G. Mode, William Warren Sweet, Clifton E. Olmstead, Jerald C. Brauer, Winthrop S. Hudson, Edwin S. Gaustad, and many other historians of American religion. All of these scholars have disclosed a serious lack of knowledge concerning the various expressions of the black religious experience. Robert T. Handy, "Negro Christianity and American Church Historiography, " in Jerald C. Brauer (ed.), Reinterpretations in American Church History (Chicago, 1968), pp. 91-112, has expressed the need for American church historians to make black religion a serious part of their agendas, and so has Sydney E. Ahlstrom, A Religious History of the American People (New Haven, 1972). My examination of the histories of the A. U. M. P. and U. A. M. E. Churches serves to provide further evidence of this need.

A few Protestant church historians have provided glancing treatments of African Union Methodism in major historical works on American Methodism, but in all cases they neglected to mention both of the denominations which fall under this banner. Bishop Matthew Simpson (ed.), in his Cyclopaedia of Methodism Embracing Sketches of Its Rise, Progress, and Present Condition, with Biographical Notices and Numerous Illustrations (Philadelphia, 1878), was the first to make significant references to the Spencer movement, but The Cyclopaedia focuses almost exclusively on the U. A. M. E. Church, giving vital statistics for the year 1876. Frederick E. Maser and George A. Singleton, "Further Branches of Methodism are Formed, " in Emory S. Bucke (ed.), The History of American Methodism, 3 Vols. (New York, 1964), I, pp. 615-617, contains an informative statement on "The Union American Methodist Episcopal Church, " but nothing on the A. U. M. P. Church. The A. U. M. P. Church is discussed in a couple of paragraphs in Frederick A. Norwood's The Story of American Methodism: A History of the United Methodists and Their Relations (Nashville, 1974), but the U. A. M. E. Church is not mentioned at all. All of these authors were apparently unaware that two denominations developed out of the Spencerian tradition.

The authors of works on general American history have demonstrated little concern for the Afro-American religious experience and have provided almost no information on Peter Spencer and the A. U. M. P. and U. A. M. E. Churches. The increased importance of black religion is acknowledged in the recent editions of John M. Blum, et al. , The National Experience: A History of the United States, 3rd Edition (New

York, 1973); John A. Garraty, The American Nation, 3rd Edition, 2 Vols. (New York, 1975); and Richard Hofstadter, et al., The United States, 4th Edition, 2 Vols. (Englewood Cliffs, N. J., 1976), but there is nothing in these sources which suggests that the authors were familiar with African Union Methodism. The vast majority of American history textbooks reflect the unenlightened approach of Samuel E. Morrison and Henry S. Commager, The Growth of the American Republic, 5th Edition, Vol. I (New York, 1962); Samuel E. Morrison, The Oxford History of the American People (New York, 1965); and Daniel Boorstin, The Americans: The National Experience (New York, 1965) in that they have not considered the black religious experience as an important facet of the total American experience.

Unfortunately, the general neglect which the Spencer Churches have received is evident even in surveys of Afro-American history. George Washington Williams, the pioneer black historian, perceived the tremendous importance of the early A. M. E. Church to black people in his History of the Negro Race in America, 1619-1880 (New York, 1883), but did not allude to the significance of the A. M. E. Zion, the A. U. M. P., the U. A. M. E., and Colored Methodist Episcopal Churches as black religious institutions. Black historians such as W. E. B. Du Bois, Carter G. Woodson, Charles H. Wesley, John Hope Franklin, Benjamin Brawley, Benjamin Quarles, Rayford Logan, Earl Thorpe, and Lerone Bennett, Jr. have displayed an awareness of the existence of the A. M. E., A. M. E. Zion, and C. M. E. Churches, but have remained curiously unmindful of the Spencer Churches. The same holds true for white historians who have done surveys of Afro-American history, among whom are August Meier and Elliot Rudwick. This disturbing lack of attention given the A. U. M. P. and U. A. M. E. Churches is not entirely surprising because so little is known generally about these bodies and because so-called secular historians have not been noted for good, solid treatments of religion in America.

Studies of black religion and the black church share in large measure the limitations common to studies previously mentioned in relationship to the Spencer Churches. W. E. B. Du Bois' pioneer work, The Negro Church: A Social Study Done Under The Direction Of Atlanta University (Atlanta, 1903), contains nothing on the A. U. M. P. and U. A. M. E. denominations. Carter G. Woodson mentioned them briefly in The History of the Negro Church (Washington, D. C., 1921), but revealed his ignorance concerning their

origins by stating that the Union Church of Africans was incorporated in 1807, and the Union American Methodist Episcopal Church in 1850. These churches were completely ignored in studies of the black church by Benjamin E. Mays
and Joseph W. Nicholson, E. Franklin Frazier, William
Banks, and Hart M. Nelsen, et al. Gayraud S. Wilmore
makes a quick reference to the early work of Peter Spencer
and William Anderson in his Black Religion and Black Radicalism: An Examination of the Black Experience in Religion
(New York, 1972). Milton C. Sernett comments on Spencer's
involvements with the Union Church of Africans and the
A. M. E. Church in three paragraphs of his Black Religion
and American Evangelicalism: White Protestants, Plantation
Missions, and the Flowering of Negro Christianity, 1787-
1865 (Metuchen, N. J., 1975), but he is wrong in his assertion that Spencer was strongly opposed to a trained clergy.
No mention is made of Spencer and African Union Methodism
in other recent works on black religion by C. Eric Lincoln,
et al.; Joseph R. Washington, Jr.; George E. Simpson; and
Albert J. Raboteau.

Most disturbing is the fact that Spencer and the
A. U. M. P. and U. A. M. E. Churches have been treated so
carelessly and cursorily in studies of African Methodism.
Spencer's views on ministerial training have been seriously
distorted by the A. M. E. bishop John M. Brown, "Richard
Allen and His Co-Adjutors, " Repository of Religion and Literature, III, No. 1 (January 1861), pp. 1ff. Important
works like Richard Wright, Jr. 's Centennial Encyclopaedia of
the African Methodist Episcopal Church (Philadelphia, 1916)
do acknowledge that the Union Church of Africans was founded
in 1813, but do not emphasize the fact that this church was
the very first branch of African Methodism to effect both de
facto and de jure separation from white Methodism. Casual
references to Spencer's presence at the A. M. E. organizing
convention in 1816 appear in Benjamin W. Arnett (ed.), The
Budget: Containing the Annual Reports of the General Officers of the African M. E. Church (Xenia, Ohio, 1881); Daniel
A. Payne, The History of the African Methodist Episcopal
Church (Nashville, 1891); John T. Jennifer, Centennial Retro-
spect: History of the A. M. E. Church (Nashville, 1916);
Charles S. Spencer, A History of the African Methodist
Episcopal Church (Philadelphia, 1922); Charles H. Wesley,
Richard Allen: Apostle of Freedom (Washington, D. C., 1935);
George A. Singleton, The Romance of African Methodism: A
Study of the A. M. E. Church (New York, 1952); and a number
of other sources on African Methodist Episcopal Church his-
tory.

Recognition of some of the early activities of Spencer and Ellis Saunders in the Union Church of Africans is given in Lorenzo D. Blackson, The Rise and Progress of the Kingdoms of Light and Darkness, or, The Reign of Kings Alpha and Abadon (Philadelphia, 1867); and William J. Walls, The African Methodist Episcopal Zion Church: Reality of the Black Church (Charlotte, N. C., 1974). Vital information and statistics on the Spencer Churches are included in Benjamin W. Arnett, et al., "History of the Union American Methodist Episcopal Church," in The Proceedings of the Quarto-Centennial Conference of the A. M. E. Church of South Carolina, May 15-17, 1889 (Charleston, 1890), pp. 229-234; and Benjamin W. Arnett (ed.), The Budget: Containing the Annual Reports of the General Officers of the African M. E. Church, 1904 (Philadelphia, 1904). The A. M. E. bishop Levi J. Coppin made scattered references to early leaders of the Spencer Churches in his Unwritten History (Philadelphia, 1919). His accounts are strengthened by the fact that he was acquainted with Edward H. Chippey of the A. U. M. P. Church and Edward Williams of the U. A. M. E. Church. J. Beverly F. Shaw devoted several pages to a discussion of the A. U. M. P. and U. A. M. E. denominations in his The Negro in the History of Methodism (Nashville, 1954). Brief comments on Spencer and the U. A. M. E. Church can be found in Harry V. Richardson, Dark Salvation: The Story of Methodism as It Developed Among Blacks in America (New York, 1976), but the author was apparently unaware that Spencer's church was organized prior to the A. M. E. Church. Carol V. R. George mentions Spencer in connection with the anti-colonization crusade of the early nineteenth century in Segregated Sabbaths: Richard Allen and the Rise of Independent Black Churches, 1760-1840 (New York, 1973), but gives no indication of being informed concerning the A. U. M. P. and U. A. M. E. Churches.

The lack of attention given Spencer and African Union Methodism by Delaware historians is especially tragic considering that Delaware was the focal point of Peter Spencer's activities on behalf of black religious freedom and black liberation. For a fleeting reference to Spencer's personality, influence, and church work by one of his contemporaries, see Elizabeth Montgomery, Wilmington: Reminiscences of Familiar Village Tales, Ancient and New (Philadelphia, 1851). Scraps of useful information on the early Spencer movement and the A. U. M. P. and U. A. M. E. Churches are available in Thomas Scharf, History of Delaware, 1609-1888, Vol. II (Philadelphia, 1888); John D. C. Hanna (ed.), The Centennial Services of Asbury Methodist Episcopal Church, 1789-1889

(Wilmington, 1889); Henry C. Conrad, History of the State of Delaware: From the Earliest Settlements to the Year 1907, Vol. II (Wilmington, 1908); Wilson L. Bevan (ed.), History of Delaware: Past and Present, Vol. II (New York, 1929); Francis A. Cooch, Little Known History of Newark, Delaware and Its Environs (Newark, Delaware, 1936); Anna T. Lincoln, Wilmington, Delaware: Three Centuries Under Four Flags, 1609-1937 (Rutland, Vt., 1937); Helen B. Stewart, "The Negro in Delaware to 1829," M. A. Thesis, University of Delaware, 1940; H. Clay Reed (ed.), Delaware: A History of the First State, Vol. II (New York, 1947); Frank R. Zebley, The Churches of Delaware (Wilmington, 1947); Carol E. Hoffecker's Wilmington, Delaware: Portrait of an Industrial City, 1830-1910 (Richmond, 1974) and Delaware: A Bicentennial History (New York, 1977); and John A. Munroe's Colonial Delaware: A History (New York, 1979) and History of Delaware (Newark, Del., 1979). Interestingly, Munroe's "The Negro in Delaware," The South Atlantic Quarterly, Vol. LVI, No. 4 (Autumn 1957), pp. 428-444, supposedly an outstanding essay, does not even refer to Spencer, African Union Methodism, or the Big Quarterly festival.

Very little has been written concerning the spectacular Big August Quarterly by Delaware historians. Brief comments on this festival are given in the aforementioned works by Scharf, Conrad, Lincoln, Reed, and Hoffecker. Of special value on this subject is Alice Dunbar-Nelson's Big Quarterly in Wilmington (Wilmington, 1932), a five-page document which also appeared in Every Evening, Wilmington, Del. (August 27, 1932), pp. 8-9. More extensive treatments of Big Quarterly are given in Lewis V. Baldwin, "Festivity and Celebration: A Profile of Wilmington's Big Quarterly," Delaware History (Fall-Winter 1981), pp. 197-211; "Festivity and Celebration in a Black Methodist Tradition," Methodist History (July 1982), pp. 183-191; and "August Quarterly: A Feature of African Union Methodism, 1813-1982," August Quarterly: An Afro-American Festival (August 1982), pp. 8-12. On page 211 of the essay in Delaware History, the figure in attendance at the 1980 and 1981 Big Quarterlies should have been listed at a combined total of 3,000 instead of the estimated 1,500. Brief corrections that needed to be made in the article in Methodist History were included on page 43 of the October 1982 issue of that same journal. The Baldwin essays on Big Quarterly should be read in conjunction with the Nelson piece.

The Saunders case, which split the Union Church of

Africans and eventually culminated in the A. U. M. P. and
U. A. M. E. Churches, has been almost totally ignored by
Delaware historians. Thomas Scharf's History of Delaware,
mentioned previously, includes a brief but informed discussion of this case. The studies of Henry C. Conrad, Wilson
L. Bevan, and Frank R. Zebley, also referred to earlier,
make passing mention to the organization of the U. A. M. E.
Church, but do not refer to the Saunders case as a critical
factor in that development. The failure of Delaware historians
to write about this case is not due to a lack of available
primary sources, because very lengthy and informative accounts are presented in Daniel B. Anderson, et al., vs. The
Union Church of Africans Before the Superior Court of New
Castle County (Hall of Records, Dover, 1852); The Union
Church of Africans vs. Ellis Saunders in the Court of Errors
and Appeals (Hall of Records, Dover, 1855); and The Case of
the Union Church of Africans, in Wilmington, Before the Superior Court for New Castle County, Comprising the Petition
of Ellis Saunders for a Mandamus, The Return Thereto; Brief
Notes of the Argument and Re-Argument of Counsel, and the
Final Decision of the Court Awarding the Mandamus, 1852-
53 (Wilmington, 1855).

　　　It is difficult to explain why leaders of the A. U. M. P.
and U. A. M. E. Churches have not compiled good, comprehensive and analytical historical studies of their churches.　　In
1920 Daniel J. Russell, Jr., president of the Philadelphia
and New Jersey District of the A. U. M. P. Church, produced
a brief history of his denomination under the title, History
of the African Union Methodist Protestant Church (Philadelphia, 1920). Russell, influenced by the fact that the rich
heritage of his church had been closed out of all synoptic
histories up until that time, began his study by citing the
need for a major history of the Spencer movement. Although
the Russell study contains useful historical information on the
early years of the Spencer movement, it reveals serious errors and omissions. There are no references in this study
to the Big Quarterly festival, the Ellis Saunders Case, or to
the U. A. M. E. Church. General statistics reported on the
A. U. M. P. Church for the year 1918, which claim 575
churches and 20,000 members in the denomination, are largely erroneous. In addition, Russell wrongly implies that he
was consecrated bishop in 1884. The A. U. M. P. Church did
not officially adopt the episcopal structure until 1967, although the titles "bishop" and "president" were used inter-
changeably by some spiritual heads of the church after 1914.
Apart from these important errors and omissions, the Russell

history is a good source and should be used as a basis for studies of the life and work of Peter Spencer. Bishop George F. Brown of the A. U. M. P. Church, a great admirer of Russell, was researching the history of his denomination when he passed away in 1975.

The first attempt to write the history of the U. A. M. E. Church began with Bishop Jacob F. Ramsey's Father Spencer, Our Founder: His Work for the Church and Race (Camden, N. J., 1914), a brief study which served as the basis for Daniel J. Russell's history of the A. U. M. P. denomination. This work is based largely on an address delivered by Ramsey to the General Conference of the U. A. M. E. Church in October 1914. It shares some of the weaknesses of the Russell study. Although it contains much on the early life and work of Peter Spencer, it affords nothing on Big Quarterly, the Saunders Case, or the organization of the U. A. M. E. Church. Only a casual comment is made concerning a few spiritual heads of the U. A. M. E. denomination who were active in the late nineteenth and early twentieth centuries. Bishop John P. Predow's A Brief History of the Spencer Movement (Wilmington, 1979) offers more substance of a historical nature, but the author's contention that a dispute over what should be the proper title of spiritual heads led to the schism within the Union Church of Africans in the period 1851-56 is not persuasive. A genuine interest in preserving the history of the U. A. M. E. Church resulted in the recent appearance of Our Heritage: The History of the Union American Methodist Episcopal Church (Hackensack, N. J., 1973). This source, which consists of individual histories of 49 of the 55 congregations in the denomination, would be of immense value to anyone concerned with writing the history of the church. It is obviously sketchy and incomplete and lacks the organization and analysis so vital to a first rate study, but it is highly informative. The presentation of three major papers on U. A. M. E. Church history at the 166th Annual Conference of the First and Fourth Districts of the U. A. M. E. Church in 1979 evidences the continuing effort on the part of U. A. M. E.'s to preserve and share their rich heritage.

This book on the A. U. M. P. and U. A. M. E. Churches is groundbreaking in that it is the first serious attempt to place these churches in their proper spectrum in the history of American Methodism generally and African Methodism particularly. Indeed, it is the first comprehensive and analytical history of African Union Methodism. It is hoped that it will serve a useful purpose in facilitating further research on this component of the black religious experience.

African Union Methodism has been neglected for so long by the academic establishment that, despite the importance of this study, a number of possible topics remain to be explored. A few recommendations for additional research in this area are given in Lewis V. Baldwin, "The A. U. M. P. and U. A. M. E. Churches: An Unexplored Area of Black Methodism," Methodist History, Vol. XIX, No. 3 (April 1981), pp. 175-178. First and foremost, we need a critical biography of Spencer. Brief but valuable biographies of this important figure are included in Jacob F. Ramsey, Father Spencer, Our Founder: His Work for the Church and Race, and Daniel J. Russell, Jr., History of the African Union Methodist Protestant Church, works alluded to already, but their hagiographic tone prevents them from completely capturing the spirit of this great leader. Lewis V. Baldwin's article, "Father Peter Spencer: Portrait of an Unknown Pioneer African Methodist Leader," The Journal of the Interdenominational Theological Center (Fall 1981), pp. 31-43, falls short of being a good critical assessment of Spencer's life and work. Furthermore, the final two paragraphs of this article (pages 42-43), which deal with the Saunders dispute and the A. U. M. P. and U. A. M. E. Churches, are not entirely correct. The errors here resulted from an oversight on the part of this author. The accurate account of the Saunders case and what transpired in its aftermath is provided in chapter three of this book.

Aside from the pieces by Ramsey, Russell, and Baldwin, other sources await those who would undertake the task of writing about Spencer. Early editions of Wilmington newspapers such as The Delaware State Journal (July 28, 1843); The Delaware State Journal (August 1, 1843); and The Delaware Gazette (August 4, 1843), which maintained close contact with Spencer during his lifetime, afford significant information on his birth, personality, and influence among his church people and race. A brief but important obituary of Spencer appeared in The True Wesleyan (Boston, Mass., September 9, 1843), which was the newspaper of the early Wesleyan Methodists. Excellent references to Spencer's anti-colonization work are contained in W. L. Garrison (ed.), Thoughts on African Colonization (Boston, 1832), pp. 36-40; and L. R. Mehlinger, "Attitudes of the Free Negro Toward African Colonization," Journal of Negro History, I (1916), pp. 283-287. For more on Spencer's life and thought, one might examine sources such as The Personal Will Record of Peter Spencer, U, Vol. I (New Castle, Del.: Register of Wills, 1841), p. 212; A Directory and Register for the Year 1814 of the Borough of Wilmington and Brandywine (n. p. : R. Porter, 1814), pp. 45-52; Peter Spencer, comp. , The African Union Hymn-Books (Wilmington, 1822 and 1839 editions); Lorenzo Dow Blackson, The Rise and Progress of the Kingdoms of Light and Darkness, or, The Reign of Kings Alpha and Abadon, (Philadelphia, 1867); and the statements of Spencer and William Anderson recorded in the various editions of the A. U. M. P. and U. A. M. E. Disciplines.

We need to know more about William Anderson, Isaac Barney, Ellis Saunders, Edward H. Chippey, Isaac B. Cooper, and others who contributed substantially to the shaping of the African Union Methodist tradition from 1813 to the present. Although source materials are too scarce to do major biographies of most of these figures, we can have brief, critical biographical sketches of them. Hagiographies, such as Isaac B. Cooper, et al. , A Short History of the Life of Rev. Dr. Daniel J. Russell, Jr. (Philadelphia, n. d.), and Daniel J. Russell, Jr. , A Short History of the Life and Death of Rev. Isaac B. Cooper (Philadelphia, 1919), will not be sufficient.

Studies of more recent figures, such as Bishops George F. Brown and Reese C. Scott of the A. U. M. P. Church, and Bishops David M. Harmon and David E. Hackett of the U. A. M. E. Church, would teach us something about the level of involvement of the Spencer Churches in the civil rights and black power movements of the 1960s. All of these men, especially Bishops Brown and Hackett, participated in these developments. Scholars who give attention to Brown and Scott would benefit immensely by doing research at the A. U. M. P. headquarters in Wilmington and at the episcopal residence in Norristown, Pennsylvania. Personal interviews with clergy and lay persons of the Mother A. U. M. P. Church, with whom Brown and Scott had close ties, would add useful information and insights. The sources on Brown are plentiful. His widow, Elizabeth Brown, resides in Wilmington and has proven to be an excellent oral source person. She has oversight of her husband's collected correspondence files, which are rich in content. In addition, one will discover that Wilmington's The Evening Journal, The Morning News, and The Delaware Defender carried accounts of Brown's social and political involvements between 1959 and 1975, the year of his death. He had served as a reporter for The Delaware Defender. The episcopal residence of the U. A. M. E. Church in Wilmington, and the church's headquarters in Camden, New Jersey, should be combed for materials on Harmon and

Hackett. One might also browse through issues of The Union Messenger, the U. A. M. E. periodical, which was published sporadically between 1950 and 1975.

The positions taken by the Spencer Churches with respect to ministerial training during the nineteenth and twentieth centuries should be studied to challenge the misguided assumption that these churches have been excessively slow in accepting educated clergy persons. Spencer's views on this issue are reflected in Jacob F. Ramsey, Father Spencer, Our Founder: His Work for the Church and Race, and in Daniel J. Russell, Jr., History of the African Union Methodist Protestant Church. For a better understanding of the A. U. M. P. Church's position on this matter, one might check The Discipline of the African Union Church in the United States of America, Third Edition Enlarged (Wilmington, 1852); The Doctrine ... of the African Union First Colored Methodist Protestant Church, Sixth Revised Edition (Wilmington, 1895); The Doctrine and Discipline of the African Union First Colored M. P. Church (Wilmington, 1927); and The Doctrine and Discipline of the African Union First Colored M. P. Church and Connection of the United States of America, or Elsewhere, Seventeenth Revised Edition (Wilmington, 1958). Information on the U. A. M. E. Church's stand on trained clergy is available in The Discipline of the Union American Methodist Episcopal Church in the United States and Elsewhere (Wilmington, 1872); The Discipline of the Union American Methodist Episcopal Church in the United States of America, the Province of Canada, and Elsewhere (Wilmington, 1892); and The Discipline of the Union American M. E. Church, Twenty-Eighth Edition (Wilmington, 1942). In addition, an examination of the roles assumed by such educated preachers as Gaylord V. Peterson, Daniel J. Russell, Jr., George N. Sheppy, and Sylvester C. Blackledge in the A. U. M. P. Church and Lorenzo Dow Blackson, Jacob F. Ramsey, S. P. Shepherd, and Orlando S. Watts in the U. A. M. E. Church would deepen our knowledge of how these denominations responded to a trained ministry. Sources like Lorenzo D. Blackson, The Rise and Progress of the Kingdoms of Light and Darkness, or the Reign of Kings Alpha and Abadon, and Sylvester C. Blackledge, An Open Book on Hidden Mysteries (Elkton, Md., 1925) would be of considerable importance in such an examination.

We also need a thorough investigation of the important roles played by women in the histories of the Spencer Churches. This is an especially interesting and fruitful area

for research because Spencer's Union Church of Africans
was the first black denomination in America to specify in its
doctrine and in the various editions of its Discipline that females could serve as licensed preachers. For references
to those black women who were active in the early Spencer
movement, one should look at the Articles of Association of
the Union Church of African Members (Wilmington, 1813);
Thomas Scharf, History of Delaware, 1609-1888, Vols. I and
II; Benjamin W. Arnett (ed.), The Budget: Containing the
Annual Reports of the General Officers of the African M. E.
Church, 1904; Jacob F. Ramsey, Father Spencer, Our Founder: His Work for the Church and Race; and Daniel J. Russell, Jr., History of the African Union Methodist Protestant
Church. Valuable information on "Mother" Ferreby Draper,
a strong spiritual force in the early Union Church of Africans,
can be found in Wilmington newspapers such as The Delaware
Tribune (May 28, 1868); The Morning News (August 26, 1889);
and The Morning News (August 29, 1927). The Union Church
of Africans' position on women preachers, which was set
forth in the 1813 and 1841 issues of the church's Discipline,
is clearly spelled out in the 1852 edition of The Discipline
of the African Union Church in the United States of America.
A. U. M. P. and U. A. M. E. sources of the late nineteenth and
the twentieth centuries yield useful information on female involvement both at the local church and conference levels.
For the A. U. M. P. Church, see the unpublished accounts of
The Minutes of the Quarterly Conferences of the A. U. F. C. M. P.
Church, November 30, 1867, and November 27, 1885 (Historical Society of Delaware, Wilmington); The Constitution
and By-Laws of the Women's Home Mite Missionary Society
of the A. U. F. C. M. P. Church (Wilmington, n. d.); The Con-
stitution and By-Laws of the Grand Body of the Daughters of
Conference of the A. U. F. C. M. P. Church (Wilmington, 1935);
and the 1895 and 1927 editions of the church's Discipline.
On the U. A. M. E. side, one might refer to Our Heritage:
The History of the Union American Methodist Episcopal
Church; The Union Messenger of the U. A. M. E. Church, Vol.
I (January 1975); The Laws and By-Laws of the Peter Spen-
cer United Daughters of Conference and the Mite Missionary
Society of the Union American Methodist Episcopal Church
(Wilmington, 1968); and the 1942 U. A. M. E. Book of Disci-
pline. The U. A. M. E. Church's stand in favor of female
preachers is made clear in the 1892 issue of its Discipline.
For more recent studies of women's involvement in African
Union Methodist history, see Lewis V. Baldwin, "Women in
A. U. M. P. Church History, 1813-1982, " August Quarterly:
An Afro-American Festival (August 1982), pp. 5-7; and

"Black Women and African Union Methodism, 1813-1983,"
Methodist History, XXI, 4 (July 1983), pp. 225-237.

A careful study of the history of the Big Quarterly
festival has yet to be written. Such a study would have to
treat this festival as one of the important and unique aspects
of the African Methodist tradition which extends beyond the
strictly ecclesiastical. Furthermore, because Big Quarterly
reflects a great deal concerning the black worship tradition
and its African background, a work which focuses on it as a
microcosm of a larger picture of what constitutes that tradition would prove especially rewarding for those scholars who
have long contended that Afro-American culture has been
greatly influenced by Africa. The richest veins to be mined
on this subject in this century, as in the last century, course
through Wilmington newspapers. Since the early years of
the nineteenth century, major Wilmington newspapers have
carried annual accounts of this festival during each week
after the last Sunday in August. Of particular significance
for what they reveal about Big Quarterlies of the pre-Civil
War years are The Delaware State Journal (September 2,
1845); The Delaware Gazette (September 1, 1846); Blue Hen's
Chicken (September 1, 1848); The Delaware Gazette (August
28, 1849); The Delaware Gazette (August 27, 1850); and The
Delaware Gazette (September 1, 1857). A great deal of information on the festival as it appeared in the late nineteenth
century is available in issues of Every Evening, The Delaware Gazette and State Journal, The Delaware State Journal
and Statesman, The Evening Journal, The Morning News,
and The Sunday Morning Star. For the twentieth century,
one should browse through editions of Every Evening, The
Morning News, The Evening Journal, The Sunday Morning
Star, The Delmarva Star, and black Wilmington newspapers
such as The Delaware Defender, The Delaware Valley Defender, and The Delaware Spectator. A great deal of history
can also be obtained through interviewing scores of elderly
blacks and whites in Wilmington and surrounding areas who
had close ties with this festival for so many years. The information provided in oral sources and in all of the newspapers mentioned would be of considerable value in a study
of Big Quarterly if used along with Alice Dunbar-Nelson's
Big Quarterly in Wilmington, and Lewis V. Baldwin's "Festivity and Celebration: A Profile of Wilmington's Big Quarterly," Delaware History, and his "Festivity and Celebration
in a Black Methodist Tradition," Methodist History.

The history of union negotiations between African Methodists is surely in need of further exploration. This topic is briefly discussed in Frederick A. Norwood's The Story of American Methodism. Perhaps the best treatment of this subject presently available is Roy W. Trueblood, "Union Negotiations Between Black Methodists in America," Methodist History, Vol. VIII, No. 4 (July 1970), pp. 18-29, but he focuses only on the A. M. E., A. M. E. Zion, and C. M. E. Churches, failing to mention the A. U. M. P., U. A. M. E., and First Colored Methodist Protestant Churches. Any complete account of union talks between African Methodists must begin with the A. M. E. organizing conference of April 1816, which marked the first attempt to unite the different strands of African Methodism. For an early reference to the ecumenical aspect of this conference, see the New York-based black newspaper Colored American (October 21, 1837). From this source one gets a deeper understanding of why union did not occur between the Allenites, Zionites, and the Spencerian group. Other references to the possible issues which separated Richard Allen, Peter Spencer, and James Varick appear in Levi J. Coppin, Unwritten History; Charles H. Wesley, Richard Allen: Apostle of Freedom; Milton C. Sernett, Black Religion and American Evangelicalism: White Protestants, Plantation Missions, and the Flowering of Negro Christianity, 1787-1865; and Harry V. Richardson, Dark Salvation: The Story of Methodism as It Developed Among Blacks in America. Important information on the 1866 merger between the African Union Church and several congregations of the First Colored Methodist Protestant Church is offered in The Doctrine and Discipline of the African Union First Colored Methodist Protestant Church, 1867; "The African Union Methodist Protestant Church," The United States Department of Commerce, Bureau of Census, Religious Bodies: Statistics, History, Doctrine, Organization, and Work, 1926 (Washington, D. C., 1929), pp. 1015-1025; and in the unpublished accounts of The Minutes of a Call Meeting of the Congregation of the African Union Church, Wilmington, Delaware, October 4, 1865 (Historical Society of Delaware, Wilmington) and The Minutes of a Call Meeting of the Official Board of Elders of the African Union Church, Wilmington, Delaware, September 26, 1865 (Historical Society of Delaware, Wilmington).

For sources that discuss more recent attempts at union between African Methodist bodies, one might examine "The A. U. M. P. and U. A. M. E. Churches: Negro Conferences Talk Merger Points," The Evening Journal, Wilmington, Del. (August 1, 1964); "A Resolution Extending Felicitations to the New York-Washington Conference of the C. M. E. Church, the

U. A. M. E. Church, and the A. U. M. P. Church, on the Cele-
bration of 'Reformation Day'," passed by the City Council,
Philadelphia, Pennsylvania (October 6, 1977); "A. M. E.,
A. M. E. Z., C. M. E., U. M. Bishops Hold First Joint Meeting,"
NOW: Black Methodists for Church Renewal, Vol. II, No. 4
(April 1979); James H. Cone, "Black Ecumenism and the
Liberation Struggle," and Bishop Joseph C. Coles, Jr., "Why
Black Church Union?" in The A. M. E. Zion Quarterly Review,
Vol. XCII, No. 2 (July 1980); and Othal L. Lakey, "The
Merger of the A. M. E. Zion and the C. M. E. Churches," and
"The Merger of the A. M. E. Zion and C. M. E. Churches:
Gauging the Improbable," in The Christian Index: Official
Publication of the Christian Methodist Episcopal Church, Vol.
113, No. 13 (July 1, 1980). The scholar who writes on this
subject should take into account the many barriers which
have served to discourage union among African Methodists,
such as personality conflicts, the willingness to maintain
separate identities, and differences in polity and style.

A study establishing a comparative context with the
Spencer Churches and other branches of African Methodism
should be undertaken. This book on African Union Methodism
is the only one available which attempts to compare and contrast the A. U. M. P. and U. A. M. E. Churches with the A. M. E.,
A. M. E. Zion, C. M. E., and First Colored Methodist Protestant Churches. The range of possible focuses for an indepth
study of this kind is broad. The similar tenets and disciplines of these various churches and their somewhat different
styles and modes of managing church matters would make
for an interesting study. Differences and similarities along
these lines between the early A. M. E., A. M. E. Zion, and
African Union Churches are mentioned in Colored American
(May 20, 1837); Colored American (October 14, 1837); and
Colored American (October 21, 1837). One might explore
the similar social and theological forces which gave rise to
the various branches of African Methodism. Another could
center on the extent to which these churches have reflected
the Wesleyan and Methodist tradition, and how they have
found special or unique expressions. Still another might
study the regional significance of the A. U. M. P., U. A. M. E.,
and First Colored Methodist Protestant Churches as compared
to the national prominence of the A. M. E., A. M. E. Zion, and
C. M. E. Churches. Scholarly treatments in these areas
would further enlighten us as to the vitality and variety endemic to African Methodism.

Various significant collections of materials concerning

African Union Methodism can be found at a number of loca-
tions in private collections as well as public or institutional
holdings. The City Library of Wilmington, Delaware, is a
major repository for sources on this topic. Enormous quantities of Wilmington newspapers dating as far back as the
early 1800s, most of which are on microfilm, are included
in its collection. One of the earliest editions of the African
Union Hymnal compiled by Peter Spencer in 1839, which is
extremely rare, is among its holdings. Rare copies of the
1852 Discipline of the African Union Church, the 1867 Discipline of the A. U. M. P. Church, and the 1872 and 1892 Disciplines of the U. A. M. E. Church are also available. A 24-
page account of The Case of the Union Church of Africans
versus Ellis Saunders, argued before the Superior Court of
New Castle County in 1852-53, can be found, along with the
aforementioned sources, in the rare book collection of this
library. Among its important papers there is vital information on the A. U. M. P., U. A. M. E., and First Colored Methodist Protestant Churches for the year 1926, relating primarily to statistics, history, doctrine, organization, and work.
In addition, this library affords one of the few available
copies of Alice Dunbar-Nelson's ground-breaking article on
the Big Quarterly festival, plus several histories of Delaware
by Wilson L. Bevan, Henry C. Conrad, Francis A. Cooch,
Carol E. Hoffecker, Anna T. Lincoln, John A. Munroe, H.
Clay Reed, Thomas Scharf, and Frank R. Zebley.

The Wilmington-based Historical Society of Delaware
has a rich and varied collection of sources on the Spencer
Churches. Numerous issues of Blue Hen's Chicken, Mirror
of the Times, Every Evening, The Delaware Gazette, The
Delaware State Journal, The Delaware Tribune, The Morning
News, The Evening Journal, The Sunday Morning Star, and
other Wilmington newspapers of the nineteenth and twentieth
centuries, which offer so much on African Union Methodist
history, are stored here or are available on microfilm. The
society's A. U. M. P. and U. A. M. E. Collections, boxes 70-76,
consist of a significant number of burial records, denominational periodicals, disciplines, deeds to church properties,
insurance policy records, loan agreements and payment sched-
ules, letters, manuals, mortgage papers, minutes of the Sunday School Associations, newspaper clippings, printed tracts
and pamphlets, records of trustee meetings, receipts for
purchases, sales agreements, statistics on active and inactive church members, tax bills, and minutes of annual,
quarterly, district, and general conferences. The Minutes
of the Female African School Society of Wilmington, 1834-

1840 and The Reports of the African School Society of Wilmington, 1853-1861, which contain several references to members of the A. U. M. P. and U. A. M. E. Churches, are also housed there. All of the important histories of Delaware which include scraps of information on the Spencer Churches, dating from Elizabeth Montgomery's work of 1851 to very recent studies by Carol E. Hoffecker and John A. Munroe, are on the shelves of this society.

Fragments of African Union Methodist history can be found in libraries and historical societies in Delaware cities like Dover and Newark; Maryland cities such as Baltimore and Salisbury; New Jersey cities like Camden and Penns Grove; and in Pennsylvania cities such as Chester, West Chester, Coatesville, and Philadelphia. In a number of small towns in these and other states, where A. U. M. P. and U. A. M. E. congregations have existed throughout the years, one would undoubtedly come across bits and pieces of useful information relative to the histories of individual congregations.

In the Delaware Division of Historical and Cultural Affairs, Bureau of Archives and Records, Hall of Records, in Dover, Delaware, there are early records of the Asbury Methodist Episcopal Church of Wilmington, which list Peter Spencer, William Anderson, and others as black members. The incorporation papers of the early Union Church of Africans, along with its Articles of Association, are accessible on microfilm at this location. Other materials at this center include papers on the free black anticolonization crusade in Delaware, with which Spencer was heavily involved; accounts of the cases involving Ellis Saunders, Daniel B. Anderson, and others, which caused a major dispute within the Union Church of Africans between 1851 and 1856; and small documents and histories of Delaware which provide some substance of a historical nature on the Spencer Churches.

Important documents are also a part of the collections of the city and public buildings of Wilmington. At the Recorder of Deeds Office in the Wilmington City Building, there are microfilm accounts of deeds to the properties of the early Ezion M. E. Church, the Mother Union Church of Africans, the Mother U. A. M. E. Church, and numerous other churches organized in the mid-Atlantic states in connection with the A. U. M. P. and U. A. M. E. denominations. The will records of Peter Spencer, William Anderson, Ellis Saunders, Edward H. Chippey, and many other A. U. M. P. and U. A. M. E. members, dating back to the early nineteenth century, are available on microfilm in the Register of Wills at the Wilmington Public Building.

Several academic institutions have important but limited supplies of source materials on the Spencer Churches. A rich variety of items are at the University of Delaware in Newark. Many of the Wilmington newspapers mentioned previously, which are loaded with information on the Spencer Churches and the Big Quarterly festival, are included in the microfilm collections of the university's library. The Special Collections Department lists a few important pieces among its holdings, such as histories of Delaware which make passing mention of African Union Methodism, and rare copies of Lorenzo D. Blackson's The Rise and Progress of the Kingdom of Light and Darkness, or the Reign of the Kings Alpha and Abadon. The same is true of the University's Black American Studies Department, which makes available on microfilm a copy of an interesting letter pertaining to the African Union Conference at Wilmington, Delaware, in September 1864. Some of these same sources are accessible at other academic institutions in the vicinity of Wilmington, Delaware, such as Delaware State College in Dover, Delaware; Cheyney State Teachers College, Cheyney, Pennsylvania; and Lincoln University, Oxford, Pennsylvania. The Lincoln University campus should be visited by the researcher who is interested in the involvement of A. U. M. P. Churches in the antislavery movement. The historic Hosanna A. U. M. P. Church, an antislavery meeting house and an important stop on the Underground Railroad, is located there. In its basement, which was a resting place for untold numbers of runaway slaves, links of chain and other items have been found which evidence its deep involvement in the history of the antislavery crusade. In the university's library there are historical studies that refer to this church which was organized in 1843, eleven years before the university itself was founded. An excellent source for information on this church is Horace Mann Bond, Education for Freedom: A History of Lincoln University, Pennsylvania (Oxford, Pa., 1976). Jesse B. Barber's short study of Spencer and the A. U. M. P. Church, supposedly completed in the 1940s, has not been found in the university's library holdings.

Sources on Spencer and African Union Methodism are amazingly scarce at academic institutions located outside of a hundred-mile radius of Wilmington. The Garrett-Evangelical Theological Seminary, a United Methodist School of Theology

in Evanston, Illinois, is the only such institution which has
a notable number of minutes, journals, pamphlets, and other
documents of the A. U. M. P. and U. A. M. E. denominations.
The Institute for Black Religious Research, operating under
the auspices of the seminary, includes among its holdings a
collection of pamphlets, tapes, and other sources which afford useful information on these churches.   These materials
were obtained through the courtesy of this author.   Among
the extremely rare items in the Garrett Library there are
single copies of the 1839 African Union Hymnal; Daniel J.
Russell, Jr. 's biography and historical sketch of the A. U. M. P.
Church; and the 1871 and 1895 A. U. M. P. Disciplines.   Northwestern University, of which Garrett is a part, makes available on microfilm the issues of Colored American which
yield important information on the early Spencer movement.
Those issues are dated February 18, 1837; May 20, 1837;
October 14, 1837; and October 21, 1837.   Copies of "'Invisible' Strands in African Methodism: A History of the African
Union Methodist Protestant and Union American Methodist
Episcopal Churches, 1805-1980, " completed as a doctoral dissertation by this author in 1980, are also on file at the Garrett and Northwestern University libraries.   A copy of the
1822 African Union Hymnal, compiled by Peter Spencer, can
be found at the library of the Union Theological Seminary in
New York City.

Most of the source materials on the Spencer Churches
are in private collections.   A number of bishops, presiding
elders, pastors, and lay persons of the A. U. M. P. and
U. A. M. E. Churches have in their possessions an abundance
of church minutes, programs, disciplines, hymnals, and other documents.   The collected correspondence files and private book, pamphlet, photograph, and newspaper collections
of the late Bishop George F. Brown, which probably contain
more on A. U. M. P. Church history and the activities of
Brown than any other single source, are under the care of
his widow, Elizabeth Brown, in Wilmington, Delaware.   The
personal files and collections of the late Bishop Reese C.
Scott and the present A. U. M. P. bishop, Robert F. Walters,
are stored in the episcopal residence in Norristown, Pennsylvania; at the A. U. M. P. headquarters and School of Religion
in Wilmington; and at the Mother A. U. M. P. Church.   Equally important for what they reveal concerning A. U. M. P.
Church history are the private correspondence collections
and papers of the Reverend George A. Woodards, the long-
time secretary of the A. U. M. P. Conference, located in Newark, Delaware; and the collected correspondence files and

documents of Edward R. Bell, the long-time mortician and treasurer of the A. U. M. P. Conference, which are at his home in Wilmington. On the U. A. M. E. side, the largest private collections of materials are housed at the episcopal residence in Wilmington, the present home of Bishop David E. Hackett; in the home of retired Bishop John P. Predow in Wilmington; and at the episcopal residence of the late Bishop David M. Harmon in Camden, New Jersey. The Predow collection consists of many of the sources once stored at the Boulden Academy and Seminary of the U. A. M. E. Church, which was destroyed in the late 1960s.

There are probably other collections of sources which are informative on Spencer and African Union Methodism at the old Asbury M. E. Church, which is now a community center, and at the Ezion-Mount Carmel United Methodist Church, which also traces its roots back to the early Spencer movement. The scholar who undertakes the task of investigating and examining such sources could perhaps add a new chapter to what is presented in this study.

INDEX

AME see African Methodist Episcopal
AMEZ see African Methodist Episcopal Zion
AUFCMP see African Union Methodist Protestant
AUMP see African Union Methodist Protestant
Abbott, Benjamin 26
Abrams, Martha 105-106
African Methodist Episcopal Church 7 (fn. 9), 28, 37-38, 50,
    59, 60-63, 65, 79-80 (fn. 97), 81, 95, 102, 105-106, 155-
    157, 159, 163, 169, 171, 173, 185-186, 190-191, 200,
    208 (fn. 61), 209 (fn. 64), 210 (fn. 74), 250-254; establish-
    ment of 3-4, 51-55
African Methodist Episcopal Zion Church 4, 28, 37-38, 50-
    51, 59-60, 63, 65-66, 79-80 (fn. 97), 81, 95, 102, 105-
    106, 117, 156-157, 159, 169, 171, 173, 185-188, 190-
    191, 200, 209 (fn. 64), 210 (fn. 74), 250-254; establish-
    ment of 2-3
African Union Church see Union Church of Africans
African Union Methodism see African Union Methodist
    Protestant and Union American Methodist Episcopal
African Union Methodist Church see Union Church of Afri-
    cans
African Union Methodist Protestant Book Room and Publish-
    ing House 174
African Union Methodist Protestant Church 5-6 (fn. 1), 102-
    104, 107-113, 115, 126, 152-187, 199-200, 241, 248,
    251-255; scholarly neglect of 1; establishment of 2, 99-
    101, 130; role of women in 105-106
African Union School of Religion 173-174, 177
Allen, Margaret 62
Allen, Richard 3-4, 9, 18-19, 24, 27-29, 38, 42, 51-56,
    76 (fn. 64), 249-250
Allenites 7 (fn. 9), 43, 46, 52, 54-55
Anderson, Daniel B. 83, 88
Anderson, Deborah 62
Anderson, Herman L. 210 (fn. 74)
Anderson, J. Harvey 2-3
Anderson, James A. 229
Anderson, William 25, 39, 48-49, 51, 55-57, 59-62, 65-66,

277